THE MUSICIAN'S HANDBOOK

Editor: Trevor Ford
Advisory Editor: Marianne Barton

R·

RHINEGOLD PUBLISHING LIMITED
241 SHAFTESBURY AVENUE LONDON WC2H 8EH
TELEPHONE 01-836 2385 TELEX 264675 GILDED G

First published in 1986 in Great Britain by
Rhinegold Publishing, 241 Shaftesbury Avenue,
London WC2H 8EH

Rhinegold Publishing has used its best efforts in collecting and
preparing material for inclusion in *The Musician's Handbook*.
It does not assume, and hereby disclaims, any liability to any
party for loss or damage caused by errors or omissions in *The
Musician's Handbook*, whether such errors or omissions result
from negligence, accident or any other cause.

The Musician's handbook.
   1. Music—Vocational guidance—Great Britain
   1. Ford, Trevor
   780'.23'41   MT10

ISBN 0–946890–10–2

Phototypeset by Oxford Publishing Services, Oxford
Printed in Great Britain by The Thetford Press, Norfolk

CONTENTS

SECTION 1 – EARNING A LIVING

SECTION 2 – BUILDING A CAREER

SECTION 3 – ADVICE FINANCIAL AND MATTERS OF LAW

SECTION 4 – BOWING OUT

EDITOR'S PREFACE

Musicians are notoriously bad at taking advice. How many of us, for example, are carrying around uninsured instruments? How many are paying too much national insurance? How many have sent out badly-designed publicity material? Nor must we entirely blame ourselves for this state of affairs: the music profession is understood by few who are outside it. Accountants are often mystified by the business transactions of their musician clients, and a pension consultant running a marketing campaign in 1984 assumed that the average professional musician was managing to earn a clear £12,000 a year.

There is another side to the coin. As any reader with outside interests will know, there is great demand from musicians for information from colleagues who are also qualified in other fields, be it as cabinet-makers or accountants, motor mechanics or legal experts. The tendency, consequently, is for our profession to become self-sufficient, with many of us running small businesses with our professional acquaintances as our customers and clients. This is all very well, provided there are enough of the multi-talented to go round. Unfortunately, there are not, and this is why **The Musician's Handbook** has been produced.

Almost without exception, the 27 chapters of this book have been written by experts with specific experience of the music profession. The aim has been to answer as many of the questions asked by musicians in green rooms, band rooms, staff rooms and common rooms all over the country as space would allow. Nor is the book aimed at any particular area of the profession: whether you are a 25-year-old instrumentalist or a 60-year-old teacher, there is valuable information here for you. And this leads me to encourage you to read the chapters which may not at first seem relevant to your particular needs. Singers will benefit from the advice to young orchestral players given by Basil Tschaikov; orchestral musicians will better understand the problems of their employers after reading Jeffrey Long's chapter on concert management; and concert promoters would do well to read of the struggle facing our composers, as exemplified by Michael Berkeley in Keith Clarke's article.

All the writers of this book have, as far as possible, avoided giving information which is likely to go out of date. However, readers do not have to look far for comprehensive lists of addresses and telephone numbers, or for current information on examination syllabuses or college entry requirements. The *British Music Yearbook* and the *British Music Education Yearbook* should be regarded as essential companions to this handbook and, for those who wish to keep themselves fully in touch with the music scene, *Classical Music* and *Music Teacher* exist to provide regular news and comment on our ever-changing profession. All are available from Rhinegold Publishing.

Finally, my thanks are due to many who have helped the seed of this book to grow and blossom into reality: Marianne Barton who, as both my advisory editor and my wife, has survived months of domestic turmoil; Jacqueline Fowler, a valued assistant; and Keith Diggle, Tony Gamble and Martin Huber of Rhinegold Publishing, without whom ... Also, thanks must go to the dozens of my professional colleagues who have suggested ideas for this publication: conductors, singers, orchestral players, music college principals, and many more.

As a post-script, future editions of **The Musician's Handbook** will only be more comprehensive if you let us know about *your* particular unanswered question. Suggestions (in writing, please) to the address below.

TREVOR FORD
May 1986

Rhinegold Publishing
241 Shaftesbury Avenue
London WC2H 8EH

ix

FOREWORD
SIR DAVID WILLCOCKS CBE MC

There has for many years been a need for a single book, containing within its covers factual information about, and practical advice concerning, almost every aspect of the musical profession. That need has at last been met by **The Musician's Handbook**, which contains 27 articles written by men and women of wide experience in their various fields.

To survive, let alone prosper, in an increasingly competitive world, a musician requires – in addition to talent, dedication, good health, and an element of good fortune – understanding of the many career opportunities, a thorough knowledge of the workings of the musical profession, and some business acumen. All these matters are fully discussed in lively fashion in this book.

The Musician's Handbook will, therefore, be of the greatest value to performers and teachers at all levels, to composers and arrangers, to agents and concert promoters, and to all those engaged in the many forms of musical administration. But it will also be of considerable interest to those who, though not in the musical profession themselves, derive enjoyment from listening to music in the concert hall, on records, or via television and radio, and who are thus the consumers of the musicians' product.

Many godparents present a bible to their godchildren at baptism or confirmation. **The Musician's Handbook** may well become the book to be presented to everyone entering the musical profession.

David Willcocks
Cambridge
May 1986

British Music Worldwide

PUBLISHED ANNUALLY

Subtitled, 'A gift from musical Britain to the World of Music', it is dedicated to the presentation of British music, opera and dance to the world. Its aim - to stimulate the employment of British people and products in other countries and to encourage artists, promoters and students from abroad to make use of facilities here.

Over 6000 copies of this A4 format book are sent as a gift to senior managers in performing arts organisations worldwide. Copies are held in the libraries of all British Council offices in the world and in the commercial posts of British Embassies and Consulates.

Its sections cover: Agents, Artists, Orchestras, Ensembles, Choral Music, Contemporary Music, Composers, Early Music, Opera, Dance, Light Entertainment, Jazz, Folk, Competitions and Awards, Venues & Promoters, Musical Education, Sound Equipment, Recording and Musical Services.

SECTION 1:
EARNING A LIVING

OPTIONS
MARIANNE BARTON

Marianne Barton is editor of the British Music Yearbook, *co-editor of the* British Music Education Yearbook, *and editor of* Music Teacher *magazine. She studied piano for four years at the Royal Academy of Music and, in her capacity as a pianist, has taught in primary, secondary and independent schools, and worked as a professional accompanist and coach. She has experience of orchestral management, promotion and publicity, and also sings semi-professionally.*

Some years ago, during a European tour, a well-known London orchestra was entertained at a lavish reception, held in its honour at the local British Embassy. In the course of a speech thanking the promoters for making the concerts possible, and thanking the orchestra for their fine playing, a high-ranking British dignitary went on to thank the players' employers for 'allowing them time off from their firms' to undertake the tour. This anecdote is a true one, and goes some way to illustrate the widespread misunderstanding about musicians' employment.

Music is not deemed to be a means of earning a living, and musicians are presumed either to support themselves through other employment (full-time teaching is the favourite assumption), or to live from hand to mouth, sharing a cold, comfortless garret with their fellow artists, the painter and the poet. As with most myths, there is a basis of truth in both these ideas: most musicians will spend some time teaching in the course of a lifetime, and making a musical career pay well can be a very difficult task.

Although such fictitious notions are primarily held by the uninitiated, a high proportion of music students (and even a few professionals) holds an equally unimaginative view of its future. The polarisation towards 'performer' or 'teacher' is fostered by course designations at music college, where students are labelled 'graduate' or 'performer' before they themselves have formed a clear idea of their musical goal. Even external diplomas are labelled as 'teacher' or 'performer' – somewhat ironically when you realise that the former carries no officially recognised teaching qualification and the latter will not even be considered by an orchestral management or concert promoter when you start looking for work.

The pages that follow cover more than a score of career options for those wanting to work in a musical environment. You may already be engaged in one particular area of the profession and feel like a change of direction; you may be nearing the end of your college or university course and be wondering what to do next; you may even still be at school and trying to decide if there *is* a career for you in music. Whichever it is, I suspect that the next few pages will reveal one or two ways of using your talents which you had not thought of. Some people will make their careers exclusively in teaching or performing, but the majority will derive their income from a variety of sources, most of them musical and complementary. As you flick through this chapter you may be tempted to exclaim 'No-one could earn a living from *that!*'. You are probably right, but if you take the view that your Monday morning session playing for that awful dance class pays the gas bill, your private teaching pays the rent, and doing the odd bit of copying for your former harmony teacher (who happens to be a composer) pays for all your postage and telephoning as you try to establish some playing contacts, you will be well on the way to understanding what earning a living as a musician is all about.

Performance

If you are likely to make a career as a *solo performer* you will have some idea well before you leave college. To be able to earn one's living from solo engagements is a mark of excellence awarded to few; if your name really is Jascha Heifetz II then you will be reading this purely out of curiosity. If you have not already been singled out, there is probably no sense in deluding yourself that you are an unrecognised genius. Your virtuosity may stagger family and friends, but if their opinion does not seem to be shared by your teachers, colleagues and critics in established musical circles, then you will save yourself much future pain and embarrassment by admitting here and now that your relations are biased. This does not mean you should give up the idea of solo work altogether – if you want to promote yourself to chamber music clubs, amateur and small professional orchestras, there is no reason why you shouldn't. Just be realistic about the market value of your talent when compared to everyone else's.

Much the same reasoning applies to *chamber music.* Many young musicians scoff at orchestral work and speak reverently of the rewards and purer musical values of playing in a small ensemble. To be blunt, the rewards are indeed musical and spiritual, but seldom financial. The *British Music Yearbook* lists almost 700 small professional ensembles. At a generous estimate, ten of these will keep their members in full-time work. If you scan the publicity brochures put out by the Wigmore Hall and the Purcell Room you might be forgiven for thinking that concerts of chamber music are very popular with promoters and, therefore, there must be a good living to be made. Don't be fooled: 75 per cent of concerts put on at the Wigmore Hall are financed by the artists themselves. By all means, spend time rehearsing and promoting your string quartet or piano trio with a view to pursuing as many paid engagements as possible, but don't presume to earn your living solely from them.

If you play an orchestral instrument, full- or part-time *orchestral work* will probably be one of your regular sources of income. Please don't harbour an idea that orchestral work is for those who are not good enough to make their way as soloists or chamber players: it is *not* an option for the less talented. Orchestral managements want the best players available – the reputations of their orchestras depend on it – and they will not take you if they can have someone better. Unless you are offered a job with one of the regional orchestras, you will need to introduce yourself to the freelance market. Elsewhere in this book, the chapter entitled **Orches-**

tral freelancing: making the contacts, will explain how to start, and it will be enough to point out here that your professional orchestral experience and your sight-reading ability will be at least as important as the way you play a prepared solo piece. Orchestras fall into two types, contract and freelance, the difference lying chiefly in the employment status of the players. Briefly, contract orchestras pay you an annual salary and may well deduct tax using the PAYE system (you are an employee of the orchestra and are obliged to play at their engagements), and freelance orchestras pay you by the concert and leave you to look after your own tax (you are self-employed and may accept or refuse the work when it is offered). The former may seem the safer approach, but speak to established players before you make any decisions – freelancing is fraught with insecurity but it can be financially very rewarding for a good player.

Session work, basically any commercial work involving recording equipment, is difficult to break into. It is well paid by comparison with most other playing work and is consequently an expensive business for the promoter. Persistent wrong notes or poor intonation can result in endless retakes: very boring for the players and very costly for the recording company if the session goes into unbudgeted overtime. With a microphone lurking by every stand, the culprit is easily identified and will not be asked back. Fixers are understandably reluctant to take risks, and will tend to book only experienced session players. If you're new to the profession, you're at a disadvantage unless you can secure a very positive recommendation from a player known and trusted by the session fixers. There won't be an audition: you will succeed or fail on your performance in the studio.

A source of professional musical training and employment rolled into one (and often overlooked) is that offered by the *armed services.* At present, each of the three branches of HM Forces maintains its own school of music (the Royal Military School of Music at Kneller Hall in Twickenham, the Royal Marines School of Music at Deal, and the Royal Air Force School of Music at Uxbridge), accepting students aged 16 and over, and offering training progressively from junior bandsman to bandmaster with an additional stipulated period of service once training is complete. Recruiting is primarily aimed at brass, wind and percussion players, but strings are sometimes required. The Metropolitan Police Band is based at Scotland Yard, and full-time training courses in band musicianship, independent of those already mentioned, are also run by Salford College of Technology.

Whilst all the above could be considered major sources of employment for players of orchestral instruments, pianists, singers and organists probably gave up reading at the end of the paragraph on solo work. Here are some ideas. Pianists/repetiteurs are needed by dance classes, choral societies, schools, opera companies, aerobics classes, singing teachers, audition panels, theatres, keep-fit classes, pubs, clubs, scout shows, amateur dramatic societies, talent contests, orchestras (occasionally), examination candidates, conductors, singers, instrumentalists, pit bands, hotels and restaurants. Organists can take advantage of any of the above, and may also consider church employment and continuo work (especially if they also play the harpsichord). For singers, the options are not quite so abundant, and they should read the special chapter devoted to the problems facing a young singer. As well as opera choruses, there are several professional chamber choirs (you should audition for deputy work even if you know there are no permanent vacancies) and church choirs (many city churches employ a quartet or octet of professional singers and it's worth 'getting on the circuit'), and amateur operatic societies will sometimes pay professional principals. There is oratorio work to consider, session work (a sizeable proportion of advertising jingles uses voices), and the field of light music.

Teaching

I have already mentioned that most musicians are likely to spend part of their working life teaching. Having said that, if you really loathe the idea of teaching, then don't. You may be short of cash, but it would be better to take a temporary job unconnected with music than grudgingly to coach half-a-dozen private pupils whose feeling for music will inevitably suffer from your lack of enthusiasm. (No damage need be done to your reputation if you have professional interests outside music, and a non-musical source of income can be reassuring. I can number an accountant, a cabinet-maker, a photographer, a secretary, a computer programmer and a freelance caterer amongst my musician friends, all with intact reputations as players.)

If you want to teach, the choice is wide. *Private teaching* is the most flexible, and you can opt to be itinerant and visit your pupils in their own homes (useful if you live in a garret . . .), or to open your own house and music room for lessons. You will need to organise your time carefully, since only a small proportion of pupils is likely to want lessons between 9 am and 4 pm. Most people's free time is after school, after work, or at weekends, so be prepared to adjust your own leisure time accordingly.

Since *school teaching* almost always requires specific qualifications, this is a branch of the profession about which you will need to decide in advance. The Department of Education and Science requirements are degree (or degree equivalent) plus PGCE (Post-Graduate Certificate of Education, a one-year course), or a BEd. Either option leads to Qualified Teacher Status (QTS) and no state school can employ you as a class teacher without this. (The route to QTS is different in Scotland, but still requires specialist training.) Independent schools are less fussy about paper qualifications (provided you are not fussy about Burnham scale increments), although they will obviously require evidence of academic and teaching ability. It would still technically be possible for a musician without QTS to rise to a senior position within the department. Visiting instrumental teachers, known as *peripatetic teachers,* work in several schools teaching individuals or small groups of children. This might suit those who like the idea of a full-time teaching career but shudder at the thought of a classroom full of children, and equally dislike the thought of opening their home and forgoing their privacy by starting a private practice. You are usually expected to be proficient on at least two instruments in the 'family' (woodwind, strings or brass), and peripatetic training courses will expect you to cover more: flute, oboe, clarinet and bassoon, for example. Not all schools require their visiting teachers to have QTS, and many established performers hold instrumental teaching posts. A fourth area of teaching often stumbled across by accident is *adult education*. Every local authority runs an adult education programme of some sort, split up into areas or 'institutes', each with a degree of autonomy when it comes to engaging staff. Qualifications are not of prime importance, and it is worth making enquiries about what classes are offered in music, contacting the existing tutors and finding out about the possibility of deputy work.

Administration

If you are hooked on music, are excited rather than appalled by the inevitable hurly-burly of musical life, and are an organised sort of person who realises your limitations as a teacher or performer, then you may find your niche in administration. This rather broad heading covers a complete range of work from the general director of an opera house to a junior assistant at an artists agency, and there is also much scope for working on your own. If administrative work attracts you and you can't type, learn *now* and try to cover word-processing skills as well. Efficient typing is expected in some administrative posts, even if there are secretaries around and, if you are setting up a scheme of your own, you must present a business-like image in order to gain the confidence of potential clients.

Large organisations employ telephonists, secretaries, receptionists, personal assistants, press and public relations staff, tour managers, concert managers, roadies, sponsorship organisers, accountants, programme compilers, promotional staff, librarians, managers, directors, and more. Look for jobs like these with major orchestras and festivals (those with a permanent staffed office, not those run from someone's private home), opera houses, music colleges, the larger agencies, broadcasting companies, arts centres, concert halls and funding bodies (Arts Council of Great Britain, regional arts associations and local arts councils), and the various large organisations serving the profession (the Performing Right Society and the Musicians' Union, for example). You don't, of course, need a musical training to be a receptionist with the Metropolitan

Philharmonic Orchestra but, if you can distinguish between the violinist asking about extra work and the violinist with whom the orchestra has just recorded the Sibelius fiddle concerto, then you will do the job better than someone who can't. You will also derive more satisfaction from your work.

Large companies can afford to employ all the personnel listed above. The services provided by these employees are needed just as much by small-scale organisations, but not on a full-time basis. A small orchestra will require the skills of a fixer, a publicist, a book-keeper, a concerts manager and perhaps others before it can put on a concert, and it will often employ freelance people to do the work. This is where enterprise comes in – if you can identify the need for a service within the profession there is nothing to stop you setting yourself up as a supplier of that service.

There is not space in the context of such general coverage to give details about all the possible options, but here are a few headings to whet your appetite: agency work, concert management, running a diary service, management consultancy, concert promotion, publicity, tour management, specialist secretarial work, orchestral contracting, computer services, brochure compilation and design, and many more.

One area of administration, *librarianship,* merits a paragraph to itself. This is a specialist area for which qualifications in librarianship may be required. Aside from local authority libraries which may have music sections, opportunities for employment exist wherever there is a substantial collection of music needing care and attention. Try orchestras, music colleges, universities, cathedrals, publishers' hire libraries, broadcasting companies and the commercial libraries of recorded music (knowledge of light and popular music would be an advantage here). Various private libraries (such as the Britten-Pears Library at Snape) will also require staff from time to time. Librarians usually have tidy, organised minds, and writing to match: if you don't feel you meet these requirements, then this is probably not the career for you.

The music trade

Anything connected with the manufacture and supply of goods as opposed to services can be described as trade, so this section deals with publishing, retailing, the record industry and instrument manufacture, and all the allied services connected with them.

There are three main areas of publishing to consider: books, music and magazines. *Book publishing* was one of the original 'gentlemanly' professions and, new technology notwithstanding, one can still feel an atmosphere of comparative calm when entering the offices of an established publishing house. There are deadlines to be met, but schedules are compiled over several months (or even years) rather than weeks or days. *Music publishing* has a similar feel to it if the publisher is one who deals with classical music. (The pop world is another matter – once a song establishes itself in the charts it has to be available pretty quickly.) The added bonus with music publishing is the regular contact with contemporary composers. A book publisher seldom takes an author under his wing in the same personal way that a music publisher would a composer. Book publishers will always promote a new title, but music publishers, in effect, undertake the role of an agent, promoting both the composer and his work and doing their best to encourage performances and broadcasts. They may even take some of the responsibility for arranging concerts, it being probably as much to their advantage as the composer's.

Magazine publishing is rather different and, with monthly or fortnightly deadlines to be met, it is not for the fainthearted or those who like a peaceful life with no overtime or work at weekends. The essential function of a magazine is to keep its readers informed of the latest in news, views and equipment. Offices are busy, littered with press releases, music and books for review, and the telephone never stops ringing. Work can be different for every issue, and there are interesting people to be met and press functions to be attended. Advertising tends to be a feature of magazines as opposed to books and, if you can combine hard telephone selling with musical knowledge, then you will be very tempting material for an advertising manager.

Publishing houses offer a variety of jobs, many of them

similar to those outlined under **Administration** and not requiring much in the way of literary talent. Fast, two-fingered typing, journalist style, is better than no typing at all, and it wouldn't be sensible to apply for editorial posts unless you had a flair for writing, a sound knowledge of grammar and an eye for spotting other writers' mistakes. Experience is needed for the majority of editorial positions, but the job of 'editorial assistant' is often advertised and can be an excellent training ground for more responsible work. Both the Publishers' Association and the Music Publishers' Association produce careers literature for anyone interested in this field. They include a warning as to the generally low level of salaries in what appears to be a glamorous profession.

On the fringe of the publishing world are typesetters, printers and designers. None needs to be musical, but a printer or typesetter (particularly the latter) who is musically literate can be a tremendous help to anyone producing music publications. Sheet music requires specialist typesetting and, although the use of hand-engraved metal plates is becoming less common, the job is a skilled one requiring more than a knowledge of the language of notation. *Copyists* are in great demand, as it is usually cheaper to reproduce hand-written manuscripts of new music than it is to have them typeset, and not all composers can produce sufficiently legible scores or have the time to write out all the necessary parts. Copyists are needed whenever the time-scale between the writing or arranging of a piece of music and its performance is too short to allow other forms of reproduction. Introduce yourself to composers, broadcasting and film companies, people who record jingles, arrangers, and all session fixers, and make sure they can see examples of your work.

Considered not so long ago to be a very obscure branch of the profession, *musical instrument technology* is currently experiencing a revival. The performing of and scholarly interest in pre-classical styles of music has led to a huge demand for copies of mediaeval, renaissance and baroque instruments, not to mention the perennial need for competent instrument technicians. Although training courses will take students from the age of 16, it is possible to switch from playing or teaching to a career in instrument manufacture, as all colleges will consider applicants up to the age of 35, and one or two will take even more senior people. To be a first-rate instrument maker requires more than a superficial knowledge of how the instrument is played as well as skill in wood or metalwork. Once trained, there is work in manufacture, repair, research, the retail trade, and museums (as a curator of instrument collections), and there are many opportunities abroad where British-trained craftsmen have a high reputation.

Not all aspects of *retailing* demand knowledge of instrument technology, but the same is true of music retailing as of any other branch of selling: the more you know about the product, and the more willing you are to be helpful, the better you will succeed. Few things are more infuriating in a music shop than to be served by a sales assistant who looks blank when asked for the Associated Board edition of the '48'. 'If it's not on the shelf then we don't have it', simply won't do. Running a shop requires business acumen and a strong aptitude for figures unless you can afford to pay a competent book-keeper from the outset.

In the *record industry,* musical qualifications are usually secondary in importance to technical knowledge. Clerical and personnel-type jobs correspond roughly to those in publishing and, where exclusive recording contracts have been signed, there is often a close working relationship between the artist and a personal manager who will undertake a certain amount of promotional work on the artist's behalf. The recording studio is a tightly organised world where demarcation between jobs is quite strict. Each person is in charge of one technical aspect, be it positioning of microphones or adjusting the balance on the mixing desk, but there is usually plenty of opportunity to learn from colleagues and to move around until you have a good grasp of the whole process involved in getting music 'in the can'. The record producer needs to know about the music being recorded, to know what sound he (or the artist) is aiming for and how to achieve it with the available equipment. Training courses in recording techniques are available (including a four-year degree course at the University of Surrey), but this is a field where you can still learn 'on the job'.

Radio and television

The BBC is the organisation most likely to spring to mind when considering work with radio and television, but there are also musical posts with independent broadcasting companies and with BBC Local Radio stations. The range of jobs within the BBC, or any other large broadcasting organisation, is vast, but almost all will have an element of adminstration. Unless you are already in a fairly high-up administrative position with the Corporation, you are unlikely to be thinking of applying for the job of Controller, Music, or Head of Radio 3, so the post requiring most musical knowledge for which you might apply is probably that of music producer. Responsibilities range from planning programmes to auditioning performers; from supervising a recording session to telephoning agents. Wide experience of music, coupled with organisational ability, is necessary. Music producers may have assistants, secretaries, technical staff and researchers working for them, and will need to call on the services of librarians, personnel officers and orchestral managers from other departments. Someone with a talent for writing and an extensive knowledge of repertoire and musical sources might apply for the job of Music Presentation Assistant, supplying the continuity announcers with all the material required to introduce the day's programmes.

Writing

You don't have to be a fully-fledged journalist to earn money from writing about music. Scope for full-time music journalists is limited: the number of salaried staff journalists with music periodicals and newspapers is quite small. Freelance contacts can be a struggle to build up, but there are several avenues to explore. The most essential requirement after a sense of style is experience, so try everything. Performers need programme notes, publicity and biographical material; local newspapers need criticism and feature articles; festivals need copy for brochures. Team up with colleagues to present evenings of words and music, arranging other writers' work in an anthology.

Work with disabled people

Full-time work with physically or mentally handicapped people normally requires additional training on top of a music degree. Courses are usually of one year's duration and, in certain special circumstances, it might be possible to waive the graduate requirement in the case of an experienced professional wishing to change his or her line of work 'mid-stream'. By far the best source of information, both for training and career opportunities, is the Music Advisory Service of the Disabled Living Foundation. The DLF publishes resource papers on all topics connected with disabled people, and those interested will find information on schemes such as SHAPE which employ 'untrained' professional musicians in workshops and courses, as well as details of possible employment for fully trained therapists.

Work in the community

There is growing concern in many musical quarters that the work of professional musicians is of little relevance to the lives of an increasing number of people. Concert- and opera-goers are a small percentage of the population, and there is a feeling that many more people could appreciate and benefit from the work and expertise of musicians if the opportunities were presented to them in a less formal fashion. The concept of the artist or composer 'in residence' is not new, but has largely been confined to higher education establishments. Now there is a move to widen this approach, to make more performing musicians aware of the necessity to take a broader view of their role within the community and to have a more open, less 'elite' approach to their work. Within the last couple of years, several posts of 'community musician' or 'musician in residence' have been created – not on university campuses but on housing estates, in schools, in regional arts areas – where the musician acts as a flexible 'resource' within the community. Teaching, performing, acting as a catalyst or *animateur* in locally created projects, working in schools, youth centres, nursing homes, would all be part of the musician's work. The job is as demanding and rewarding as you make it yourself, and might well embrace all the other career options mentioned in this chapter.

The concept is still very new, and there are no firm guidelines to offer those who are attracted to community work. People worth approaching for funding could be regional arts associations (many of whom now have community arts officers), local education authority music advisers, local arts centres offering a broad base of community interests, and local industry. You will have a better chance of success if you have a package worked out in advance: the people you approach may know very little about what you are suggesting and you will get nowhere with idealistic theories and woolly propositions.

Generally speaking, earning a living in the music business is hard work, especially if you are a performer, and professional musicians who are also parents sometimes do all in their power to dissuade their offspring from taking up a musical career. Nevertheless, if you are really bitten, you will have to fail very dismally indeed before you can be persuaded to try another profession altogether. With the number of options outlined above, you should be able to find at least one outlet for your musical talent. If nothing seems to suit you, might I suggest motorcycle maintenance . . . ?

'CJ, CJ, I do believe I've got it!'
'Got what?'

'SRAAMAIV'

Europes Specialist Flute Centre.

'Let's think of a name for our new Company' said the Boss to his colleague. 'O.K. CJ, anything you say' said the colleague. 'Have you got any good ideas?' 'Well', said the Boss, 'I thought we could make a name from the initial letters of all the services that we provide.' 'Super idea, CJ. How do you do it?', said the colleague in an appropriately admiring tone. 'Let's make a list'.

S ales of fine instruments, Student & Professional, from the most comprehensive range and at the best prices.

R epairs, modifications & customising to the highest standards.

A dvice and expertise from knowledgeable and experienced staff.

A ccessories of all types for your instruments.

M usic available from a collection of several thousand titles.

A ffiliated items like tuners, metronomes, panpipes, recorders etc.

I nsurance facilities for your valuable instruments.

V aluations for insurance and sales purposes.

'Great, CJ', said the colleague, showing due enthusiasm for his master's idea, 'Let's see what names we can make from those'.

'We could call ourselves...er...AARMASIV, or...hmmm...MASIVAAR, or...what about...er...VARMISAA. I know, this one's got a ring to it. What about VSMRAAAI?'

The boss sighed deeply and examined his colleague's head for evidence of the tragic accident that must surely have happened to him. 'I think', he said after some thought, 'that we should call ourselves ALL FLUTES PLUS'.

'Great name, great name CJ', came the simpering response. 'That really says it all'.

'You know', said the boss, 'I really think it does'.

'Right, CJ, leave this to me, I'll turn this into a great logo for us'. And so he did.

For all your flute requirements, come to

TALL SLUF PULSE

Europe's Specialist Flute Centre, 5 Dorset St., London W1H 3FE
Telephone 01-935 3339

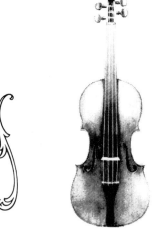

ORCHESTRAL FREELANCING – MAKING THE CONTACTS

TREVOR FORD

The telephone rang again. I picked up the receiver and gave my number. 'Hello,' said a rather cross-sounding young female voice, 'I wrote to you two months ago about work – I'm a violinist'. I asked if I'd replied. 'Yes,' she said, sounding surprised that I wasn't sure, 'and you said you would put my name on your list'. This sounded ominous. 'And I'm telephoning,' she continued, 'to see what's happening. It's been weeks now and I haven't heard from you!' I explained, as I had done so many times before, that things were quiet and that I couldn't guarantee work to everyone who contacted me. There was a pause. And then: 'How many violinists are there on your books?' I thought for a moment and guessed at five hundred. Another pause, a disappointed 'Oh . . .', a click and she was gone.

This true story illustrates the wrong way to follow up a letter and I could easily fill many pages simply quoting from correspondence and conversations which have been disastrous in the extreme. So, how should you go about making yourself known to those of us who are responsible for booking orchestral personnel? First, please remember that we fixers, like you, are human. Most of us have been, or are still, orchestral players and many of us have written exactly the same type of letter which you are now trying to compose. Generally, we understand your problems and are just waiting to be convinced that you are the genius we have been looking for.

Identifying the target

There really is very little point in making up a giant mailing list by adding together the orchestras and fixers sections in the *British Music Yearbook* and sending everyone the same letter at the same moment. An hour or two of intelligent research can save you a small fortune in postage and can also make the whole operation a little more worthwhile. On many occasions I have received five copies of the same letter, four of which have been forwarded to me from the offices of the orchestras who employ me. First, therefore, knock out the duplicates; if Sid Honeybucket fixes for half-a-dozen orchestras, you will achieve little by writing to him at six different addresses. And if he is called Sid (or John or Peter or Ann), please don't start with 'Dear Sir or Madam' as did a letter I received recently. It doesn't get you off to a good start.

Then, establish what sort of organisation you are contacting. Orchestras are, on the whole, contract or freelance and I would be inclined to treat the four London symphony orchestras as being contract orchestras for the purpose of this chapter. Additionally, many fixers only contract for commercial organisations, such as record and TV companies. Unless you are already well established or can secure a personal introduction you will be wasting your time by writing to them. The contract orchestras will usually have some sort of system for dealing with applications to get on the extras list. Often, a copy of your letter will be passed to the section principal and he will decide whether you should be called for audition. And, since they audition, they are worth writing to, even if your professional experience is very limited.

Things are quite different with the freelance orchestras. Usually, the fixer is far too busy to spend time reading your letter over and over again looking for the good points and will have to rely on your ability to show that you are already a trustworthy and reliable professional. The chances are that there will be no auditions and, therefore, there is an element of risk for the orchestra if you are booked. If you have no professional orchestral experience at all and had a mediocre career as a student, why bother writing at all at this stage? You would probably be better off waiting a few months until you have played in a few concerts and actually have something worth writing about. If you really are an absolute beginner, speak to professionals you already know, either as teachers or as friends, and try to get them to recommend you. Alternatively, see if you can play to some established freelance principal players with the same objective.

What to say

The golden rule is: *be brief*. Fixers bore very quickly. The fat letter bursting from its envelope at the breakfast table rarely reveals a list of international solo engagements but more often details of ten O-level passes (with grades) and a directory of all the pieces played by the writer since she was 12 years old. Handwritten. On lined paper . . .

Your job, as I said earlier, is to convince me that you are just the player I am looking for. Your primary school, Sunday school, secondary school, O-levels, weight-training classes and ability to crochet an electric blanket are of no interest. Equally useless is a list of conductors you have played under (anyone can pay to go on a music course and my youth orchestra was once conducted by Sir Adrian Boult), a list of orchestral repertoire (are you implying that you can only play these pieces or that we should plan our programmes round you?) and (ladies) a very sexy photograph. And don't say you are a regular extra with an orchestra which booked you once and didn't call again: we often find out.

What we do want to know is:

1 Where and with whom you studied.
2 Awards and prizes at college and since you left.
3 Concerto appearances, recitals and responsible positions while a student or after (e.g. principal second violin).
4 Professional orchestral experience. Deputising with the Sprongthorpe Symphony Orchestra is *not* professional experience. Neither is getting together with a couple of dozen unemployed ex-students. Generally, if you weren't paid for it, don't mention it.
5 What you play – guess how often you forget to tell us!

6 Where you can be contacted easily. Easily doesn't include a deaf grandmother who can't write or a permanently engaged telephone at a student hostel. If you are living with your parents, warn them that you may be telephoned at odd hours. I was once abused by a parent for attempting to telephone his daughter at 10 p.m. He hung up on me and I didn't bother to try again.

The letter

Having decided what you want to say, you now have to write a letter. On the face of it, this seems easy. In theory, I would agree. Experience has shown that many of you don't know where to start.

First, decide if you are going to enclose a curriculum vitae or if you are going to incorporate everything into the letter. Then establish to whom you are writing and make sure you can spell his or her name. Establishing sex is also a good idea. Don't use (a) ruled paper, (b) file paper, (c) torn paper, (d) paper with flowers or pictures of cats on it, (e) toilet paper (the off-white highly absorbent stuff from Woolworths). Then simply say what has to be said as quickly and as neatly as possible. I will give some actual examples of bad wording later. Don't address the fixer by his Christian name unless you really know him well. Don't say that you are an undiscovered genius or you will remain one. Don't say how brilliant you are – you might be lying.

If you have references, by all means enclose copies. Please make sure they are in English and are legible. If you are listing referees, it helps if you spell their names correctly – you will, of course, have asked their permission first. Enclose a stamped, addressed envelope; it doesn't guarantee a reply but it can help. However, an envelope four inches by three inches isn't much use. Or why not be really nice a say that you don't need a reply? If someone who works regularly for the orchestra to which you are writing (and who, preferably, plays the same instrument) has told you to write in, mention his name, but only if he is really prepared to recommend you.

Finally, 'yours sincerely' is acceptable; very few other things are. And, please, sign or write your name legibly at the end of the letter. Then check it carefully, put it in an envelope, address it correctly, put a stamp on it and post it. This all sounds terribly obvious but at least three of these last points are often neglected.

The CV

Personally, I rather like a well-produced, typed CV. It can be the most efficient way of conveying what you have to say and the reader can easily find the information he wants. However, the majority of CVs are far too long and contain quantities of irrelevant information. Go back to the list of things to say and, if you are tempted to include something which does not come under one of the six headings, think again and (usually) leave it out.

Set out your single page of A4 in chronological order with your name, address, telephone number and instrument at the top. Please don't write it like a programme biography ('she then spent an enjoyable three years in historic Vienna studying with . . .') but keep to the facts. If you photocopy five hundred and then move, change your name or decide that you have missed something out, start again. Crossings out, comments in boxes with long curly arrows spidering their way across the page and stapled-on scraps of paper are not a good idea.

Last of all, if you know you can't spell, get someone to check it for you. If you can't type, don't try – ask (or even pay) somebody who can do it properly.

The telephone call

Some people insist on telephoning, usually during lunch, mainly when I am not in the office and, inevitably, when I don't want to be disturbed. The conversation usually starts with 'You don't know me, but . . .' or with a long silence. Someone once said 'a number of people have told me to phone' and, when I asked who, couldn't think of anyone.

Unless you really have a wonderful way on the telephone, it

is usually better to write; the recipient of your letter can read it at a time which is convenient to himself but he can't choose when you are going to telephone. If you do decide to telephone, think of what you are going to say first – long silences are embarrassing for everyone. Make sure you know who to ask for, preferably by name, and then establish if you are calling at a convenient time before beginning your soliloquy. Don't stay on the phone too long. Ask if you should follow up the call with a letter.

Keeping in touch

First, don't be too disappointed if you don't receive a reply to your letter. An orchestra can easily receive five hundred letters in a year from aspiring musicians and the cost of answering these in both time and money is considerable. From a small organisation, at best a duplicated reply may be expected; many just don't answer as a matter of course. This doesn't mean that your letter hasn't made an impression.

Letters are usually filed away by instrument and referred to when necessary. This may be months, or even years, after your original communication and all your work will have been wasted if you have moved house without telling anyone. The fact that you have not had any response from an orchestra does not mean you never will and you should retain your original mailing list and update it regularly. Then, if your address or telephone number changes, you can easily notify everyone who might be interested.

A change of address can also be a good opportunity for updating your CV. If you are now working regularly for the LSO and have recently recorded a concerto with the Berlin Phil, say so (as briefly as possible), but don't send any information which was in your original letter. However, if you really have nothing new to say, don't try to make something up but just send a postcard, either handwritten, printed or incorporating a stick-on address label.

Following up your original letter with a telephone call achieves very little. For one thing, you are implying that your letter was incomplete. If you are expecting to be told what sort of impression you created, then forget it – we are all far too polite to tell you what we really thought. Don't call to complain if you aren't offered any work. There may not be any.

Diary services

Just a brief word about these. The original diary services were for session players but, in recent years, the idea has spread to the freelance orchestral fraternity. A diary service exists to take messages for you. It does not (and should not) promise to get you work. You should only consider joining a diary service when you have enough established freelance contacts to justify the expense.

A number of rather misguided younger players seem to think that the appearance of their name on a service's clients list gives them some sort of professional status. This is far from true and, in fact, the opposite can be the case. Writing to your fixer and letting him know that you are now a proud client of David Bakersmith's diary service can simply imply that you are getting no work and are becoming desperate.

If you do decide to join a service, first ask around to find the one best suited to your needs. Speak to the proprietors and see what they can offer you. Don't be talked into joining a service by offers of a sudden rush of concerts – it won't happen. Make sure that their telephone is manned at all times – I recently called one of the newer services and was greeted by an answering machine.

Once signed up as a client, make sure you can be traced at any time – don't disappear for a week without leaving a contact telephone number. Keep your diary up to date by phoning in any work which comes direct to you and also take out holidays, personal engagements and your great-aunt's funeral otherwise you may find yourself double booked. And remember to call in daily.

Getting asked back

The longed-for telephone call has come and you have a date in your book. How do you make sure that you get asked back? This, of course, depends to a large degree on the impression you create at that first rehearsal. Naturally, your technique and musical ability have a lot to do with it, but you are probably no better than a dozen others. Here, then, are the ten commandments:

1 Be on time. If you are late, the chances are you will never be asked back.
2 Make sure you can sight-read well. Rehearsal time is very limited and if we have to wait while you try to practise a difficult bit in your bars rest, we will become a little disillusioned with you. Remember that the BBC often starts rehearsing at 10 o'clock and recording by ten past. And you won't have seen the music before.
3 Don't practise concertos in the bandroom or sit in the orchestra with a book of impossible-looking fingering exercises on your stand.
4 Don't complain about being bored during the rehearsal; the rest of us have learned to put up with it and so will you.
5 Don't practise someone else's part where he can hear you – even if you think you can play it better.
6 Don't tell the person sitting next to you that he is out of tune.
7 Unless you have been booked as a principal player, don't ask the conductor questions. Refer them via your principal.
8 Don't deliberately play at a different pitch, in a different style or at a different speed to the players around you, even if you are sure that they are all wrong. They have probably been in the profession for years and may, by now, know what they are doing.
9 Be friendly, but not patronising.
10 Don't tell everyone how short of work you are. We may all be in the same position.

I hope you don't mind me writing to you like this

Finally, for amusement but really as a warning, I quote from some letters I have received. All are genuine, as is the heading to this paragraph, but I have changed names where necessary. Don't be too annoyed if you find your letter to me quoted below . . .

I would be grateful for any work, even in the Midlands. I have relatives I visit regularly up there.

Orchestras for whom I hope to work in 1986:

I am enclosing a tape of my playing some arrangements for up to four clarinets with myself playing each part. Please take the bass playing with a pinch of salt as when I recorded the pieces it was the first time that I had played a bass clarinet as I do not own this instrument. The recording machine was not of a very high standard and there is some distortion every now and then.

I recently got married and would like to have a job in an orchestra.

If you require any more information, please let me know and I will gladly fill you in.

I have practical experience of symphonic, solo and session work along with other musicians who have aspired from within the Royal Marines: Arthur Smith, Fred Bloggs and his brother George, and Bert Jones to name a few.

I am now learning Hebrew.

Dear Sir . . . Bye for now

I am now from October working in a warehouse, 27 hours for £34 per week, Mon to Fri, 11.30am to 5pm every day, so if I only had one concert per week it would be a great help although I would like a full-time job playing rather than working in a warehouse.

I also play the saxophone rather badly.

I have played for one week in Cornwall with the Southern Ballet. I was only filling in for someone who was ill. I also did one concert with the Plymouth Mozart Orchestra. I have had no work since then.

I have recently returned from overseas where I was first horn for five years.

Other posts held:
   Percussion and cello teacher, Milthorp School
   Barman, Truman 1980–81 Bass Charrington 1982

P.S. I travel well.

from a cellist I took Grades 4 5 6 7 & 8 piano and gained distinction in them all. I gained Grade 7 theory with distinction (96 marks out of 99).

I would like to offer my self as a timpenist or percussienist with your orchestra. I have all my own insruments. 3 pedal timpeny, Vibraphone, Xylophne Glok, ect.

You can phone me any morning Monday to Friday from 9am to 11am and anytime after 5.30pm also anytime Saturdays and Sundays. If you cannot get me on my phone, you can phone John Smith & Co of Sheffield and leave a message with Eric Jones a friend of mine or his office girl, his phone is Sheffield 12345 anytime from 9 to 5 Monday to Friday.

British Music Worldwide

PUBLISHED ANNUALLY

Subtitled, 'A gift from musical Britain to the World of Music', it is dedicated to the presentation of British music, opera and dance to the world. Its aim - to stimulate the employment of British people and products in other countries and to encourage artists, promoters and students from abroad to make use of facilities here.

Over 6000 copies of this A4 format book are sent as a gift to senior managers in performing arts organisations worldwide. Copies are held in the libraries of all British Council offices in the world and in the commercial posts of British Embassies and Consulates.

Its sections cover: Agents, Artists, Orchestras, Ensembles, Choral Music, Contemporary Music, Composers, Early Music, Opera, Dance, Light Entertainment, Jazz, Folk, Competitions and Awards, Venues & Promoters, Musical Education, Sound Equipment, Recording and Musical Services.

TO RESERVE ADVERTISING SPACE CONTACT MARTIN HUBER, ADVERTISING DIRECTOR, RHINEGOLD PUBLISHING LTD., 241 SHAFTESBURY AVENUE, LONDON WC2H 8EH (Tel.01-836 2535)

IN MEMORIAM: STEFANIA NIEKRASZ

Written in homage to Professor Stefania Niekrasz, President of the Association of Polish Musicians Abroad.

When candle drippings fall upon the floor
As wicks that once were long are all too brief
And sostenuto chords are heard no more,
Then, then we fill an abbey with our grief.
The Queen is gone from Court; what will become
of those proud lords whose medals made it gleam?
The polonaise, to sound the martial drum,
Mazurka's poem, etude's fragile theme?
But while we mourn, still others weep for joy
For what is great and good can never die–
The gifted girl, the talented young boy
Will some day with their anthems fill the sky.
   She's left a Royal legacy unseen;
   The Queen is gone, and yet – long live the Queen.   LARSON L. HOEL

Stefania Nickrasz / 1887-1973/, a distinguished concert pianist, a scholarly authority on many aspects of music, and an indefatigable organizer of musical life and activity in many countries, was indeed "an irreplaceable artist of world stature", and it would probably be true to say that she did more for Chopin's music than any other person in the world since his death.

Born in Warsaw, she easily gained widespread acclaim as a performer of Chopin and Polish music in general. She also founded Conservatoires at Thorn, and in Eastern Poland.

In post-war period she was the President of the Association of Polish Musicians Abroad. She established the Chopin School of Music, and in 1963 instituted the International Chopin Competition.

Due to her initiative a statue of Chopin now stands in front of the Royal Festival Hall, unveiled in 1975 by Her Royal Highness Princess Alice, Duchess of Gloucester

THE STEFANIA NIEKRASZ PRIZE

for the best performer of works of Frederic Chopin.
The first prize was given to K. Zimerman in 1975.
To fulfill the wish of Professor Stefania Niekrasz, the late President of the Association of Polish Musicians Abroad, there are plans to continue her work in helping young musicians, especially to encourage the young pianists by giving also a prize for the best performer of works of Frederic Chopin in every country. Certain projects are in mind to raise necessary funds.
Hon. Sec., 30 Eaton Rise, London W.5.

THE YOUNG SINGER
TERRY JENKINS

Terry Jenkins sang in the Westminster Abbey choir as a boy chorister and later obtained an engineering degree at London University. While studying part-time at the Guildhall School of Music, he met the director of the London Opera Centre who engaged him for Opera for All. After further study at the LOC, he worked as a freelance for many years, undertaking session work, singing in the Glyndebourne chorus and taking leading roles with the smaller opera companies.

Since 1972 he has been a principal tenor with English National Opera. He made his Covent Garden debut in 1976.

Many people setting out on a career as a professional singer have been fired in their original ambition by a natural talent. This may have been evident at school, where they acquired a reputation for 'having a voice worth teaching', or later in life, through singing with local amateur societies as a hobby. But, in considering a professional career, they will be entering a much wider pool of talent where individual capabilities might not be as great as was first thought. Indeed, if anyone were to ask me whether to take up singing as a career, I would advise the utmost caution.

Most singers enter the profession dreaming of a solo career leading to international stardom. This is quite different from instrumentalists, who generally see their careers in terms of joining an orchestra or playing in smaller groups. But every singer wants to be a soloist: indeed it is considered a sign of failure by people outside the profession (and, unfortunately, by some within it) to be anything else. A realistic appraisal will show that there are very few international singers, and that the qualities which set them apart are usually obvious. Very often, this is purely and simply the timbre of their voice; they possess a unique sound that is both instantly recognisable and is also what the public likes to hear. A Gigli or Callas can be identified by one phrase of music! If this is you, then you are indeed fortunate, for it is a quality given to very few. But there are many other ways to build a successful career and the first essential is to have a clear knowledge of your own particular talents and shortcomings. As an amateur, you can remain a large fish in a small pond; as a professional, you will never have a satisfying career if you are always yearning for the unattainable.

Obviously, the first requirement is a voice, but natural ability is not enough: a firm technique is essential. Indeed, a singer who has always sung 'naturally' can experience far greater difficulties when things start going wrong than one who has always been aware of technique. Acquiring a technique takes time, and many singers, finding the process lengthy and irksome, rush into work for which their voices are ill-prepared and then suffer the consequences. Nobody would expect to pick up a bassoon and play it instantly, but many a singer expects to do just this with a voice.

Your voice is an integral part of your whole metabolism, and when your body is not in perfect health this will be reflected in your singing. Actors and dancers often push themselves to the limits of endurance in a desire to perfect their performance, but this is a very dangerous way for singers to work. A good technique, which can also cope on those 'bad' days, is essential; but as the voice is an internal organ, it is not easy to recognise and eradicate faults. A teacher is, therefore, generally necessary: someone who not only gives advice but who also listens dispassionately to the sounds you are making which, of course, are not the sounds you yourself can hear. One needs to continue working in this way throughout one's career, with a teacher who can spot the insidious faults that creep in gradually and of which one is not aware. Conductors and coaches generally listen to the music, not the voice, and may well be unaware of these faults: they probably do not have the time or expertise to correct them and should not be expected to do so.

It is debatable whether or not there is only one way to sing correctly; what is certain is that the methods used by singing teachers to achieve this end are innumerable. All teachers employ a different use of imagery to explain to their students what they should be doing and one approach may suit one student better than another. In order to progress, you certainly have to trust the teacher you have chosen, but against this you have to balance a blind belief that the teacher is some kind of Svengali who alone knows the magic formula which you have to swallow wholesale, even though your voice is suffering in consequence. Many students get into worse difficulties through a misunderstanding of what the teacher is trying to achieve. Surely, any method of teaching should try to eradicate the stresses and strains which will eventually wear and damage the voice. Unfortunately, there are teachers who attempt to impose a quality on the voice which they like to hear, rather than allow it to develop its intrinsic individuality. Some appear to be unaware of the effect they are having. It must always be the pupil's ultimate responsibility to realise this and to make a change when necessary, although it is not always easy to recognise what is happening. Singing is a physical activity, but the effort needed has to be carefully learnt and controlled; then you may acquire the ability to sing difficult and taxing music and enjoy a long career.

It is not only vocal fitness that is important, but also physical fitness. A singing career is hard work, and you must be able to cope with the late nights and early morning rehearsals, the travel and the meals snatched at odd moments. As relatively few singers work on a continuous contract, illness can mean having to cancel work and, therefore, losing money. It can also lead to a reputation for unreliability. I have often wondered whether entertainers have bio-rhythms that peak in the evening, but recording sessions are just as likely at ten in the morning, so you must be able to cope with those as well. A factor which can limit your progress, but over which you may have little control, is physique. This is especially true in opera: gone are the days of overweight sopranos and short, fat tenors (though they do still exist!). If it is only a question of weight, then you will need to diet. Singing is not merely a matter of producing the notes: the whole manner of presentation is crucial. Two points are of equal importance: care of your body

I have already mentioned, the other is personality. One sees examples of singers with good voices and no personality at all, not just on the opera stage, but in concert and recital work. No audience wants to look at a singer who feels embarrassed and ill at ease. To communicate with an audience, you need to develop a confident manner which you can use as a basis for stylistic interpretation. This will, of course, grow with age and experience, but it is a requirement very often not given due attention by the student.

And it is this inner confidence which will help you to control nervousness. If you find the mere thought of performing makes you sick and a nervous wreck, then I would question whether a career as a performer is for you. Of course singers get nervous, but it is rather the nervousness that comes from wanting to perform to the best of their ability. You have to enjoy performing, although it is never the easy satisfaction that the public believes. Even though you are doing something you like, you will always be dissatisfied with the results you achieve.

Many singers regard the ability to read music as relatively unimportant; they somehow think it is below their dignity to be bothered with such trivia. However, you do not find many instrumentalists unable to read music. At the early stages in a career you have to seize the opportunities when they arise. If you can learn quickly – and reading music is only the first stage in doing this – this could tip the balance in your favour. If, however, you are reliant on someone else even to teach you the notes, then it could well be another opportunity missed. It is often said that people who can easily read music have more trouble memorising it. I do not believe this: memorising is boring and time-consuming but necessary, and continues right through the career. The established singer reaching the end of a career will still be learning and memorising new repertoire.

Now, how do you start to find work? People will only offer you an engagement if they know your voice and capabilities. As a student, you will meet many young conductors and singers who can help you, either by directly offering you work or by telling you of opportunities. A useful way of getting known can be to enter competitions, some of which offer engagements as prizes. Whereas it appears that virtuoso pianists need to win a competition to start their careers, the same is not true of singers and there are many successful singers who have never won a competition in their lives. But at an early stage it will be necessary to do many auditions. You will find out about these by looking on notice boards or in the musical journals. Beware of choosing only very well-known arias to sing – the panel will have heard them many times before and will either be bored or hypercritical. Far better to choose something lesser known and let them concentrate on your abilities. Foreign opera houses, however, prefer to hear familiar arias, so they can immediately classify the voice and place it in the appropriate *fach*. Never be too ambitious in your choice of arias: you will have a better chance of demonstrating your potential if you sing something well within your capabilities. It is always advisable to rehearse with the accompanist before the audition. Either take your own, or arrive in sufficient time to rehearse with the accompanist provided. Most singers find auditions daunting, and draw comfort from the popular belief that people who give good auditions give bad performances. Many of the singers at English National Opera even claim to have given poor auditions when they were engaged, so never get discouraged; but there is no escaping the fact that you will have to audition many times in order to make the essential contacts.

The more people know about you, the more chances you have of finding work. The majority of people in the profession are freelance, and obtain work from many sources: job security is a very rare commodity. Although West End musicals may run for many years, this type of work is not predictable, and the only area of guaranteed continuous employment is in a chorus – either with a major opera company or with the BBC. Ours can also be a lonely profession: travelling round the country, always working with different people, leads to many acquaintances but few deep friendships. There is a ready camaraderie working in a chorus, an easing of financial worries, and still the fulfilment that comes from being involved in music-making of a high standard. For these reasons, many people find chorus work a satisfying way to make a career. Indeed, a chorister of long-standing with a wide repertoire is probably more use to an opera company than a young soloist making his debut. There are usually opportunities to sing and understudy parts as well, and there is no reason why a singer should not join a chorus for a time to gain experience and then leave. At one time, it seemed to be a virtual necessity for all operatic soloists to have sung in the Glyndebourne chorus at the start of their careers.

Nevertheless, 'chorus' can be an emotive word. 'I'm only in the chorus' is often said with an expression of regret, as if accepting second-best. But there are many operas which depend on the choral contribution for their success: Boris Godunov and Aida are examples which immediately come to mind. Alternatively, the BBC Singers require excellent musicianship to tackle the varied choral repertoire they perform, and the small professional choirs are setting standards of performance and authenticity that have never been heard before.

Many of the London churches maintain a very high standard of choral singing through the use of professional singers. The requirements vary with each church: it may involve services during the week or only on Sundays. Some, especially the cathedrals, will have their own choir schools to sing the treble line, but there are opportunities elsewhere for women as well as men.

A lot of chorus work, however, is arranged on an ad hoc basis. This can include the need for extra choristers in the opera houses or with the BBC Singers, or session work for individual chorus masters and fixers. Most singers are not the snobs that the public, or even the critics, might expect and enjoy the versatility to be found in the musical world. Well-known, established singers will happily accept session work, whether it be commercial recording, film scores or TV jingles. Whereas, in solo work, the individual characteristics of a voice are crucial, in chorus work there is room for all. You need the ability to sight-read well and to be familiar with many different styles of music. For modern music, you will need to be able to cope with the extreme complexities of rhythm as well as pitch, although it is rare for perfect pitch to be a necessity. You will also need a telephone number where you can be easily contacted and which you can give to anyone you think may be useful.

Before starting to look for solo work, singers must have a much clearer idea of their voice: they must know its qualities, its strengths and its weaknesses. Is it light or heavy in timbre, for example? Is it youthful sounding or dramatic; is it clear and pure in tone or does it possess a vibrato; is it flexible and good at coloratura; where are the upper and lower extremes of range, and to which styles of music is the voice best suited? In these days of small, portable tape-recorders it seems surprising that most singers only use them as an aid to learning music. Although the standard of recording thus achieved is poor and not to be compared with professional quality, it can be useful to hear yourself as others do. Sometimes it will be a salutary shock! You may have a predilection for one type of music more than another and this will be where you would hope to channel your greatest enthusiasm. However, it may well be that your voice is not suited to this style of music, and then you will have a difficult decision to make. You have to face up to the reality that your talents and ambition are irreconcilable and accept a career doing what you are best suited for, rather than what you hoped for. Five-foot soubrettes very rarely get cast as Wagner heroines!

As a soloist, the whole business of agents arises. It is always useful for a young singer to have an agent: he will have many useful contacts, know of work that is on offer and have more experience of financial affairs. But the agent does not need you as much as you need him. It serves very little purpose if the agent is only collecting clients and does no work on your behalf; you can then find yourself in the invidious position of paying commission on work which you find yourself. These days, the oratorio business is not dominated by a few agents as it once was: choral societies are just as likely to book artists through personal recommendation. They are all in financial difficulties and it is wise to be flexible in the matter of fees; it is better to accept work for a lower fee than to have no work at all.

A few years ago, there were many more small opera companies than there are now; companies which could offer a young singer the opportunity to sing leading parts in smaller theatres away from the glare of national critics. Many of today's established artists learnt their trade in this way. But again, economic pressures have altered the position. However, there are still more opportunities than one might realise. A brief list that immediately springs to mind includes Opera 80 and Opera Factory, university societies, groups in various towns that use an amateur chorus, and the occasional performance in a country house. Reading the musical journals will tell you of forthcoming events and auditions, and may carry reviews of past performances.

The larger, full-time companies generally have a small nucleus of contract soloists, but English National Opera regularly uses over 100 different soloists in a season, and auditions are held all the time. Opera, of course, requires other talents than purely musical ones: it is necessary to be able to act, and this can add to the difficulties of the music. You may well be encumbered with a heavy, awkward costume and suspended on a wire! It is, therefore, wise to be cautious and only accept roles suitable to your stage of development: it would be dangerous, for example, for a young singer to sing Sarastro in the Magic Flute, as not only is the music deceptively difficult, but the whole character of the role needs qualities that only a fully mature person can bring to it. The operatic world has been a minefield for young voices, many of which take far longer to develop than their owners realise.

The BBC is probably the largest single employer of musicians in the country, offering work throughout the whole range of music. To be accepted by them, you will need to pass a rigorous series of specialist auditions (light music, for example) although personal contacts can be useful. Like the opera companies, they have departments which co-ordinate and arrange auditions. The first step, therefore, is to write and request an audition, stating the areas of work in which you are interested and telling them of your previous experience. In general, it it not necessary to make and send a demonstration tape unless you are thinking of working abroad, when it may be necessary as a first step, preparatory to going to audition in person; although there may be a delay, with perseverance they should eventually hear you as it is in their own interests to discover new talent.

Never forget self-promotion. It is soul-destroying work to write to all the music societies and local authorities listed in the

British Music Yearbook, yet it can lead to a solo recital or, more probably, to a concert with two or three other singers based on some theme – a Victorian evening or a Viennese concert, for example.

I would, therefore, advise any young singer to gain experience wherever and whenever possible; regardless of the obscurity of the music or of the venue, regardless of the fee offered, or even for no fee at all. You never know who may hear you and where. Singing is a practical occupation and not a subject over which you can theorise. To start with, you can evade the issue by simply talking of your intentions, but eventually you have to commit yourself to a performance and be judged; even the least knowledgable member of your audience will have an opinion on your performance, and why not? We are not just here to perform to the *cognoscenti*, but to anyone: as a professional, you are a member of the entertainment industry.

However, opinions on the sound of a voice are always subjective, and what one person likes, another can hate. This is just as true of managements as audiences; indeed, very few managements understand voices or even listen to them as other singers do, leading to exploitation of voices that are not able to cope. This is not necessarily management's fault; singers must always preserve their own interests. After all, it is the singer who gives the performance, not the army of advisers, coaches and teachers standing in the wings. You must be aware of your limitations and ultimately take all the responsibility – and glory!

Like all artistic pursuits, there are always more people striving to make a career than there are places for them to fill. If the caution I recommended at the outset is sufficient to deter you, then you probably do not have the commitment to succeed: if my warning simply serves to strengthen your resolve, then that can only be a good thing, for much resolve and belief in your own abilities is needed. At times, all may seem to be purely a matter of luck; you may well find other people achieving early successes which, in your opinion, they do not deserve. However, in the end, genuine talent will always be recognised.

PRIVATE PRACTICE – THE INDEPENDENT TEACHER

TANYA POLUNIN

Tanya Polunin's Pianoforte School was concerned for many years with the training of concert artists and teachers. Students of the School, from all over the world, have won scholarships to study in the USSR, Poland, Hungary and Czechoslovakia and have been finalists in many national and international competitions. Tanya Polunin was Warden of the Private Teachers' Section of the Incorporated Society of Musicians and is a founder member of International Piano Teachers' Consultants (IPTEC). She has been on the jury of BBC TV's Young Musician of the Year, and adjudicates frequently at leading music festivals.

So you have decided to teach independently, either a few hours a week, or full time; what does it take? Ask yourself the following questions and, if the answer is even a qualified 'yes' to most of them, you are in business.

1 Do you have faith in yourself as a person, as a musician and as a teacher?
2 Do you have talent, training and some experience?
3 Can you communicate easily; are you articulate?
4 Have you business acuity and organisation, or the ability to acquire them?
5 Do you love people, especially children?
6 Are you enthusiastic about music itself, and about musical skills and knowledge?
7 Are you keen to enthuse others and to pass on your joy and experience in music?
8 Have you had a thorough basic training and are you well qualified?

If you *are* in business, get going without hesitation. Much of what follows may seem complex, but it is possible to make a sound and gradual beginning with only the most basic equipment – a studio, an instrument, a telephone and a business-like approach. It is necessary to charge realistic fees (see below), and to be informed and well organised in your approach. It makes no difference whether you intend to teach for 5 or 50 hours per week.

Acquiring pupils

The best method is by personal recommendation – hard at first, but it is self-generating in time. Advertising in local papers and the musical and educational press needs to be continuous to be effective, but so can be a simple but nicely displayed card: 'Piano Tuition by Qualified Pianist'. Name, qualifications, address, telephone. One new pupil from this will pay for many insertions. Leave your professional card or printed notice in libraries, music shops and music clubs, in social clubs, schools and colleges. Playing for festivals and dancing classes as accompanist, giving recitals at local institutions, teaching part-time in a local school or college, will all help to get you known and talked about. Occasionally it is posssible to buy a teaching practice from a retiring teacher, but this often means buying the house as well as the goodwill.

A practice takes time to build up, but eventually you will reach the envious stage of being able to audition and choose your new pupils, and gently to shed those who have not the talent or industry to benefit from your specialist work.

Adult beginners

Adult beginners, or 'begin-againers', often have to trudge round from teacher to teacher until they find one who will accept them; they are brave people, pitting themselves to learn what children learn with comparative ease.

The advantages of adult beginners are that they possess
(a) a love of music which has driven them to seek lessons,

(b) a long-term view of their aims, and the patience to work and progress gradually,

(c) greater musical experience to draw on,

(d) the ability to be more outspoken about their playing, and

(e) expertise and superiority in their own fields, giving them self-confidence.

Their disadvantages are stiff muscles and inflexible joints, laborious learning of skills a child can acquire, poor co-ordination, visible and intractable nerves, and the expectation that, because they are adult, they should progress very quickly. However, their love of music is so great that they persevere, and are tremendously worth while to teach; you will learn so much from them.

Adults are often ambitious in the music they wish to study, and may have to accept a modest standard of playing at first. They frequently wish to take examinations but I would never enter an adult for an examination under about grade 5. Remember that they can be among your best ambassadors.

Your brochure or prospectus

To give accurate factual information about yourself and the services you offer, it is necessary to have a brochure or prospectus. This should be well laid out using only the most expensive paper and printing you can afford. It is desirable to look successful from the start, however diffident you may feel. Quite a basic lay-out can be used, which hardly varies, even when the prospectus becomes glossy later.

The simplest form is a sheet of A4 card or good quality paper folded in half; this gives four pages. On page one, the name of your school or studio, your name and qualifications, address and telephone number. Page two contains your musical curriculum vitae, excerpts from press notices of your work and from letters of recommendation, and brief details of pupils' successes. Do not be modest; be factual, but write in glowing terms: if you do not blow your own trumpet, no-one else will. Page three: clear descriptions of the courses available and the subjects of lessons and classes. Mention special tuition for children and adult beginners. Page four can contain a brief resumé of business terms. The fees list should be a separate insert of a different colour (which changes when new fees come into effect) stating current charges (on an hourly basis and pro rata) for consultation lessons, courses of lessons and classes. On the back of the fees list, give your business terms in full.

Setting up the practice

The most ambitious plan is a separate studio block or wing comprising a large studio, one or more smaller studios, a waiting room or area, toilet and kitchen facilities and an office. However, if you are using your house, you can have a more modest arrangement, although a studio, a waiting area, an office and facilities are essential. The studio should be seen to be a *music* studio, not a hastily or temporarily converted family room where you have to turn out the family and the cat and deprive them of TV – but a studio used only for your work, and fitted up and sound-proofed as such. The decor should be light, airy and positive with close carpeting and pleasing curtains and pictures, generally music-orientated. The best piano you can afford should be well lit, free from dust inside and out, with clean ivories. You will also need an adjustable piano stool, a footstool for tiny pupils and a strong, efficient, adjustable music stand. Amenities should include shelves for your library, tapes and records, recording equipment, a music centre and an office with a desk, filing cabinet, telephone and typewriter (learn to type!). Also have a telephone extension (with a very soft bell) within easy reach when you are teaching.

These first essentials can be expanded gradually to include the use of several studios, or a house for your School of Music. More and better instruments (two grand pianos in your main studio are impressive and practical) and good pianos in your other studios. A waiting room or hall, warm and comfortable, with music books and a table where waiting pupils can do last-minute theory or homework, and can meet and talk. A library of books and music, and a lending library for sight reading. Recording equipment, records and tapes; business stationery and a part-time secretary.

Noise nuisance

Music entails the production of sounds which may annoy neighbours, and it is important to do all you can to minimise this. In a semi-detached house, choose a room on the other side from your neighbours which has no party wall. Sound-proofing may mean only keeping windows and doors shut during practice and teaching times. Secondary glazing can be effective where there is a gap of at least four inches between inside and outside windows. Reflective acoustic panels can be used on walls and ceiling. Small rubber pads, up to one inch thick, underneath piano casters, close carpeting, thick curtains, all can help to insulate the sound. Prove to your neighbours that you have done a great deal, and spent money too, considering their comfort – state the times you teach each day and promise that there will be no music making before 8 am or after 10 pm and none on Sundays. Do not set up a practice next door to a bed-ridden granny.

It is wise to scan the local bye-laws on noise nuisance, as they can vary from council to council. Consider also the Town and Country Planning Act which designates areas which may not be used for business, and bye-laws affecting the 'change of use' of a house. A mean neighbour can report you to the council as 'running a music school' and the council is bound to investigate. It could even prevent you from continuing your business.

Business matters

For clear understanding of the terms and conditions under which you will accept pupils, it is wise to have printed agreement forms which are signed both by the pupil and/or parents and yourself; this means two copies which are exchanged after signature. Make sure these terms are under-stood by the pupil or parents, and invite questions before signing.

It is important to cover the following points:
  (a) The pupil wishes to study and the teacher agrees to teach.

(b) The number of lessons in a course (usually ten) and the length of lessons.

(c) Teaching terms according to the school calendar, with holiday breaks and public holidays.

(d) Payment of fees in advance, at or before the first lesson of a course.

(e) Notice for the cessation of lessons: notice of at least one full course to take effect at the end of that course.

(f) Missed lessons, which will be charged for unless a month's notice is given. Lessons missed by the teacher are carried forward; the pupil does not lose them.

(g) Examinations, competitions, and public performance: the teacher will not enter a pupil without the pupil's or parent's consent; the pupil will not enter an examination or competition or perform in public without the teacher's consent.

(h) Increase of fees: the teacher reserves the right to increase fees from time to time, (to reflect increasing costs of overheads and inflation and the teacher's added experience).

How much to charge

You are not a benevolent institution – you are earning your living by your profession, and your fees need to reflect a realistic return on your investment, your talent and experience, and your devotion to your work. It is essential to charge realistic fees which bear comparison to what your colleagues earn per annum at universities and schools.

When deciding what fees to charge, consider the following;

(a) The value of your talent, years of study and training, your musical and teaching experience.

(b) The fact that you will not be earning during holiday periods. Thirty to forty weeks' work has to show a profit on 52 weeks' living. No holiday pay, no sick leave, no unemployment benefit, and you must pay your own national insurance, self-employed pension and insurance.

(c) Find out what is charged by experienced, qualified teachers in your district (the others do not count).

Consider how many of them earn their full living from teaching, and *charge more*. Alright, *be* the most expensive teacher in the district. *You* know you are worth it. You might even become fashionable!

(d) Start high; you can always lower fees, but it is much harder to raise them (except as a direct result of inflation, and that is *not* progress). Start high, but remember that 'high' is relative. What do dentists, lawyers, medical consultants and solicitors charge? Like you, all have had long, arduous, expensive training. How much do you pay the plumber or electrician?

(e) People plead poverty, even when they have two cars in the family, a second home or two holidays abroad a year, and colour television. *People will pay for what they really want and people value most what costs them most.*

(f) Experience is invaluable, is worth paying for, and should be reflected in your fees. Most recommended fees are for young, beginner teachers with little or no experience.

Once you have decided on your fees, make sure you have an effective billing system and keep clear accounts. You will be respected for your strict code of business practice.

If you have an agreed code of business conduct you can then, *as a concession only*, be a little flexible if *you* feel the pupil's situation demands it. There should be no concessions regarding fees, except insofar as you, the teacher, wish to help a talented and really needy pupil by giving a bursary. Remember that it is *your* livelihood, and you can only be as generous as you can afford to be. Bill pupils in full each time, and then deduct a proportion of the bursary. It is desirable that this should be a confidential arrangement, unless bursaries are awarded by open competition.

Accounts should be sent out to arrive at least two weeks prior to the end of a course of lessons. Bill forms should also carry a resumé of the business terms relating to payment and notice.

Do not accept payment per lesson (except for single consultation lessons charged at a higher fee). Do not give lessons without prior payment, or you lay yourself open to abuse and find yourself giving presents to unscrupulous people.

Finances

Consider your finances in two stages. First, those concerning your school activities: your income from teaching, and the cost of the day-to-day running of the studio and practice. Remember all expenditure, including rent or mortgage repayments, rates, heat and light, domestic help relating to the parts of the house used for your business. Don't forget the upkeep of your capital investment, the depreciation of assets, insurance of the studio and effects.

Second, you will have to submit annual accounts to the tax-man. There are many allowable expenses for running the practice and it is wise to use an accountant from the beginning.

Consider your self-employed status and the resultant benefits and drawbacks. Consider national insurance payments and a self-employed pension. Consider insurance, house, fire and theft, and list separately instruments and valuable assets. Consider life and accident insurance, public liability, income protection; consider medical insurance which will enable you to *choose* to go into hospital in a holiday period and not lose too many fees in term time.

Running the practice

Get used to the idea, from the start, that much of your work will be at rather unsocial hours; from four to nine or ten in the evening when school children and working people are free, and on Saturdays. Many teachers take Sunday and part of Monday off, starting at 4 pm. A few adults can come during the day, and some people have half-days free.

When planning your timetable, consider the age and school commitments of child pupils, the distance they travel and their homework (Fridays are therefore popular for lessons); also the early dark during winter.

Make a timetable that is reasonable for *you,* and does not impose the strain of over-long hours, otherwise your last pupils of the day will not get a fair deal – you will have little brain or patience left.

Length of lessons can vary according to pupils' ages and

standards – 30 minutes for age 5 to 9, 45 minutes for 10 to 13, and one hour from 14 years onwards. Also consider the standard of work: to try to give a broad musical and instrumental education in 60 minutes a week at grade 8 standard is not realistic. Teachers may, and do, try to get by on less, but instruction can hardly be detailed and thorough, and we owe our pupils this. At this stage, two separate, one-hour sessions a week might suffice to cover everything.

Keep broadly to school and college terms, but there is no reason why you should not teach most pupils for up to 40 weeks a year, and this may be wise if you have a family to bring up. It is possible to have four ten-week courses of lessons a year running continuously across pre-arranged holiday breaks of, say, two weeks each at Easter and Christmas, five weeks in summer, and three separate weeks when schools have their mid-term breaks.

New pupils can begin lessons at the beginning of any ten-week course of lessons. Some teachers prefer to adhere to school terms, but they still have to live for 52 weeks – and take a holiday.

Courses and classes

The aim is a course of musical instruction and education, in the broadest sense, together with specialist instrumental instruction. 'I only teach piano – you must go to Mrs Bloggs for aural training, sight reading, theory, history, general musicianship and so on.' This is not good practice, dividing the indivisible. It took me years as a child before I realised that my classical pieces were full of cadences, or that the hymns I played at school prayers were traditional harmony . . . You need to be a jack-of-all-trades, though specialising in your main subject. If you feel you cannot teach the so-called 'fringe subjects', jolly well learn how to, at least up to a moderate standard; obviously you need educating. Only at an advanced level should you need help from specialist colleagues.

How are you going to fit it all in? The answer is with Saturday classes for much of the instruction. Groups of three to ten pupils of related standard can learn very fast, from you and from each other, and much fun can be had in the process: to the subsidiary theory, keyboard harmony, extemporisation, score reading, written harmony, part writing, chorale singing and aural work contained in the general musicianship classes I also add teachers' classes, technique jamborees, scale and study competitions, performance prizes (with outside adjudicators) at students' recitals, and progress prizes.

The courses of study need individual planning for each pupil, to suit their ability and needs and individual rate of progress.

Lesson content

Each lesson requires planning on a simple basis, with a clear idea (in your pupil's mind, too) of what you hope to achieve each term and in the long run. Each instrumental lesson can be divided into –

- (a) *Aural skills* A few minutes as the pupil comes in the door!
- (b) *Sight reading*
- (c) *Technical skills* Scales and arpeggios, exercises and studies
- (d) *Interpretation skills* How to study; study of works; performance; memory

and, for beginners:

- (a) *Aural skills*
- (b) *Reading skills, notation and timing* later combined into sight reading
- (c) *Exercises, scales, arpeggios, short studies*
- (d) *Pieces*
- (e) *Playing old pieces from memory*

If any important part of the lesson is omitted for lack of time, arrange with the pupil to *start* the next lesson with it. Punctuality is vital both for you and the pupil. Start in time and finish in time. Just 'finishing the movement' steals time from the next pupil, or runs the whole day late.

Classes should have the same organised basis, and the same main principles apply.

Performance

Encourage the corporate life of the school by getting groups of pupils to play to each other frequently, starting in groups of three or four to avoid shyness, and later developing this into a gentle criticism class where they can help each other with suggestions and get used to playing to an audience. Informal in-house competitions can foster keenness, as can recitals, with parents and friends present and, finally, the more formidable end-of-term concert, all of which is a direct preparation for the important aspect of playing, freely and easily, for other people's pleasure. Have tea and cakes and a social gathering after the more informal events and get to know something of the family backgrounds of your pupils; parents can meet and can discuss their children – and you!

You will also gain a valuable insight into how your pupils react under performance conditions and a chance to see how well your lessons in platform deportment have stuck.

Parents

Parents are ambitious for their children; it is difficult for them to think objectively, and emotional ties confuse matters. Take the parents into partnership with the pupils and yourself. Discuss aims, progress, practice, the importance of examinations and competitions and all matters relevant to the progress and enjoyment of their particular child. Do not pronounce on prospective progress until you know something of the talent and application of the child; do not patronise parents, rather, share with them. Communication is vital here, your attitude is always attentive and concerned. Occasionally, parents are not very interested in the child's music and, if so, the pupil needs extra support and encouragement from you. Arrange a time each evening when parents can telephone you – not during lessons . . .

In your business dealings with parents, keep strictly to the business code; do not be persuaded or cajoled into lowering fees or accepting late or part payment. We can all plead poverty.

Examinations, competitions, public performance: as mentioned above, there will be a clause in your business terms and agreement about these.

Regular grade examinations are a way of life for some teachers and pupils. Sadly, progress is linked to, or judged by, success in examinations, or pot-hunting in competitions. But you know better, and value them for the incentive to work and progress that they generate. Taken in passing, in the pupil's stride, they can be valuable and tangible assets, and the resulting certificate a source of pride.

A diet of examination music only is to be deplored, nor is it necessary. Keep it all in perspective, bearing in mind those examinations that are qualifying grades for O and A level or college entrance. If a child wants to enter competitions, the competitive spirit is to be realistically encouraged but certificate collecting is to be deplored and has nothing to do with music. Parents often suggest that their child *should* compete or take an examination. Discuss future plans so that all realise you are being constructive and not negative, but do not be bullied against your judgement. Some young people thrive on examinations. However, others of different temperament should rarely, if ever, do them, and should not be allowed to think themselves second class. They need to be allowed to go at their own pace.

You, the teacher, should have the final say; good results will reflect on the pupil (rightly); bad results reflect on you, the teacher (wrongly).

Qualifications and the music profession

Ambitious pupils who do well in final grade examinations often like to consider taking a diploma, or even entering the profession. Advise them to consider these facts:

Grade 8 is still an amateur examination, where the examiner will do his best to give good marks. Diplomas are *not* grade 9 or 10; they are totally different and are several years' study in advance of grade 8, and are the first professional examination. You have to *prove* to a panel of examiners that you are good enough. A diploma syllabus is also far more advanced and far-reaching in its demands. A brilliant grade 8 has little bearing on professional musician material, unless you are 12 or 13 years old – or less!

If a diploma is really desirable and, in your realistic view, attainable, then the pupil who has largely grown up within your comprehensive course can be well prepared by extending the various aspects of study towards the requirements of the syllabus. It may be advisable to ask for additional help from specialist colleagues if, say, your knowledge of history of music is not sufficiently far-reaching. Also, an adult musical approach is needed and your brilliant young pupil may take time to grow into this.

O and A level music can be valuable, but it is essential to co-operate with the pupil's school head of music and to agree how to divide the tuition. Extra time for lessons with you is essential to cover your part of the syllabus and to provide practical training as well, in the time the pupil has remaining after school work. How many hours a week does the school give to maths A level, for instance? Music will take just as many.

Your answer to 'shall I take up music as a profession?' is generally 'to be realistic, I would not advise it'. It is not a soft, easy option, it is an overcrowded profession and very tough. There is room at the very top, but not for many as soloists. Is your pupil top-class material? It is misleading to foster hopes which may lead to struggle and frustration. So many talents are required of a professional beyond just outstanding ability – above all, the determination not only to survive but also to make an individual niche for himself.

College entrance and diplomas are the first hurdle. A performing talent if you wish to teach, and a teaching talent if you wish to perform. Immense musical ability with a well-founded and developed technique and resilience are required, and a great dedication to work.

Professional associations

It is wise to belong to at least two national professional associations, one representing musicians as a whole, and one covering your special interests as an instrumentalist and teacher. Both these can give you invaluable advice and support in all aspects of your work, and even legal assistance. It is also helpful to join local music associations, clubs and festivals; these will help you to get better known and to meet colleagues.

I would particularly suggest the Incorporated Society of Musicians, International Piano Teachers' Consultants (IPTEC), and the European String Teachers Association (ESTA).

As you build up your teaching practice, gradually work yourself into a consistent organised system which suits *you*. If your basic methods are clear, sound and strict, you can afford to be a little flexible. Try to create a corporate image of your school so that pupils identify with it with pride, and younger pupils have a clear idea of how they can progress in their music.

Here, then, is a brief outline of how to set up and run an independent teaching practice. You will have many ideas to try out, but this is a method that has worked for me and for my past students for over 30 years – I, for one, have found it to be the most satisfying and fulfilling work in the world.

BRITISH MUSIC EDUCATION YEARBOOK

EDITED BY MARIANNE BARTON AND JACQUELINE FOWLER
THE DEFINITIVE GUIDE FOR TEACHERS, STUDENTS, PARENTS AND MUSICIANS

CONSERVATORIES, UNIVERSITIES, COLLEGES, POLYTECHNICS · Which course should I choose? How do the various establishments compare? Performer, teacher, administrator, instrument-maker - what options do I have?

TRAINING TO BE A MUSIC TEACHER · What kind of courses are there? Where are they and how much emphasis does each place on music? What in-service courses are available for trained teachers?

LOCAL AUTHORITY MUSIC GUIDE · What does the state system provide for music education in my area? How many orchestras, wind bands or courses are organized and what levels of ability do they require?

INDEPENDENT AND SPECIALIST SCHOOLS · Where can my child receive a specialised musical education? Which schools will waive part or all of their fees on the strength of a child's musical ability? Do the armed services offer music training?

SCHOLARSHIPS AND GRANTS · Is financial support available for music students? Where should I apply? Which universities offer scholarships?

EXAMINATION REQUIREMENTS · HOW CAN I COMPARE THE SYLLABUSES OF THE VARIOUS EXAMINING BOARDS?

INSTRUMENTS AND MUSIC · Where can I obtain instruments and sheet music produced specifically for educational purposes? How wide is the choice available? What computer music software is available for my school micro?

MUSIC AND SPECIAL NEEDS · What musical provision exists for disabled people? What courses exist in this subject? Where can I train to be a therapist?

CONCERTS IN SCHOOL · How can I get in touch with groups and soloists who offer specially prepared school performances?

MUSIC FOR ENJOYMENT · How do I go about finding a teacher? Are there holiday courses and competitive festivals organized in my area?

PRICE: £8.95 Postfree in the UK   (Overseas: add £2.50 for surface mail; airmail Europe £3.50, Outside Europe £5.50)
Send to: Book Sales Dept.,
Rhinegold Publishing Ltd.,
241 Shaftesbury Avenue, London WC2H 8EH

THE COMPOSER
KEITH CLARKE

*This article was written after a series of conversations
with the composer, Michael Berkeley.*

Meeting a successful composer like Michael Berkeley, it is easy
to fall into the trap of believing that a composer's life is a
highly attractive existence – a comfortable home, freshly-
brewed coffee and reams of virgin manuscript paper. He is
quick to correct the impression. The best advice to offer most
would-be composers, he feels, is to put them off the idea
altogether. The hard facts are that a composer will almost
certainly have to do something else to make a living – there are
very few in this country who live solely from writing serious
music – and that it is an incredibly competitive business.
Unless a prospective composer has a burning passion to write
music and cannot conceive of doing anything else, he had
better keep composing for his spare time – he may be a little
frustrated, but at least he will be financially secure.

If a student is prepared to accept this rather daunting
prospect, he or she should set out to find the best composi-
tional training available. Clearly, that depends on the student's
qualifications but, if there is a choice, it is best to find an
establishment where there is a composition professor who is
interested in the kind of music that the student writes. It is then
vitally important to acquire a really sound technique – some
sort of contrapuntal training, some knowledge of the serial
system – even if it is finally rejected completely. No-one can
break the rules with any confidence without knowing what
they are: people like Turner were great painters because they
were first great draughtsmen. So, a student should try and find
a university or college where there is a thriving composition
course and then start to organise music making with fellow
students – writing for the players immediately at hand. Often,

this is the only way to get any performances. Then, with someone to play one of his works, the young composer should ask permission to make a tape of the performance to send to suitable people. Performers usually agree, provided the recording is not exploited in any way and is just used for promotional purposes.

At this stage, it is a good idea to think about competitions. Some people have mixed feelings about them because they can sometimes produce purely competition winners rather than really talented composers. But a young composer certainly has nothing to lose by entering. An important competition is the Guinness Prize. This is a creative competition offering not just prize money but also a commission for another piece to be performed by a professional group in the following season.

However, no competition win is going to bring the commissions flooding in, and sitting in a garret thinking how awful the world is won't help much either. Getting commissions is very much a self-help process and involves the composer in establishing good relationships with players that he knows and trying to persuade them to commission pieces. The Regional Arts Associations (to which the Arts Council devolves commissioning below a certain financial threshold) will give commissions to composers so long as they are not completely unknown, and provided their works are being played by established groups who are prepared to give more than a single performance. Of course, this is something of a vicious circle – until a composer has had a performance he probably will not be offered a commission. Here is the first barrier to break through – building a reputation. The importance of the composer getting involved with players he knows cannot be over-emphasised: naturally, it carries more weight if a performer is telling the Regional Arts Association or the BBC that he thinks a composer has got something than if the composer is going round saying it himself.

If a composer really believes in himself, he will have the urge to write music with or without a commission. However, getting commissions is the aim. To summarise, therefore, the composer should persuade musicians he knows to play his pieces, arrange to put on concerts, try to get a reasonably important venue for the first performance, and follow it up with two or three subsequent performances. Then he should write to his Regional Arts Association and ask for an application form for a commission. If he is unknown to the association, he should obtain some references from well-known musicians or teachers.

It is pointless approaching orchestras in the hope of receiving a commission. Nowadays, it is possible to find that an orchestra is not playing a single work by a living composer in an entire season, so the chances of their commissioning something from someone they have never even heard of are not worth mentioning. However, it may be worth his while approaching a festival, especially a small local one, with the idea of their putting on one of his pieces. Composers should get to know local people and be flexible in their approach to what they want to write – it may be useful to start by composing something for local children to perform.

Composing music for musicians with whom the composer is acquainted suggests that there is little point in producing huge orchestral pieces – the chances of getting them played are remote. It makes much more sense to start off on a fairly modest scale and hear the results, learning from experience. One mistake that many young composers tend to make is to write too much music; it is better to restrict the output and write for the forces available. Let us suppose that a composer is friendly with a gifted clarinettist and has persuaded the Regional Arts Association to commission a piece. The next thing is to try to make sure that the clarinettist takes the piece around on several performances. At that point, the composer should try to get the BBC interested, telling them about the performances, sending them a score, and asking whether there is any possibility of a producer coming to hear it. Composers living in the regions should write to the senior music producer in their area, again asking if a producer can come along. And no composer should ignore local radio; sometimes that can be an easier opening. For one thing, local radio cannot afford large-scale pieces and is more likely to be interested in chamber works, which is what a composer will be writing at this stage. For another, local radio producers are usually quite keen for items of the 'local boy makes good' variety. The composer should use his wits a little: not just ringing up to say he has a new piece which he would like broadcast, but trying to find an angle that makes it interesting to them. Perhaps he has set words by a local poet, or maybe local people are involved in the performance – it pays to try and think in advance about how a producer could put together an interesting item about the piece.

How a composer makes a living while all this goes on is really up to him. Some people like the idea of working in a university or of teaching; others try to get into music journalism or broadcasting. One or two write film music, jingles and commercial music. Whatever the choice, the composer is going to have to think of himself as a slightly schizophrenic character, partly making a living and partly writing music.

Film and television music are among the most exclusive areas. Everybody would like to write a movie score but film directors tend to use people they have used before. By the time they get round to thinking about the music they are often at their wits' end, facing all sorts of problems and financial pressures; they need someone they know they can rely on to write the music at short notice. The only way into this field is by getting to know the people who work in it, and the same applies to music for radio, television and commercials.

A composer may *never* make enough from composition to support himself. Even if he is lucky enough to win a commission (unless it is for some huge orchestral work) he is unlikely to be paid more than £2,000 and can hardly live off that, especially as he is not likely to be offered more than one commission in a year. The sensible attitude is to reconcile himself to doing something else to start off with, and then be very pleased if he ends up making enough money from composition to live on.

While he is doing something else to support himself, it is very important that the time left for composition is carefully structured. A composer has to be very disciplined about this – there must be certain times when he is always going to compose. In Michael Berkeley's case, he keeps the mornings for composition, and any other work – broadcasting or writing scripts – he tries to save for the afternoons. If there is any time left over, he sometimes does some scoring in the evening. Very few composers are able to write solidly all day without a break; composing is physically exhausting work. That is one reason for keeping the mornings for writing – it would be difficult to do a day's work and then try to write afterwards. To start with, a composer might have to get up early and compose for just a couple of hours a day before leaving for work and then try to do more at weekends. One thing he must never do is to give in to the feeling that he has no ideas on a particular day, that the inspiration is lacking. If that is the case, he should work at something regardless, even if he later decides to reject it. Until the composer makes himself sit and work, the ideas prob-ably will not come. If he waits for the god-given moment when suddenly the rainbow appears and heavenly choirs start singing, he will probably wait for ever and never finish anything. Most composers agree that one of the hardest things is being selective and throwing material away. Com-position has to be thought of as a job of work which is done between certain hours, irrespective of how full the waste-paper basket is at the end.

Young composers should always aim to produce clean, tidy scores, written in pen with ruled bar lines, and completely intelligible to a conductor. Nothing is more likely to put people off than something they can't decipher, especially as most contemporary music is quite difficult to hear in the head from looking at the score anyway. If it is difficult to read, it will just go straight to the bottom of the pile.

Another huge benefit of producing tidy scores is the possibility of their being published in facsimile form, a method very much in favour with publishers these days. It is more in a composer's interest that the music should be circulated and played than that huge expense should be incurred in setting it in print. The popular image of a composer covering the manuscript with illegible scrawl in a frenzy of inspiration no longer holds true. These days, most composers take a pride in the way the music looks, and many produce scores that can be used in performance. Any would-be composer who fails to see the importance of this is going to have a tough time.

Producing scores from facsimile is obviously a much cheaper process, and this is especially relevant to composers who want to try self-publishing. Getting a publisher to take on new composers is quite difficult at the moment, most having fairly full lists. Self-publishing is a natural solution, and is quite feasible. Additionally, when the music is performed, the composer receives all the royalties, but he will have to be prepared for a lot of administration, including getting all the parts copied and sending them out. As far as copyright is concerned, once a composer has written something and put his name to it, that is his copyright. But, for someone who is self-publishing, it would probably be wise to lodge copies somewhere like the British Music Information Centre so that he can prove that the music was his from that date. Clearly, there is more to self-publishing than simply taking the music to the local print shop and getting some copies run off and it is a venture that needs careful consideration. The Association of Professional Composers has issued a guide to publishing which goes into all the advantages of finding a publisher and self-publishing.

A composer who is determined to get on to a publisher's list should send in scores and, ideally, get recommendations from established musicians. If the composer has a performance of one of his works coming up, he should see if the publisher will send someone along to hear it. It is most important not to be put off: many publishers will say that they are quite interested and want to see how the composer develops and simply ask him to keep in touch. This is worth pursuing; new composers cannot expect to be taken on at once. If a composer is accepted and has produced good clean scores and parts, he can probably work out a reasonably advantageous deal to cover the costs that he has put into the music. Of course, it is easier for a publisher to promote music than for a composer to do it himself.

When it is so difficult to find *any* publisher it may seem hair-splitting to talk about finding the *right* publisher, but it is an important consideration nevertheless. Most publishers have a composers' list with a specific emphasis, and it pays to do some homework by studying these lists and getting a feel of the kind of composers that may interest them.

There are several organisations that can help the young composer. If he has got to the point where someone may have heard of him, and people are beginning to talk of him as someone who has a certain gift, then players or festivals which may want to produce his work can apply to the Regional Arts Associations for financial help, or direct to the Arts Council if the piece is substantial. The Composers' Guild of Great Britain and the Association of Professional Composers are two bodies which are certainly worth joining once a composer has begun to establish himself; there is an annual subscription and a small percentage of royalties to be paid up to a certain maximum, but they are well worth the money. These two organisations argue composers' cases with the BBC, the Performing Right Society, the Musicians' Union, the Arts Council, orchestras and so on. They also send out information which can be very useful for someone who is just starting, including details of competitions and of people who are looking for a composer to set words for them. The Composers' Guild is the older organisation and has quite a large clientele. The APC has a stronger commercial membership, including many film composers. It was set up to promote composers' rights from a different angle, to be a little more hard-edged, and its selection procedures are slightly more rigorous than those of the Composers' Guild. It is a good idea to get details from both groups and see which one is appropriate – there is nothing to stop a composer being a member of both. Certainly, if he wants to be part of the composers' movement in this country, joining one or the other is essential.

The Society for the Promotion of New Music is another useful body. It has a wide-ranging panel which regularly reads scores, and anyone can submit works for consideration. The Society also mounts performances of new works. The BBC has a reading panel, too, but there is a long wait before the composer hears if the piece has been accepted and then there is another lengthy interval before it is broadcast. Acceptances fall into two categories. In one, the BBC offers to broadcast the work if it is performed; in the other, the BBC will promote a performance itself. The second option sounds preferable but, in practice, the piece will usually be broadcast sooner if the composer can set up a performance himself. There is a third way on to the air if a composer is lucky enough to know a producer who will argue fiercely on behalf of a piece he believes in but, generally speaking, the reading panel is the best bet.

There are a few trusts which can help young composers. It is difficult to be precise about them because their objectives tend to change, but certainly it is worth keeping an eye open and seeking out information at local libraries. It always pays to be curious.

To sum up, there are two important things to say about composition. First, a composer should realise that he is probably going to have to make a living in some other way. Second, he must believe that composition is something without which he just cannot live. If he decides he simply must devote his life to writing music, he should just be himself, be honest to his voice and not jump on a band-wagon. It is often imagined that composers fall into two categories: those who have a wonderful technique and those who don't, but those who have a voice of their own and can actually say something in music are the ones who stand a chance of success. The technique can follow, but no amount of technique will make up for a lack of talent or individuality.

All in all, it is quite a bleak picture, and it would be very unfair to try and paint it any other way. Composers have to reconcile themselves to a really hard life, hours and hours on their own, constant ups and downs. They have to learn to cope when someone writes something unpleasant about them. But, while it may all sound very depressing, it can be a wonderful way of earning a living. Anyone with a strong-enough character to deal with the problems should not be put off. If he has a voice, he should let it be heard, even if it is a long time coming. Michael Berkeley's father, Sir Lennox Berkeley, was really an amateur musician until he went to Oxford where he read French. It was there that Ravel went one day to receive an honorary doctorate and Sir Lennox, because of his knowledge of French and love of music, was deputed to take him round. He seized the opportunity of showing Ravel one or two of his pieces. Ravel said that they were very good and showed promise but he thought that a proper grounding was needed and suggested that he should go to Nadia Boulanger. This he did, and Boulanger would not let him write a note of his own music for a year or two but simply counterpoint and nothing else. It is not the end of the world to be a late developer. Becoming a composer is something that can happen in all sorts of ways – a person *can* change direction in mid-stream and become a success.

Whether a composer finds his voice early or late, if he is prepared to do all the spadework then good luck to him. But he should go into the profession with a realistic idea of what it is he is taking on.

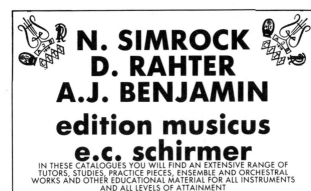

FORMING AND RUNNING AN ENSEMBLE
ODALINE DE LA MARTINEZ

In 1976, Odaline de la Martinez, together with the flautist Ingrid Culliford, founded Lontano, *a chamber music ensemble committed to the performance of twentieth-century music. She is also a prominent composer and conductor.*

Almost anybody can start an ensemble. All you need is good players, a bit of organising, a few good press reviews and you're off . . . Well, not exactly. *Starting* an ensemble is not so difficult, but keeping an ensemble going requires persistence, courage, creativity, enterprise, belief in what you're doing and endless sacrifices. A lot of input, I know, but if you are successful it can also bring a great many rewards.

However, there are several mistakes that one can avoid from the beginning and, if one learns a few tips early on, then one has a better chance of survival. Here are some of them:

Finding the players

Finding the right players for an ensemble is not an easy task. No doubt you've worked with several people and found out that you work better with some than with others. But, whatever you do, *never* choose players because they're your friends. If they're good players and happen to be your friends, that's fine, but when you're giving a concert or making a recording, you want to feel confident and play well, and not worry about the mistakes of the 'friend' sitting next to you.

If you find early on that someone whom you thought was good has not developed as quickly as the rest of the ensemble, don't let it pass by. Talk to him in private and discuss the situation; give him a chance to improve noticeably over a period of time. However, if that member doesn't get any better, sort it out early on. The longer you leave it, the harder it is to remedy the situation and you may well end up with a weak link in your ensemble. Remember, if you try to cover up for the weak player or pretend there is no problem, you will harm the ensemble, not help it.

Forming an organisation

When forming an ensemble, open a bank account using its name. To do this, you must have some sort of document which shows that the ensemble exists. Do not deposit cheques for concerts in the account of one of the members of the ensemble because it may complicate that person's tax return as well as making him liable for VAT registration.

It is important to have a document that says you exist. My advice is to form a *company limited by guarantee*. It is also advisable either to turn the ensemble itself into a charitable organisation or to form a charitable organisation which, among other things, will sponsor concerts by your ensemble. Let me first explain something about two terms which I have just used:

(a) A *charity* is usually a non-profit-making body. Having charitable status is an important requirement if you want to raise funds for putting on concerts. The Arts Council, for example, will probably not consider your ensemble for any grant or guarantee against loss unless the body making the application is a charity. Other grant-giving bodies also prefer giving money to charitable organisations, although it is not a requirement. Also, charitable foundations are quite often required by the terms of their deeds to give to charities only.

(b) Becoming a *company limited by guarantee* means that if, due to unforeseen circumstances, the organisation incurs debts beyond its means, then the individual members are not personally responsible for those debts. In this day and age, when sudden turns of fortune can occur, it can be very wise to take such a precaution.

Both forming a charity and a limited company cost money and require the services of a knowledgeable solicitor. If possible, employ a solicitor who has formed a charitable organisation before. In addition, if you know of a charity with aims similar to yours, you can get a copy of their deed by requesting it from the Charity Commissioners. However, a word of warning: the definition of a charity is looked at every few years, so to get a deed from a charity that has been formed recently.

VAT

At the present time, businesses whose turnover is greater than £20,500 a year are required to register for VAT. (This is the 1986 figure and it tends to increase with each new tax year.) Performance of music is considered a VATable service and, therefore, if your organisation's turnover nears this amount, you should consult your accountant about registering for VAT. If you don't have an accountant, ring your nearest VAT office; they are very good about giving advice on the telephone. Grants from the Arts Council of Great Britain, the British Council and other bodies are 'exempt'. So, for example, if in one year the organisation received a £4,000 grant or guarantee against loss from the ACGB and earned £19,000 from concerts given for music societies, the £4,000 received from the ACGB would not count towards the VAT limit. However, grants from other organisations may not be exempt and, therefore, you and your accountant should keep a close watch on your turnover totals. Don't take this advice lightly: if you go over the limit for a period of time and fail to register, the likelihood is that the VAT office will find out either when you eventually register or via the ensemble's tax return. Not registering when required means that your registration can be back-dated and you are liable to pay VAT from the date *on which you should have registered.* VAT registration require- ments have been toughened in the last year and those who hired you before you registered are not required by law to pay your back-dated VAT. In the early years of an ensemble, failing to register for VAT on time could do terrible harm.

When one is beginning one's career in the music business,

the amount of time spent trying to get work and money for the ensemble is incredible. That doesn't even take into account all the time spent organising the concerts, booking the players, and *practising*. At the end of the day, the last thing anybody wants to do is work on the books. However, a few minutes (or hours) spent every once in a while keeping an up-to-date account of what has come in and gone out of the account is very valuable. If you're absolutely hopeless with figures, then it's worth paying a little money every week to employ someone who knows how to keep your books in order. This must be better than having to pay hundreds to your accountant for putting your annual accounts together from scratch!

How to promote your ensemble

There are many ways to do this. In the early days, you probably want to attract the right kind of attention and the best way to do this is to put on interesting concerts of a very high standard. 'That's fine' you say, 'but how do we tell the world we exist?' In other words, how do you get the press and general media to mention and review your concert?

There are two ways of getting attention. One is to make a big splash: put on a programme with something interesting in it (a newly-found work by a well-known master, a newly-commissioned work by a British composer, the revival of a lost or neglected masterpiece, the UK or European première of a foreign work) or employ a big-time soloist or conductor. This will give you the limelight for a while but, when you run out of ideas, you run out of splashes. The other way, and the more solid way, is consistency. Be consistent in your quality of programming, balancing programmes of classics with interesting new ideas, featuring some of the most outstanding members of the ensemble and being innovative with what you offer. Don't try to do the same thing that brought somebody else attention because, by the time you do it, it will be old hat. Always provide and aim for the highest performance standards. Consistency coupled with innovation can go a long way.

Publicity is very important when beginning to build your

audience. Adopt a logo for your ensemble. Compile a list of magazine, newspaper and media people who would be likely to mention your concert and send them a press release at least four weeks before your performance. Print a leaflet. At first, your means will be modest, but that doesn't mean your leaflet cannot be attractive. Send leaflets to your friends and anybody else whom you think might be interested in coming.

There are many mailing lists which you can buy into. In contemporary music, there is the Contemporary Concerts Co-ordination mailing list together with their music diary, which lists all the twentieth-century events in London each month of the year. Magazines like *Classical Music* will enclose your leaflets in their subscription magazines for a fee. Virgin records is now sponsoring a fortnightly musical events diary, published by Rhinegold, in which you can buy an entry for a very reasonable price. There is also a relatively cheap way to get your leaflets around town: get someone to spend one or two afternoons visiting the colleges, universities, hotels and libraries and leaving your leaflets there. However, make sure that you don't do it just *once:* the leaflets have to be replenished and, if you carry sellotape, blue tack, or drawing pins, you can display them in useful places.

Don't be afraid to sell group tickets at lower prices. An audience that looks healthy is good for the morale of your players. There is nothing more depressing than playing to an empty house! You might wish to advertise in the newspapers, although personally I don't think that it makes much difference to your audience.

Agents – pros and cons

Many young artists coming out of college think that, if they don't get an agent right away, they will never have a career. I don't agree with that at all. You can be lucky and get a manager or agent who will push your ensemble and get work for you *or* you can end up as just one of many ensembles represented by an agent and something may occasionally filter down to you because the better-known artists were too expensive for the interested promoters.

Agent or no agent, the best way to generate work is to do it yourself. Have a good-looking brochure of your ensemble produced and send it to the many promoters here and abroad. The National Federation of Music Societies publishes an annual directory with the number of members each society has and contact addresses. You can get lists of arts centres and music clubs from the music officers of each Regional Arts Association. The Arts Council also publishes a book of music festivals with dates, descriptions and names of festival directors and organisers. Also, do not underestimate the *British Music Yearbook:* the amount of information it contains is incredible! Brochures, postage and all publicity is *tax deductible* – take advantage of it. Whenever I feel lazy about mailing publicity material, I always say to myself 'if you send out a thousand brochures and one per cent of the music promoters come back to you, that's ten gigs'. If you keep tabs on your mailing costs, you will see that sometimes even *one* concert can pay for all your mailing. That is what I call a good return for the effort involved!

Another possibility, and to me a very good one, is to have an administrator; he is either paid commission or for so many hours work plus expenses. Of course, if you're just starting out, you won't be able to hire an administrator, but there are a lot of people out there who are trying to get into arts administration and who would love to have some experience. You never know, they might agree to help you out as long as you pay their expenses. However, my best advice is to put a lot of work into it yourself: you can learn a lot about the business so that, when you do have enough money to pay someone, you will know exactly what kind of person you are after and how things can be done. Remember, when you are estimating how much money to charge for a concert, always budget an extra ten to twenty-five per cent to pay for administration costs. You'll be surprised how much money you can spend on telephone bills, music, and postage.

Scores, parts and props

Any performing ensemble will play from music that it will

either hire or buy. During your student years, you might be able to borrow music and parts from the college music library. However, once you leave college and no longer have this facility, you will have to buy scores and parts. The question is, who buys the music? You might want to start a fund for the purchase of music which will belong to all of you. But, of course, what happens when someone leaves? Do they take part of the music or do they get a refund? My advice is to arrange for the music to belong to the ensemble. When you prepare a quotation for a promoter, always add on a small amount for music purchase and, if music has to be hired, let them know how much it is in advance. If you didn't have to spend any money on music purchase because one of the players already owned the parts, use that small amount saved towards buying more music. The owner of the parts may want to use them with another ensemble and your bowings, fingerings, and other markings might be erased; or the player may leave your group. Always try to have a set of parts that belong to the ensemble, not the players. Then you will always be able to go back to the markings on the parts and save rehearsal time *and* a few headaches.

With small ensembles, it is perfectly acceptable to ask the players to bring their own music stands. They usually own at least one which they use for practice and, if they put their name on it, there's no reason why it should get lost. There are certain pieces of music where you need props which are an essential part of the performance but are not necessarily for playing. Examples are works like Peter Maxwell Davies' *Eight Songs for a Mad King* where an extra fiddle (to be broken as part of the work) is required. Sometimes, ping-pong balls to throw inside the piano or wine glasses which are rubbed to create a whistling sound are needed. Again, I think it's better if they belong to the ensemble. These objects, together with scores and parts, should be kept in a 'library'. In the early days, one of the players should be happy to be librarian. Later on, as the ensemble grows and becomes busier, the job can be assigned to the administrator (if he has any spare time) or to a part-time librarian.

A final word

By this time, you may have realised how much time and
money it takes to run an ensemble. And, above all, how much
sacrifice. But, if you stick to it and do not become discouraged,
you can survive and even begin to do well. Just remember, you
are not competing with anyone but yourself. Concentrate on
your own work. Believe in yourself and what you have to
offer. Don't worry about anybody else. If you're too busy
looking around, you might miss your own goal.

Building the Future On the Past

"Master instruments by master craftsmen" has been a Yamaha trademark for a century. Since 1887, skilled artisans at Yamaha have been crafting outstanding instruments that are recognised as masterpieces all over the world.

The superior quality of Yamaha is the result of experience and dedicated craftsmanship combined with technical expertise. Highly trained engineers, skilled craftsmen and gifted musicians work together to produce the finest possible instruments. Traditional skills are enhanced by scientific excellence and musical artistry. We build the future on the past.

SECTION 2:
BUILDING A CAREER

FIRST IMPRESSIONS:
THE SOLO CAREER
MICHAEL KAYE

Michael Kaye was director of the Peter Stuyvesant Foundation and the Rupert Foundation from 1961 to 1976, and managing director of the London Symphony Orchestra until 1980. Subsequently, he was appointed general administrator of the South Bank Concert Halls and artistic director of the Greater London Council. Since 1983, he has been general administrator and director of the Young Concert Artists' Trust, and is also director of the City of London Festival.

Although the transition from studentship into professional performing is very difficult – perhaps never more so than today when many promoting bodies are in financial difficulty – it is, nevertheless, a leap that many do make successfully. It demands a high level of performance skill and the ability to communicate to an audience – not necessarily the same thing – but the major problem for the young performer lies in getting the goods to market. And that means finding out what the market is, and where it is, and what it wants.

I make no apology for reducing the subject to marketing terms, although of course there are other important aspects, and we shall return to them later. But at the first crucial stage, that of securing work, what is called for is a clear assessment of one's advantages. Then follows a consideration of how to deploy them. Last, but equally important, one must have the initiative, energy and determination to do what is necessary in a lively and co-ordinated way, and to keep on doing it for as long as it takes.

All this need not be quite as daunting as it sounds, and I shall try to break down the plan of action into manageable components. Nevertheless, the crucial question that must be answered at this early stage is whether the artist is prepared psychologically to tackle the whole issue of self-promotion and self-selling as a commitment that may last quite a long time. There must follow the understanding that a lengthy campaign requires the proper material and preparation. It is better to spend a few weeks on these preliminaries than to start off in a random or unco-ordinated way. There is, after all, no reason why at least some of the steps should not be taken while the artist is still in full-time study.

Let us look first at the intended market. While a very small number of artists will make an effortless transition to the big time by winning a major competition and being snapped up by an important concert agency, it is not these we are concerned with here. Therefore, we are not – primarily – aiming for securing concerto or solo performances with major orchestras, here or abroad. Rather, we are directing our approach to music clubs and societies up and down the country, to every type of organisation offering a chance of performing – Live Music Now! lunchtime concerts such as those organised by the Royal Festival Hall, Barbican and many regional halls, young artists platforms, concerts in stately homes, and so on . . . and on.

Rather than attempt a definitive list of these possibilities, which could only be correct at the time of writing and would rapidly become out-dated, it is more helpful and realistic to advise constant alertness to what is going on. Make sure you get one or more music magazines on a regular basis, and read everything systematically to see what is happening at lunchtimes and during the day. Study every item of literature that comes your way – National Trust leaflets, giving details of concerts in Trust properties; stately homes material; concert hall programmes (and not just the big ones); SPNM material; festival prospectuses. Pay an occasional visit to your local library – and others – to see what leaflets they are displaying. Do not pass a wayside church without at least a glance at the notice pinned to the tree by the entrance: one sees surprisingly distinguished names figuring thereon! More important to us, of course, is the context in which they are appearing: where? when? every Tuesday? every other Sunday? who is promoting the concert?

How should one deal with the information so gathered? As I shall emphasize the importance of being systematic, let us start right here by advising the keeping of an orderly note-book of references. It goes without saying that you will be keeping a diary, with clear and unambiguous entries of possibilities, pencillings, firm engagements and fee agreements, if any. Yet some artists, surprisingly, do not, and without exception suffer from the deficiency. It is almost equally important to maintain a careful record of leads and the sources from which they are picked up. Perhaps I can illustrate the importance of this point by giving an example of a concise and fully informative letter of approach to a concert organiser:

> I have pleasure in enclosing my personal details and repertoire and I would be grateful if you could consider engaging me for a recital in the lunchtime series you are planning for next season in the crypt of St. Dracula's Church. Mr Thistlewaite, who is on your committee, heard me perform in the early evening series in the Mae West Theatre foyer last week and suggested I should approach you.

This is so much better than a telephone call which, as luck may have it, will often arrive at an inopportune moment.

This illustration will also serve to highlight a few other important points. First, always put yourself in the position of the person you are approaching, and ask yourself what he or she will want to know. Second, always sound and look well organised and efficient, without giving the impression of aggression and bossiness – or even being too smart for words. Third, do not try to carry out business by telephone that is better conducted by letter. The concert promoter, for all you know, may, on any given day, be trying to cope with artists cancelling, his hall burning down, or a child with measles. Your letter, supported by appropriate printed material, will be welcomed or, at the very least, read and filed. One hopes it may be answered, and perhaps positively. Your telephone call will usually result in an invitation to send your details anyway. I know it is easier and cheaper to lift the telephone, but take a moment to consider: your reluctance to marshall the facts in your favour puts on the organiser the obligation to put pen to paper, perhaps on the back of a handy envelope that may go astray. If you are listened to, you will not, in the course of a reasonably short telephone call, be able to say everything about yourself that should be said, and you will not be able to show how attractive you look at the harpsichord! Why put yourself at a disadvantage to start with?

All this leads to a consideration of what printed material should accompany a letter of application. As a general rule, it need not be expensively or lavishly produced, but it should be distinctive, well laid out and well printed, and on decent paper – preferably a rather heavy stock. Flimsy sheets are too easily overlooked in the voluminous files that organisers rapidly build up, and often they do not take print and illustrations successfully. I am not unrealistic – I know that expense is a major consideration and that the cost of good print design can be very high. But perhaps you know someone who is studying typography or graphic design who can give you a hand, and who may know a printer who can be relied on to do a conscientious job at a reasonable price.

Include a good photograph in your leaflet: not, please, one taken on an *instamatic* in the back garden on the first sunny day of spring. Take a deep breath and pay to have a good set taken by one of the photographers who specialise in musical portraits. Ask the photographer to avoid heavily over-dramatic effects and, particularly if you are young, excessive use of soft focus. Try to get photographs which make you look alert, unpretentious, charming and (a bit!) artistic. And don't be the final judge yourself; we all have a preconceived idea of what we look like, or want to look like, which does not necessarily reflect either reality or what the world is seeking. Check the results with your friends, rather than your family, before deciding which of the proof set to choose for use.

Your leaflet should obviously present all relevant information, particularly prizes and scholarships and competitions you have won. It should include reviews, but beware of quoting ones which are not likely to impress but may, indeed, have the reverse effect. A quote from a *Times* or *Telegraph* review of a concert, even if only one in which you were a component rather than a star, is useful: an extract from an unknown local free-sheet comparing you to Callas or Horowitz (or both) is not.

The run-on costs of printing are an attractive trap which should be avoided. Typically, it will cost, say, £50 to produce 250 leaflets and only £75 to print 1,000 because the initial typesetting and plate-making charges are covered. Resist the temptation to go for the larger quantity if you are not certain of your plans or where you are going to be living in three months' time. Old print material easily gets a tatty look before it is used and rapidly goes out of date. Your repertoire may expand; you may win more awards; your address and telephone number may change. Certainly, promotional litera-ture amended by pen and modified by stick-on labels is unimpressive. Avoid such expedients if you can. One way of doing so is to embody changeable information in a covering letter, as far as possible. On the same topic, reviews or extracts are better dealt with on a separate photo-copied sheet, so that they can be constantly updated. It is impossible to over-emphasise the importance of this point, for good reviews are independent testimony to your claim to be an artist worthy of engagement. They are what good references are to a job applicant. Finally, make sure that the style of presentation of your leaflet is attractive and that the copy is easy to read. Avoid busy, indigestible paragraphs. Highlight salient points, such as the winning of important scholarships or awards.

To whom should the artist send this attractive material? It is not too difficult to build up a very large mailing list based, let us say, on the total membership of the National Federation of Music Societies, the British Arts Festivals Association, the Association of British Orchestras' membership list, and so on. But let us be realistic. The cost of a mailing of this scope, which can easily run into two or three thousand addresses, is high. Also, these bodies receive many such mailings every week. Of course, if you fire enough shots you may eventually wing a bird, but the volume of work and the costs entailed in an operation of this size are likely to daunt most people, and a comprehensive job which is not completed or carried out carefully and thoroughly is beaten every time by a more considered and selective approach that is well and truly followed through.

The artist should consider first what factors are on his or her side. Consider, for a start, locality. It is demonstrable that, for example, a Yorkshire artist will command a sympathetic initial response from societies in that county. This local patriotism seems to get stronger the further one goes from London. Did you win an award in Tunbridge Wells or in Truro? That might be a useful starting point. Reflect, also, that no-one starts down this road totally without history. You have recent fellow students, tutors, professors, judges who may have heard you in auditions or competitions, or people you have met while taking part in master-classes and who may be directing a festival. There are appreciative people (whose names you noted as soon as possible thereafter) who came back to congratulate you after your final college performance. All these should be sent your literature. While at college you may have taken part in chamber music recitals or opera performances. Maintain contact with your fellow performers and with the conductors and repetiteurs. Above all, be around, be seen, keep in touch.

It may be that it will take some time, perhaps a very long time, before engagements start to flow in rewarding numbers, and the need to support yourself in some other way will become urgent. There is no shame in that, and no-one will hold it against you if you earn your income by teaching, by freelancing, by writing concert programme notes, working in a contract orchestra, or whatever occupation your talents lead you to. But, unless you persist in maintaining old contacts and developing new ones, you will find it terribly easy to lose the impetus to build a career as a solo performer. Nor is it a grave sin to do so. Only the artist can sort out his or her ultimate goal and determine whether the effort to achieve it is worthwhile and can be sustained.

But if the drive is there, there are any number of steps which can be taken to keep the career pot simmering. There are BBC auditions to be applied for, there is new repertoire, preferably including some contemporary music, to be mastered. While it is unlikely that an emerging artist with no major competition win will be taken up by an established concert agency, there is no reason why anyone eligible should not apply for an audition by Young Concert Artists' Trust which, if successful, will lead to professional management and representation. Live

Music Now! also provides many openings for young artists, and other bodies offer similar opportunities. Standards are quite high in most such schemes, but this in itself is no bad thing. A favourable audition will be a valuable help to morale. A series of negative results should not necessarily totally discourage, but should give pause for thought.

When engagements do start to flow from all this hard work, the young performer should feel that no opportunity is too small or insignificant to yield exposure and experience. This may, in practice, sometimes present a difficult choice. Does one turn down a £25 lunchtime foyer recital if there is a chance of something more lucrative coming up in the way of work as an orchestra extra or perhaps in a TV jingle recording? I do not need to answer this question. The individual who has correctly analysed his or her qualities and found a firm career aim will be able to make the correct decision quite easily.

Certain it is that if an engagement is accepted it must be fulfilled with total professionalism. Better by far not to accept a date because it is too far, too unimportant, too poorly paid, than to approach it in less than a wholly committed and enthusiastic manner. The performer has a serious duty to the public, and that duty extends to every facet of his or her appearance and to the business as well as the musical preparation for it. In the absence of a manager or agent, it is necessary to be punctilious in committing engagements to the diary and confirming them by letter or – if appropriate – acknowledging such confirmation as may be given by another party. It must be very clearly (but politely) established what the fee is, and whether it includes travel costs (and if so, on what basis) and/or accommodation. Does the fee include the accompanist's remuneration? Is the accommodation offered in a private house or as a sum of money? Where exactly is the performance to take place and when will the hall be available for a warm-up? What piano will be provided? If music stands are necessary, should the artists bring their own? Will the musicians be met at the station? If not, when and to whom should they report?

There is, on the other hand, no need to make very heavy weather of these points, or to make a society secretary feel that she is being interrogated. In many cases, a telephone call will be the appropriate way to resolve any matters that are not covered in the initial letter of engagement and, providing a clear understanding is reached on peripheral matters, not everything need be spelled out in black and white. But fees, expenses, concert dress and any other items on which misunderstanding might lead to later awkwardness should be set down clearly.

There is obviously nothing I can say about musical qualities of an engagement but it should be pointed out that, although the actual performance is the kernel of the presentation, it can be marred or enhanced by incidental factors which are under the control of the artist. It would take much more than a paragraph or two to deal with the complex and subtle ways in which the artist's comportment and appearance affect the audience's enjoyment. But there are some simple acts of folly which are obtrusive and which can and should be pointed out. Appearance is one area that deserves more attention than it sometimes commands. Dress should be appropriate, clean, well-pressed and not distracting. Stage deportment is also important. The artist should walk on to the platform, not hurry, stumble, slouch or loiter. Do not try to walk while turning your face to the audience and smiling: you will fall over and probably miss the piano! Walk to centre stage, turn to the audience, smile and bow. Try to look confident and pleasant.

When performing, do not stamp your feet, sway excessively or make funny faces. Rostropovich can get away with it and maybe some day you will too – but not yet. I have heard audition judges comment many times on pianists who try to convey the marking *espressivo* with body movements but not in the notes played.

After the performance, receive all who come backstage to see you. Thank those who have helped you to appear and be naturally and unaffectedly polite to everyone. When you have returned home, a letter of thanks to those who invited you and the hosts who put you up will be appreciated and leave them with a pleasant and positive recollection of your performance. Never forget that the relationships you establish during your visit will either help or hinder your further progress. Word of mouth is still the most potent form of publicity for the emerging artist.

PREPARING FOR THE ORCHESTRAL PROFESSION

BASIL TSCHAIKOV

Basil Tschaikov, at present Director of the National Centre for Orchestral Studies, was for nearly 40 years a clarinettist with the London orchestras. Starting as a member of the London Philharmonic at the age of 17, he later joined the Royal Philharmonic under Sir Thomas Beecham and finally, the Philharmonia Orchestra, remaining a member for many years and becoming chairman of the board of directors. He was a professor at the Royal College of Music for 20 years and is the author of several books and tutors.

I suppose we all hope to be successful – but success can mean such different things. For some it is money, for some prestige, for some security and for others the fulfilment of playing the kind of music they enjoy with like-minded people. Having started out on the path towards a career in music by going to music college or university, it is sensible, long before the study period ends, to consider what your intentions are, what will give you satisfaction and what being successful means to you.

There are two facts that everyone aiming to be an orchestral musician should bear in mind. First, that there are far more people wanting to earn their living from music than there are jobs. Second, that being a good player, or even a very good player, will not guarantee you a job. Entering the profession successfully and maintaining a career within it depend to a considerable extent on the following qualities:

(a) the ability to play your instrument and to demonstrate your talent on your own
(b) the ability to play your instrument with other people, in a variety of circumstances
(c) an ability for self-assessment
(d) the determination and resourcefulness to hold out until you establish yourself
(e) the ability to survive the inevitable ups and downs that a career as a performer will bring.

No amount of know-how will get you a job – but it can help you to present yourself and your talent in the most effective way.

The qualities required

Very few other occupations call for the degree of self-discipline required of a musician; you will need the mind of a businessman and the heart of an artist. Making responsible arrangements for your transport, for example: excuses such as 'the train was late', 'the buses weren't running' or 'my car wouldn't start' are not much use to recording, broadcasting or concert managers. Playing in different venues, going on tour, arranging deputies, and a hundred and one other things you may not even have considered, require intelligence, quick thinking and a sense of responsibility to others.

As a player, you will find yourself faced throughout your career with demands on your tolerance, understanding and patience. Sometimes the music you are playing is music you love but the way you are asked to play it is not to your liking. Sometimes you don't like the music, or you have an uninteresting or undemanding part to play – and the conductor spends a great deal of time rehearsing it. Sometimes you have to listen to someone playing the part *you* would like to play, and playing it badly – or worse still, perhaps, playing it much better than you could. Sometimes you don't feel like playing at all, you feel unwell or you are not in the mood. Sometimes you have to sit with someone you don't like or whose playing irritates you. Worst of all, there are times when these ills all descend simultaneously. If you want to be a professional, rather than an amateur who plays for his own entertainment and pleasure, you will have to learn that your responsibilities are to the composer and to the audience.

Starting your career

We are now at the point from which you are setting out to earn your living. You are probably scanning the advertisements from the orchestras and looking for any freelance work you can get. For the moment, let us turn our attention to the full-time jobs on offer.

Before applying for a job, you should ask yourself if it is a position for which you are suited and which really interests you. Sometimes young players are told to do auditions simply for experience: this can be unwise. Nowadays, there are so many applicants for most jobs that orchestra managements just cannot afford the time or money to hear everyone.

To listen to fifty or sixty players will take a couple of days, even giving each one only ten minutes. Also, there are considerable administrative costs involved in engaging auditioners and accompanists and in booking a venue. Often, managements will have to make arbitrary decisions as to whom they will actually audition, so as to reduce the numbers to manageable proportions.

So, don't apply for a job if you are unsuitable for the position on offer – there is little point in auditioning for the no.3 first violin position if you are only good enough to sit at the back of the seconds. In fact, you will make it harder for yourself should you apply to that orchestra again later, when your playing standard may well have improved.

Find out as much about the job as you can: the orchestra's work programme and repertoire, style, conductor, and about the members of the section you wish to join – what are *their* priorities and styles of playing. If they are wind players, what kind of instruments do they play? There may be little point in auditioning for an orchestra where the players have quite different musical intentions from your own.

Your curriculum vitae

You will probably be asked to apply in writing and to send a CV. Your letter of application and CV will probably be the first impression an employer will have of you, and it is important that it should be a good impression. The letter should state the position you are applying for and should only give any additional information that cannot sensibly go on your CV. It should not be 'chatty', nor should it say how wonderful you are. Type the letter if possible; otherwise write clearly, so that it is easily legible. Write on white paper, unlined. Lay out the letter attractively so that it is neither all squashed up at the top of the page nor squeezed in at the bottom. Use a size of paper, A4 or A5, suitable to the length of your letter.

Your CV should be typed on white A4 unlined paper. If your name is one used by both men and women, you should add which sex you are. Give STD codes for all telephone numbers, including your own, and take great care to spell names correctly, especially that of the person to whom you are writing and also those of your referees. Give addresses for your referees, and telephone numbers, if known. If your referees are not famous, nationally-known names, and are not mentioned as having taught you, give their instrument, position or status; you should always have permission from referees before giving their names.

Here is an example of the layout you should use:

CURRICULUM VITAE

Name Daphne Bowarm

Instrument Bozouki

Home address
   21 Any Road
   Sometown
   Whereshire
   A1 1AA
Telephone 0999 41414

Present address
   16 This Road
   London
   SE14 8AB
Telephone 01–858 1000

Marital Status Single

Nationality British

Date of Birth 12.2.62

Age 23

General Education

   Thornton Grammar School
     7 O-levels
     3 A-levels (including music)
     Highgrade University BA (Hons) Music

Musical Education

   Royal Conservatoire of Notegetting (1981–85)
   Studied with Charles Virtuoso
   Private lessons with Frank Blower and Jane Wellknown

Orchestral Experience

   National Youth Orchestra of Briwalsco
   University of Highgrade Orchestra
   College Symphony Orchestra (section principal)
   Bolson Symphony Orchestra
   Freelance engagements for concerts and shows

Referees

Charles Virtuoso   17 Staccato Road
                   Lipville
                   Therewhite   AZ1 4QQ
                   (0567 12345)

Jane Wellknown   6 Legato Street
                   London   NE1 3RR
                   (01–123 4567)

Preparing for the audition

You should always have a few pieces on hand ready to play should you be called for audition. Do not wait until you apply for a position before starting work on something suitable: auditions have a habit of coming at inconvenient times. Your choice of music is important. Choose a piece about which you are enthusiastic and which shows your talent to the best advantage. However, a standard work is preferable to a showy piece that does not display basic techniques – off the string bowing for strings, staccato for wind, for example. Will your piece require rehearsal? Will a poor accompanist wreck it? Can it be played effectively without accompaniment?

Since you are applying for a job in an orchestra, the orchestral extracts will be the most important part of the audition. In Britain it is not usual for the orchestra to send music to prepare, though this is a common practice overseas. Consequently, the ability to sight-read and a knowledge of the standard repertoire for your instrument are essential. Most young players, especially string players, find sight-reading difficult and frequently this causes them more anxiety and nerves than anything else. This is because they do not practise sight-reading regularly. Shortly before the audition, panic sets in and some attempt is made to catch up on lost time. Usually it is too late, and the wrong music is selected – orchestral extracts. These are difficult to play and are, therefore, quite unsuitable for use as sight-reading, even by experienced players.

A method I suggest you might try is to use music well within your technical grasp (say Grade 8 standard) that has no changes of time- or key-signature. Play, without stopping, three lines of music. When you can do this fairly well, try to play six lines and then a whole page. As your ability improves, use more difficult music: music with some rhythmic complexity and more accidentals. If you spend ten minutes each day in this way you will find that, by the end of a few weeks, your reading will have improved greatly and your confidence will have increased in proportion.

You may find that establishing a system for dealing with any music you are given will help. Don't be flustered. Look at the music carefully. Note (i) time-signature (ii) key-signature (iii) tempo (iv) dynamics. Never start till you have checked these and set a pulse for yourself. Look out for changes of key, time-signature and tempo. Play rhythmically. *Don't stop, even if you miss notes or make mistakes.*

Practise the well-known orchestral passages for your instrument. It is worth knowing the kind of repertoire played by the orchestra you want to join, though they may go outside this repertoire at the audition.

The people listening to you will be musicians and they will be listening to hear if you are the kind of musician they would like in their orchestra. Your choice of tempi, observation of dynamic and other marks and sense of style for each piece of music will be as, if not more, important than getting the notes right. Technical mistakes are much more likely to be overlooked than unmusical and insensitive performance. Be ready to play at different tempi, if requested, or louder or softer. You may be asked to make more or less crescendo or a bigger accent. Respond quickly and sensitively; this is not a time for argument or discussion of your ideas on interpretation.

Prepare yourself in every possible way. You need everything in your favour during these few minutes; they may well make a decisive difference to your entire career.

Visualise the audition as you practise at home and ask others to listen to you. Try to create the audition conditions beforehand so that it is not a novelty when the day arrives. Wear the clothes you will wear for the audition. Play as for a performance. Create stress and discover the amount of endurance you will require. Establish a sense of occasion and try to experience the tension involved in having to get something right first time. Breathe slowly and deeply. Do not be rushed. But keep a sense of proportion – if you pin everything on the result of your audition, you will simply inhibit your performance.

Be sure that your instrument is in good condition: strings, reeds, pads, valves, mutes, cigarette papers, pull-though, repair equipment all need to be with you – not at home. Try, if possible, not to use new equipment or borrow an instrument just before an audition. Even if you prefer it to your own, it can let you down under the stress of the moment.

Collect all you need before starting out – have a bag or holdall if you have extra things to take into the audition room as well as your instrument. Don't stagger in, arms full and flustered: it may amuse the auditioners, but it probably won't help your chance of getting the job.

An audition is certainly not the ideal way of assessing a player's suitability for a job, but usually it is the essential step to getting a trial. It tells the auditioners something about you: whether you have the necessary technique, can play with good tone, have rhythm, a reasonable ear and a feeling for music. Players will usually perform well below their best, but something will always come through. One only needs to hear a few notes with good tone or a feeling for line and texture to know if someone is musical. Even poor rhythm and pitch, bouncing bows, fluffed staccatos or split notes will not disguise real talent – if it is there. You need to achieve a standard whereby you will be good enough even if you only play to 60% of your capacity.

The audition

Auditions are held in a variety of venues: be prepared for them not to be ideal. Always be sure you know where the audition is to be held, what time you are expected and what you are to play. Be on time, early if possible, but not so early that you have to hang about getting nervous. If, for any reason, you are going to be late or are unable to attend, let the orchestra management know as soon as possible, – you don't want to get a bad reputation, even before they have heard you.

You may have to play as soon as you arrive (maybe earlier than you were expecting because someone else has dropped out) or you may have to wait around. Be prepared for either. If you are travelling any distance, do not leave too late and don't just allow enough time by taking the very last coach or train: the room or part of the building in which the audition is to be held can sometimes be difficult to locate.

Don't be affected by other players. Some may show off in the waiting room. Ignore them. Concentrate on what you can do. Take care not to tire yourself by playing too much before the audition.

When you go in to the audition room, play a few unhurried notes to get the feel of the acoustics. Then concentrate on the music. Don't worry if you make a mistake – keep going! Don't be distracted by movements or discussion between the auditioners – they may be saying how good you are.

You may only play for a short time. This may mean that they like your playing and can make up their minds quickly, or that they do not, and want to get on.

Be firm and pleasant – neither timid nor surly. Remember that the auditioners are on your side – after all, they are looking for what is good in your playing. If you make a few mistakes, even serious ones, it will not matter if they hear that the essentials are good.

After the audition

If you are one of those chosen, you will be offered a trial lasting a few days or maybe a week or so. Try to gain as much as possible from this experience. You can learn from eveyone, even from those who are not such good players as yourself; they will probably have had more experience than you. Remember that an orchestra is a group. If individual members misbehave, the whole orchestra is likely to suffer. Do not be led into 'larking about' by others.

You may attend a number of auditions and not get a job. This may *not* mean that you are no good but only that they liked someone else better. There are a number of possible reasons for this:

(a) your style was not what that particular orchestra was looking for

(b) the position was not the right one for you

(c) there were several good players, all suitable, but only one could be appointed. Other factors – age and personality, for example – will have been important.

If you played well but were not chosen, you may be offered some deputy or extra work and then, when they next need someone full-time, you will be ahead of the field. Your main concern should be that you have done your best and done yourself justice. Try to assess how you can do better. Be ready to take the next audition – it may take time, even if you *are* a good player, for you to gain the necessary courage and experience.

Freelancing

Some players earn a better living from freelancing than they would from a full-time job. Whenever and whatever you play can add to your reputation. Play as well at an out-of-town, ad hoc, semi-pro date as at the Royal Festival Hall: you never know who may be listening and watching. How you look can be as important as how you sound. It is more noticeable if you are working hard at the back of the section than at the front. You may be bored; reading a newspaper tells everyone that you are. High motivation and persistence, resourcefulness and always being in good playing condition are often more valuable than talent alone.

As a freelance player, you will be very dependent on the telephone. Always keep a diary by the telephone, as well as on you. If you do not have someone to answer the telephone for you when you are out, you should consider an answering machine or one of the diary services. The diary by your telephone, or the one held by the diary service, should always match your own. A double booking or misunderstanding with an engager caused through carelessness can be very much to your disadvantage.

Your reputation for straightforward dealing and efficiency – always being in the right place, wearing the right clothes, with the right instrument, remembering the details of the engagement so that you do not have to telephone at the last moment to find out the time of the train or coach – will give those employing you confidence and will encourage them to book you again. Never take on another date when you have already accepted a previous engagement without first asking to be released. Be prepared for a refusal. However much better the second date may seem, to let someone down or send a deputy without the engager's permission is professional suicide. If you have permission to send a deputy, send someone as good or even better than yourself and certainly never anyone less than entirely capable. If the person you send does not satisfy your employer, your reputation will suffer.

Fancy cards and stationery are not necessary. However, be sure that when you give someone your address or telephone number it is legible and makes it easy for them to contact you.

Overseas engagements

You will, of course, already be a member of the Musicians' Union. You have an obligation to report all overseas engagements and submit the contract or agreement to your local branch before you sign it. If you have not done so and something goes wrong, it is unlikely that the Union will be able to help you. Find out as much about the job as possible. The following information can be very important:

(a) the rate of exchange
(b) the cost of food – that is, the food you will want to eat, rather than the local food, which is often inexpensive
(c) the cost of accommodation to foreigners – this can sometimes be more costly than for residents
(d) the cost of transport
(e) the amount of work you will be expected to undertake
(f) the repertoire – advertisements can often be misleading in this respect.

Finally, instrument and personal insurance, national insurance and income tax; these are all important matters for you as a professional musician. See that you are fully informed both of your needs and of your responsibilities.

FINDING YOUR WAY ROUND THE ASSOCIATIONS

SUSAN ALCOCK

Susan Alcock is the Events Organiser (formerly the Assistant Secretary) of the National Trust and was the General Secretary of the Incorporated Society of Musicians from 1973–1983.

The 1986 edition of the *British Music Yearbook* listed nearly 300 associations. Should the professional musician consider joining them all? Of course not, but perhaps half are joinable by certain kinds of musicians or music-lovers with particular interests. Of these, the two main groups are *trades unions and professional associations* and *special interest societies* (by instrument, period, nationality, teacher and so on). In this chapter, I am going to concentrate on the associations which are of particular interest to *professional* musicians at the 'serious' end of the business, including performers (concert, recital and opera), teachers, church musicians and composers. The special interest societies and groups I will come back to at the end.

Performers

To represent the interests of players and singers there are three main organisations. Two are unions: the *Musicians' Union,* which all orchestral players are obliged to join, and the *British Actors' Equity Association* (known simply as 'Equity'), which is obligatory for opera singers, and especially chorus members; and one is a professional association: the *Incorporated Society of Musicians,* with its broad professional base which, through its Solo Performers' Section, gives special support to chamber music players, soloists and conductors.

These three are recognised by the broadcasting corporations as the negotiating bodies for minimum fees and conditions and, in their several ways, seek to promote and protect the interests of the profession. Together, the ISM and MU, with Equity on occasion, can be a formidable force when a real matter of principle is at stake.

Teachers

Musicians who teach in schools, colleges and universities are also expected to join a trades union, such as the *National Union of Teachers,* the *Assistant Masters' and Mistresses' Association,* the *National Association of Teachers in Further and Higher Education,* and the *Association of University Teachers,* but there is none devoted specifically to music teaching other than the MU, which takes an interest in the teaching aspirations of its player members. Here again, the ISM, through its Music in Education and Private Teachers sections, strives to protect members' interests as teachers of music. Apart from the ISM, associations for musicians in education tend to be specific to a particular group, such as the *Music Advisers' National Association,* the *Music Masters' and Mistresses' Association* (for teachers in independent schools) and the *Society for Research in the Psychology of Music and Music Education.* Additionally, particularly in the past ten years or so, instrumental teachers have found it valuable to found and support specialist groups which exist to enable their members to share knowledge and enthusiasm. A glance through the *British Music Yearbook* shows a wide range of these, including the *European String Teachers' Association,* the *Association of Woodwind Teachers,* the *Association of Teachers of Singing,* the *European Piano Teachers' Association,* the *National Association of Percussions Teachers* and the *National Early Music Association.*

Musicians involved in teaching might, therefore, find it sensible to join a trades union if they teach in a school, college or university, a broadly-based professional association like the

ISM, and a specialist group directed at their particular interest. The services that these will be able to offer should be complementary.

Church musicians

Most organists or singers combine their work in church or cathedral with other professional activities, but here again it is worth giving some thought to membership of an appropriate organisation.

Larger cathedral choirs look to Equity to negotiate their basic fees and conditions for broadcasting and television; the ISM fulfils this function for professional singers in other choirs. Organists also look to the ISM for this service (whether they are members or not, as it happens) and are also encouraged to join the *Cathedral Organists' Association* (if they qualify), the *Incorporated Association of Organists* (which helps, in particular, the amateur church musician), the *Royal College of Organists* (which is responsible for the professional diplomas) and the *Royal School of Church Music*. It is perhaps fair to say that the major father-figure in this world is the Royal School of Church Music where the Director, Lionel Dakers, in particular has done much to encourage co-operation between the associations in order to improve the lot of church musicians.

Composers

Increasingly, composers are finding it worthwhile to join and create associations to draw attention to their work and protect their interests. Elsewhere in this publication is a lengthy chapter on the various complications of copyright which I will not, therefore, touch upon here, but I will take this opportunity of mentioning the stupendous work of the *Performing Right Society* which, on behalf of composers and their publishers, collects the fees due every time one of their works is performed. The *Mechanical-Copyright Protection Society* undertakes a similar task in respect of a composer's work which is broadcast or recorded.

For many years, the *Composers' Guild of Great Britain* strove to promote the interests of all British composers from the humble to the great but, perhaps because the Guild opened its doors so widely, some of the more successful composers recently founded a new professional association – the *Association of Professional Composers* - to take a rather firmer line in what has become a somewhat hard-nosed world. The ISM, too, takes an interest in composers, and the MU has an interest through its Composers, Arrangers and Copyists Section.

Apart from the professional associations, a good many other organisations exist to encourage new music, including the *Park Lane Group,* the *Society for the Promotion of New Music* and, possibly also appropriate in this category, the *British Music Information Centre* (though the latter would not profess to be any kind of association).

The principal professional associations and unions protect their credibility by setting qualifications and/or standards for membership, and only those who are professionally eligible will qualify. It is also worth noting that subscriptions to certain accredited professional associations and unions are tax deductable as a professional expense. Neither of these criteria, however, is likely to apply to the many other associations and societies which are open to those (professional and amateur) with a special interest. There are dozens, most of which depend for their success upon the enthusiasm of their leaders. Just a few examples will suffice to show the range of interests.

Instrument based
British Flute Society
Clarinet and Saxophone Society of Great Britain
Lute Society
Plainsong and Medieval Music Society
Steel Band Association of Great Britain
Viola d'Amore Society

Nationality based
Welsh Folk Song Society
Scottish Pipers' Association
Association of Polish Musicians Abroad

Composer based
Schubert Society
RVW Trust
There is an umbrella organisation to which a number of these belong, the *Association of Composer Societies and Trusts,* but nearly all are independently listed in the *British Music Yearbook.*

Conductor based
These range from societies to honour the work of the dead, (the *Sir Thomas Beecham Society,* for example) to fan clubs to celebrate the living, such as the *André Previn Appreciation Society.*

All of the above are for the enthusiasts, even the fanatics, and can be immensely rewarding.

Charitable institutions

And what about the benevolent organisations – those which try to help professional musicians in times of need? Chief of these is the *Musicians' Benevolent Fund* which, as well as making substantial grants to individuals, runs three excellent retirement homes and a convalescent home for musicians. You can't join the MBF (though you may contribute to it) but any musician faced with dire need may qualify for its kindly help. Professional associations and unions, too, will have benevolent funds (usually fairly small) to help their members, and there is one remarkable society, the *Royal Society of Musicians of Great Britain,* which was set up in Handel's day to provide pensions and charitable help for elderly musicians and their dependants. This *is* joinable and membership can be fun, though I doubt whether the financial reward can replace a commercial pension scheme – don't take my word for it though!

Let me end with one other godfather to the profession, the *Worshipful Company of Musicians.* Musicians and non-musicians with certain qualifications are invited to join this venerable body whose main aim is benevolence. The Musicians' Company also administers a number of trusts through which it helps young musicians in particular.

In this short chapter I have described some 40 organisations which may be of interest to the professional musician (some of which cater even more for the amateur or simply the music-lover), but still there are dozens more which I have not covered – maybe an opportunity for your own research.

MUSICIANS' UNION

Working For Today's Musicians

Regional District Organisers

London · Maurice Jennings 01-582 5566
South East · Stan Martin 01-582 5566
South West · Ken Cordingley 0272 265438
East/North East · Dennis Scard 021 622 5361
Midlands · Terry Yates 021 622 3870
North West · Tony Lucas 061 236 1764
Scotland · John Fagan 041 248 3723
North/North East · Jack Jenkins 0912 325 741

Session Organiser · Don Smith 582 5566

General Secretary
John Morton
National Office,
60-62 Clapham Road,
London SW9
01-582 5566

The only Trade Union for
all musicians in the UK

MUSICIANS' UNION SAYS KEEP MUSIC LIVE

COMPETITIONS
SIMON MUNDY

*Simon Mundy is a well-known author and journalist.
From 1980 to 1983 he was 'young artists' correspondent
of* Classical Music *magazine, and now regularly contributes articles on radio and television.*

However much one regrets that, all too often, applause is
linked to prize money rather than performance, the competition system now dominates the international music world. In
this country alone, there are some fifty competitions organised, and around the same number of competitive scholarships. The help they offer is as varied as can be devised and
some are very much more helpful than others.

At its best, the system can speed up the rise of a musician
from the ranks of the unknown-but-talented to those of the
notorious-and-employed. Because of the fickle nature of the
public memory, winning is no substitute for the dull business
of self-promotion, but it can jolt a career into life. The lucky
winner – and it should be stressed that luck can play as large a
part as talent in this murky field – can walk away with extra
finance, head-bulging publicity, a full diary and the chance of
exotic travel.

For all the performers, not just the ones who take home the
pots of gold, there can also be less tangible benefits. The
process of public audition which is, after all, the basis of most
competitions, allows artists to hear and measure themselves
against the standards of their contemporaries. Too often,
soloists spend a disproportionate amount of time, once they
have left college, studying and practising in private; only dimly
aware of standards in the rest of the profession when they turn
up to concerts given by friends.

At the beginning of a career, *any* concerts can be hard to

come by. A listless lack of direction can grip the musician without an immediate goal. The competition can provide that goal, delineating repertoire that needs to be learnt and giving a deadline. It may not amount to a proper engagement, but at least there will be a sense of occasion and a chance to be heard. At a time when performing may still cause a feeling of panic it enables the artist to get the feel of the platform. If the rounds are held somewhere like the Wigmore Hall or the Purcell Room (or a television studio) the familiarity with the backstage of major venues can be thoroughly reassuring later on, when the time comes to give a debut recital or a first broadcast. At this stage, even after a successful competition, many musicians will have an unappetising and rather blank curriculum vitae. A couple of placings in the upper reaches can do much to plug the gaps and bolster the confidence of promoters inundated with pleading brochures.

However, for all the help a competition is able to offer, there are many caveats which cannot be ignored. There is no doubt that, although most events are planned with excellent intentions and a genuine desire to benefit the arts, there are some that do more harm than good, both to the development of the musician and to the audiences' intelligent understanding of the profession.

Too often the competition has little to do with musical quality and more with the sort of spurious attributes celebrated in boxing or 'Miss World'. The notion of 'better' in music, except where applied to the few empirical details of technique (intonation, dexterity, breath control, etc.) is a pernicious one. What is deemed 'best' in one country or tradition is often anathema to another. If prizes were openly awarded on the basis of subjective favour (rather than insisting, as many sponsors and publicists like to do, that one person was 'the best' and therefore could be dubbed 'Young Singer of the World' or whatever) the public might be less titillated, but it would be encouraged to trust its own judgement of quality. It is too easy just to count the trophies on a performer's mantlepiece before deciding to attend his concert. Sheer laziness and the wish to have a 'selling-point' makes the promoter rely increasingly heavily on 'winners' for those dates when a sop is tossed at 'duty to emerging talent'.

For the artists themselves, the effects of devoting too much time to the competition circuit can be dangerous. In order to win, contestants may have to develop a limited repertory of 'show-off' pieces unrelated to any normal ideas of concert planning or operatic casting. The experience gained will have more to do with knowing how to produce bland technical wizardry (and upset the least number of people) than to move and satisfy an audience artistically.

For the artist who does not win or come close, the resulting feelings of failure, frustration and rejection can be traumatic. It can be an expensive lesson in misery. By the time tuition has been taken, clothes bought, tapes recorded, accompanists hired, travel and accommodation booked, the bill can be considerable. Unless there is a fair chance that a considerable amount of the cash can be recovered, it is probably not worth entering.

An increasing phenomenon is the competition which is merely an excuse for upmarket advertising, with executives and PR representatives of the sponsoring company treating artists as irritants who should be excluded from everything except the stage. There are also other competitions set up by ambitious groups or municipal authorities purely for the sake of self-aggrandisement, with no thought given to the needs of the profession which they purport to serve.

In a system geared to youth, flashiness and the latest *wunderkind,* there is little room for the late developer; the artist who takes time to mature. The competition circus should not be the sole means of throwing up talent. Disproportionate press coverage and no allowances made for the professional fouls committed by judges (whether through prejudice, jealousy or ignorance) will not only ensure that the wrong artists win but also hamper the performer without the temperament for public degredation. He/she will be over-looked by a publicity machine that sells music in the same way as cosmetics and frequently confuses the uses of both.

Sadly, it is probably now inevitable that every soloist will have to enter a competition at sometime in his/her career. The main concern should be to extract as much from the arena as possible, while limiting the damage. So pick your competition carefully.

The first task is to establish what you want out of winning. Money, engagements, training, publicity or all of them? Having decided that, and picked a contest that looks promising, examine its conditions and track record closely. Is the prize realistic? Does it pay out enough to compensate for the work and expenditure involved in entering? If there is only one major prize, even if it be £50,000 and a gold-plated Steinway, but you are asked to submit an hour-long programme on tape, professionally recorded, and then fly to Mogadishu for the finals, then I suggest you forget it unless expenses are paid. It is assumed by many competitions that they are merely in the business of doing you favours. But, while this may be fine in the foetal days of a career, it is thoroughly patronising when one is professional. Competitions are tools of the trade, not seaside talent contests. If there is only one prize and an entry of fifty, it follows that there will be forty-nine also-rans, most not necessarily any more ghastly than the eventual winner. Without adequate reward for runners-up, the competition organisers are making capital out of your work for no payment.

It is advisable to ask yourself whether the event you are entering is the right one for you at that stage in your development. It is all very well knowing deep down that yours is the voice that will stroll into Covent Garden, but should it be asked to just yet? Musicians develop at different paces. The genius at twelve may be the rather ordinary fiddler in his thirties, whereas the gawky twenty-two year old with a pretty but rather weasly little voice may become the chesty thumper of forty. Do not enter a competition until you know, and your teacher confirms, that you are ready. It is a waste of time, money and goodwill. There is always a chance that you will come up against the same judges again later, and it will not help your cause if they remember you as the twit that dried.

If the prizes suit you, the next stumbling block is the status of the event. It may be called the Piltdyke International World Cello Competition, but has anyone heard of it or its prizewinners? If the reaction from other professionals and agents is a combination of amusement and disgust, or if two-thirds of its champions are complete unknowns five years after conquering Piltdyke, leave the place alone. There is no point in going through the nervous agony of competing for the sake of oblivion. Here again, make sure that you are sufficiently aware of your own current standard so that you do not enter a contest for which you are not ready. There is equally little point in being thrown out at the paper application stage; far better to come third at Piltdyke.

Having entered, make sure you have the right repertoire. In almost all cases this should be a combination of the pieces that you know best (and are sure of to such an extent that if called to play them underwater with an accompanist playing backwards there would be no effect on your performance) and those that show your ability to its greatest advantage. If the piece is plainly too hard and you are only having a bash, nobody will be impressed. Similarly if you are ducking the issue by picking something too easy, the assumption may well be that you cannot do any better.

Who are the judges? Do you value their opinions and trust their impartiality? If the chairman is somebody who regularly only gives prizes to his own students and has loathed your teacher and all her works ever since being jilted at college, it might be worth bearing in mind when you peruse the final results. Conversely, if the jury consists of six people you have always admired, then their ideas may well be worth listening to. Make sure that they really are the judges, however. Organisers often slip in the phrase 'the invited members of the jury include Joachim, Casals, etc.' The fact that they have been invited is no guarantee that they will accept or turn up. Beware the jury with one dominant member and five sleepers who, although brilliant in their field, are incapable of holding their own in an argument. If, after a harrowing defeat, you are approached by a judge saying that, whatever the result, they all thought you were the best *really,* your reaction should be 'Then why didn't I win?', not 'How nice of you to say so!'

Read the small print. Make sure you fill in the forms properly, enclose all the documents, photographs, references and information requested and lodge the application with plenty of time to spare. That way, if something has been forgotten, there is time to rectify the mistake. It may seem an obvious point, but it is surprising how many competitors never get past this stage because of sheer inefficiency. One administrator told me that up to a quarter of all applications she received were incomplete or late and went straight into the waste-paper basket. They may have been fine violinists, but they could not read.

If you do win, the problems may be just beginning. You will have to cope intelligently and graciously with press interviewers who may ask stupid questions and candidly tell you that your success amazed everybody. Reviews may be aimed to take you down a peg or two. Do not be put off. Musicians have a terrible tendency to remember only the demolition job, not the sensible and helpful notice. There will be sponsors and mayors to meet and charm, a rather forced air of congratulation from your beaten colleagues and, inevitably, a flat morning after when the telephone fails to ring and the gas bill still looks unpayable. But any lasting exposure will be up to you to generate.

Make sure you are given full credit for your achievement. Tell the press. Phone your agent. Have photographs circulated and write a new publicity brochure. Bombard the promoters, the radio stations and impress your next audience. Blow your own trumpet, because no-one else will do it for you, and nobody knows about you unless they have been told. Remember that, if you are the flavour of the month at the moment, there will be a time when you seem old hat. When that happens, it is your professional reputation, not your past publicity, that will count and consolidate your career. The competitions will then take their rightful place as the early chapters of your biography, exhibited proudly but in the end irrelevant.

If, as you will most of the time, you lose, do not despair. Ask yourself first if your position was a realistic assessment of your performance. If it was, then work out what the winner did that meant victory. If it was not, then feel sore but philosophic. A decline into misery helps no-one but your rivals, unless it spurs you to greater things. Competitions may be a cynical rat-race and symptoms of the reduction of the arts to the same level as *Jeux sans Frontieres* but, if they have to be tolerated, then they must be used with your eyes open. They may have little to do with your vision, your ability or the enrichment of an audience, but your future command of a pay-cheque may depend on them.

12,000 parts
133 years
88 notes
11 models
1 name...

 STEINWAY

See one, touch one, play one, own one.

Steinway Hall, 44 Marylebone Lane, Wigmore Street, London W1.
Telephone: 01-487 3391.

Steinway pianos can also be seen in Belfast, Bolton, Chester, Edinburgh, Glasgow, Huddersfield, Liverpool,
Manchester, Nottingham and Oxford.

MARKETING YOURSELF
KEITH DIGGLE

Keith Diggle is the Marketing Director of Rhinegold Publishing Limited and author of the book, Guide to Arts Marketing. *He was a promoter of music and the performing arts when director of Merseyside Arts Association and was co-founder of the English Sinfonia. In his work with Rhinegold and* Classical Music *magazine he has counselled many young artists on how to set about promoting themselves.*

The product and the market

If there is one essential, never-to-be-forgotten rule in the marketing of individuals or groups of individuals, it is 'always put yourself in the shoes of your customers'. Just as writers have to learn to be readers if they are to assess their work effectively, so the performer must develop the objectivity that will enable him to see himself, his professional colleagues, his programmes and performances, even his style of dress and speech, clearly and unemotionally. Most important of all, the performer must assess where he stands in his profession, how he is rated as a performer (by those who can influence his career) and how well-known he is (by those whose interest he seeks to arouse). Only when we can 'see ourselves as others see us' can we begin to apply the concepts of marketing to a career.

We must take this even further and imagine what it is like to be a person who, for pleasure or professional reasons (I grant that the two are not mutually exclusive) employs, engages, or in any other way makes use of the services of, musicians. What is he like? How much does he know about music? About your kind of music? About you? Under what pressures does he labour? Is he motivated towards achieving success? What does 'success' mean to him – is it a full house, irrespective of the artist engaged or the music played, or can 'success' mean something else? At the heart of who he is and what he does, what does he really want?

I have started by touching on the first and most important considerations in marketing: the *product* (that's *you*) and the *market* (that's *them*). I have made the point that your assessment of both must be ruthlessly honest; you must see things as they are and not as you would like them to be. Note that I have not defined the market as being those blessed people with good ears and good sense that make up your audiences. They would be your market if you were yourself promoting music (either your own or someone else's). For the moment, let us assume that the promotion of your performance is being handled by someone else, so your task is to sell yourself to those people, the promoters, whose responsibility it will be, later on, to market you to the public.

What does your market know of you?

Consider what passes through the mind of a promoter as he opens an envelope and takes out a brochure. Secretaries of music clubs, local government officers in departments of arts and recreation, university music societies, all tell us how many of these brochures they receive every week. Some say they just throw them in the bin without a second thought (sometimes unopened) and others say they give them a second thought and *then* throw them away. How many are opened, read carefully, acknowledged by post, filed away for future reference, we shall never know. Yet, artists *are* engaged and concert seasons *are* booked. How?

The temptation to refer to the parable of the sower is very strong at this stage. The sower accepted the random nature of what he was doing. However, when we consider the concepts of marketing, we are trying to keep the element of chance to a minimum: we have to seek out the fertile soil and set about creating more, not being able to afford to waste the seeds that are our advertisements on the rocky ground.

When the promoter opens an envelope and takes out a brochure, or opens a magazine and sees an advertisement, he relates what he sees to what he already knows. His state of *awareness* in relation to you and/or what you have to offer is crucial to what he does next. If nothing strikes a chord with him, nothing is what he does in response (apart from reach for the waste-paper bin). If the promoter has already heard of you, or if what you are offering is something which is of *interest* (preferably both) your brochure or advertisement will be given the benefit of closer examination and may result in action – or a decision to take action at a later date (so you go in the filing tray rather than the bin).

The part played by the brochure

Does the brochure itself not play a part in this? Surely, a well-designed, well-written, attractive piece of print will stand a better chance of making an impact than one that is plain, lacklustre and boring? Indeed it does, but it will go no further than attracting attention (that is, it will attract for no more than a fraction of a second) unless it is attracting attention to something that the reader knows something about, is interested in and, preferably, has need of. Are *you*, the reader, not constantly receiving through the post wonderfully well-designed, expensively-printed sales brochures for things in which you have no interest and for which you have no need? And what do you do with them?

Am I saying that, if one is a complete beginner whom no-one knows, a brochure posted to a promoter has no chance at all of obtaining an engagement? Not quite, but I *am* saying that there is only a very small chance. The promoter's awareness of you is non-existent and his need for you is probably non-existent as well – unless he is looking out for beginners.

So, goodbye to brochures? No, not at all. But, if you are a beginner, goodbye, perhaps, to investing all your hopes and a fair amount of your savings in a mailing to every known promoter in the land in the belief that engagements will immediately follow. You will still need a brochure because, as you create awareness of yourself and as you learn more of what individual promoters are doing, you will require a piece of paper that tells people who you are, what you do, how well you do it, and how they may make contact with you. You will need to revise that piece of paper regularly as you add to it news of your developing career and remove from it that which is out of date and, one hopes, now unworthy of you. And, as we shall see, these pieces of paper will play a part in creating fertile soil for your subsequent advertising.

Publicity – how to become famous

These considerations are all concerned with your *publicity,* a word which is often very misunderstood. Publicity comprises two closely-related activities: *public relations* (not a very helpful term unless you remember that your public in this instance is made up of those who may engage you – a better expression might be *market relations* or *promoter relations*), and *advertising*. Advertising (sending out brochures, for instance) only works if the ground has been prepared, if the people to whom you are aiming it know something of you, and if there is a good chance that they will believe what you are asking them to read. More than that, what they know about you already must be essentially favourable.

Most artists only ever concentrate upon their advertising. Once a career has matured, this may well be enough but, at the start, PR is crucially important: you are attempting to build a favourable awareness of yourself in the minds of those who can give you work. The various opportunities that exist for young artists to display their talents, the competitions, awards and 'platforms', do not necessarily create work instantly, but they make the artists better known: they create 'fame'.

It is worth dwelling briefly on this word 'fame', which literally means 'to be spoken of'. Fame is not a matter of being either famous or not-famous; it usually builds slowly with each exposure in the media gradually being added to by each successive appearance, until eventually an artist becomes someone who is known by many more people than he knows himself. Of course, there are the exceptions: those wonderful occasions when someone wins a major international competition and becomes a star overnight with every promoter in every civilised country clamouring to offer engagements. Mainly, however, it happens over a period of time. As one famous actor commented, 'it took me at least ten years to become a star overnight!'.

Promoters need audiences, and that is why fame is important to them and why it is important to you. You need the promoter to know of you and you also need the promoter to believe that you are known to enough people to make an audience.

Building one's fame is a matter of making the most of every opportunity. If, by hook or by crook, you have obtained an engagement (whether paid or not doesn't matter) you should spend as much time exploiting this as you do rehearsing for the performance. Your first interest will be with music critics in the hope that they will say good things about you and your performance, but the chances are that they will all be far too busy to come to hear you. As a general rule, music critics only show interest if they have already heard something good about you on the grapevine (you have to face the problem of awareness with these folk just as you do with the promoters). Start with the people you have met in the business, preferably people who engage musicians and people whose opinion counts with them (don't forget your own friends in the music world). Call them, get them to come along, make sure someone meets and greets them and gives them an interval drink. Afterwards, write to them and ask them what they thought of it all. If they say anything complimentary, see if you can quote them in your letters and brochure.

Weeks before the event, start thinking if there is anything about you and what you do that might interest the newspapers and radio. If you were born in Bristol, write and tell the Bristol papers and local radio what you are doing – even if your performance is going to take place in Southend. Are you planning to play anything written by a person with local connections? What about the Bristol music clubs? Why not invite them to attend? Why not hire a coach and suggest that they come along to support you? Then telephone the local radio stations (at both Southend and Bristol) to tell them that your supporters' club is about to descend on Southend. Make sure that you have some photographs taken of the occasion, not just of you performing but of you with the music club members (laughing), you with the local government entertainments manager who booked you (still laughing), you with a group of local children who are studying music (still laughing) – and then have enough prints made to send to the local papers (in Bristol and Southend) and to magazines such as the 'county glossies', those monthlies that are devoted to local activities. A brief reference to you in a local publication, with a picture, will not make you a star but it will give you something to copy and send on to other promoters. *And* it will add to their perception of you, making you more than just a name at the bottom of a letter.

Obviously, I do not mean that you should slavishly follow this example. I give it as a simple illustration of how you can be creative using a straightforward engagement that would otherwise be over when the last note had been played. Read the national newspapers and you will see how bright ideas are constantly being used to put artists into the public eye.

Degrading and time-consuming?

To the serious musician this will all feel rather degrading and, in a sense, it is: you are a musician because you want to be a musician and not a buffoon desperately seeking attention. But such is the nature of the world in which we live that the majority of people, even very talented people, have to develop a knack for attracting attention. It is desperately unfair, but it also helps to be physically attractive: when you are wholly unknown, the people whose attention you are seeking need something to latch on to. You must help them do this by paying attention to how you look. Make the most of yourself! Most people's first sight of you will be in a photograph (this tells us something about the importance of your professional photograph). Only later, when you become better known, will it be your talent that comes to mind first rather than your appearance.

Marketing yourself will also strike you as being very time consuming. It is. Perhaps one of the only advantages of being a beginner is that you will tend to have time on your hands (when you are not practising, naturally) and the task should not be overwhelming. Later, it would be wise to consider paying someone to do this work for you. A PR specialist can say things about you that you would never dare say yourself and he will also know far more people to say them to than you do. A good agent (see the chapter entitled **Tackling the Agency World**), should you be successful in persuading one to take you on, will carry out many of the PR functions for you because, at this later stage, telling people about you and selling you to them is pretty much the same thing. But, if you are failing to make your career live up to your talent, consider taking on a PR specialist who knows the music world.

Advertising – using your fame to obtain engagements

Try to think of advertising not as something separate from PR, but as an activity to be practised together with PR. It is an inseparable companion to the process of making people aware of you. The brochure you send out may not find you an engagement immediately but, if it is well conceived and executed, it is playing its part in helping your market know you are there. As you develop your own fame, so your advertising will become more effective. What advertising methods are open to you?

The multi-purpose brochure is clearly an essential. It can be used to introduce you to a large number of people who, up until that time, have never heard of you. As I have said, it will not yield much in the way of engagements initially but it builds awareness. It can be used to leave a permanent reminder of you with people that you have met – people who have attended one of your performances, for example. If the telephone is used as a means of seeking engagements, it can be used to accompany the letter which follows up the conversation. As your fame grows, it becomes more and more an instrument that will sell you.

How, then, does one set about creating a good brochure? Keep at the forefront of your mind the thought that the brochure has to carry three basic pieces of information: it must convey a clear and attractive impression of who you are and what you do, it must carry information that gives you credibility (so that people will believe that you are good at what you do), and it must provide the interested person with a means of making contact with you.

People who work in advertising tend to apply the mnenonic AIDA when planning advertisements and sales literature. *A* stands for *Awareness* - the instant that the piece of paper is seen it must make people aware of it; it must be eye-catching. *I* stands for *Interest* – once you have caught the reader's eye you must then hold his interest. *D* stands for *Desire* – then the reader must begin to want what is advertised. *A* stands for *Action* – the reader must then be encouraged to do something, preferably pick up the telephone to see when you are free.

Good copywriting and design contribute enormously to all four parts of the process.

Copywriting and design

The best thing to do at this stage is to disregard every other artist's brochure you have ever seen and try to think of original ways of describing yourself that will excite the reader. Most people start with their name. But why? Unless their readers already have some awareness of them, why should a name excite them? They also slap a photograph immediately under their name. Wonderful! Now we know what this unknown person looks like. Where's the waste-paper bin?

You are a double-bass player, your name is Eric Smith and your appearance, although neat and tidy, is not striking. (If double-bass players of unstriking appearance, called Eric Smith, read this, their time will not be wasted.) The envelope is opened and what do we read? All by itself, on the first part of the paper that we see: LOW NOTES ON A HIGH LEVEL – that is all. The letters are printed in an unusual typeface in bright orange on a buff coloured background (or buff on a bright orange background, or in any other striking combination of colours that are compatible with legibility). What does it mean? It means we are made *aware* and, because the statement does not tell us enough, we are *interested*. We need to know more so we turn the page. And what do we see? A sketch of a small person, holding a double-bass, apparently playing it on the top of a New York skyscraper. There are more words alongside the sketch: A DANGEROUSLY ENTERTAINING EVENING IN THE COMPANY OF ERIC SMITH AND HIS AMAZING TALKING, DANCING DOUBLE-BASS. Beneath these words there are more words, written smaller (now your attention is held, the words do not have to shout at you):

'Dragonetti would have loved every minute of it' *The Manchester Gazette.*

'He held his capacity audience enraptured – and the double-bass was good as well' *Peterborough Post.*

'Thank you Eric Smith, you brought life to this tired old town' *Councillor John Jones, Chairman of the Entertainments Committee, Borough of Oldville.*

The brochure goes on to tell you what Eric Smith does for his money. Having caught you, it does not waste any more of your time; it tells you that Eric Smith does a light-hearted lecture recital on the history of the double-bass, illustrating it with a wide variety of music, old and new, and any amount of amusing anecdotes. It tells how long the entertainment lasts and what sort of facilities are needed (for example, if an accompanist is used, a piano might prove useful). It mentions some of the more interesting places visited in recent times. It also adds credibility by quoting at greater length some of the laudatory comments that have been made by promoters, musicians and music critics. Because Eric Smith is not very prepossessing – no photographer has ever taken a halfway decent picture of him – no picture appears in the brochure apart from one or two more sketches.

The interested promoter will now need to be told how much Mr Smith charges for his services and how to contact him. It is hard to say when a fee should be stated in print and when it should be left to emerge in a subsequent discussion. As a general rule, only the very famous need to be coy about how much they charge (either because they are embarrassed about how large the fee is, or because they do not wish to pre-empt a discussion that could result in it being even bigger). It helps a promoter to know where you stand on the matter of fees (and expenses), so say what you want.

Whether or not you should invite a response directly back to you very much depends on your personality. Eric Smith, as you can tell, is quite happy to deal with enquiries himself – indeed, he rather enjoys it. If you are a quieter sort of soul then you might, in the absence of an agent, obtain the assistance of husband, wife, father, mother or friend who lives in the same house. I know one musician, a guitarist, who performed under a stage name and acted as his own agent under his real name. He kept the bluff going for years.

But what about the *design* of the brochure? First do the real spadework: decide who you are, what you do, and how you want people to perceive you. Reject all the conventional approaches and invent something for *you* which is true, original and most likely to attract. The brochure has to convey as persuasive a picture of you as possible and that means that it must immediately make you stand out from the crowd.

Consider giving a title to your performance. Or devise your programmes on a thematic basis and give them titles. If you are part of an ensemble, choose a good, original title for the group, a title that will stay in people's minds. See how memorable are titles like The King's Singers, The Scholars, Sheba Sound, Trio Zingara and Fortune's Fire.

Once you have decided how you want to present yourself and, by implication, the style of your presentation, the matter of design becomes relatively simple. It is a mistake to present yourself unprepared to a designer in the expectation that a personality will be created for you – you must do this work yourself. Then it is simply a matter of producing an original piece of paper so designed that it will immediately create *awareness,* arouse *interest* and so on. Look out for different ways of folding the paper to tempt the reader into the brochure; decide which words will shout and which words will speak quietly and in more detail. The best brief that you can give a designer is the *copy* – the actual words you want to use. From your words, the designer can create design using the tools of typography, illustration and colour. And if you cannot afford a designer? Do it yourself – it is not impossible.

Design leads to printing and this is expensive for most people. It is a necessary expense, however, and provided you have done the preparatory work before you approach a designer, and given that the designer knows that you want to keep printing costs to a minimum, it should give value for money.

Advertisements

Advertisements in magazines such as *Classical Music* should be approached in exactly the same way as the brochure. If you just stick down your name and standard photograph, do not expect huge results. The only difference between brochure and advertisement is that the advertisement is almost always in black and white, is flat (that is, no folds), is always in the company of other advertisements and is printed and distributed by someone else for you.

Using the telephone

An advertisement or a brochure cannot do any more than project its message. It cannot respond, answer questions or steer the reader into a more productive frame of mind. If the advertisement or brochure tempts the promoter into calling you, or the person you have deputed to act as your intermediary, then there is the opportunity to turn the interest into a commitment of one sort or another. The commitment may be an agreement to engage you on a certain date for a certain fee; that is the ultimate as far as you are concerned. A commitment to attend one of your performances, to meet you afterwards for a drink and a chat, is the next best thing. The aim must be to obtain one sort of commitment or another from the caller. If this cannot be done then and there, note the telephone number and name of the caller and arrange to call back – and call back within a few days with a better reason why they should engage you or come to see you.

Should one ever take the initiative and call promoters before they think of calling you? Again, it depends on your personality or that of the person acting for you. If you can do it well, you will ultimately find it very rewarding: even if you do not get engagements at first, you will learn about the promoters, how they work, how they make their decisions. Be systematic. List your targets, names and telephone numbers (Rhinegold's *British Music Yearbook* is an excellent source) and make out a file card for each. As you telephone, check that you have the correct person, address and telephone number, and make notes on each call. Find out and note the best time of day to call. Summarise your reception and record what action you agreed would be taken: 'send brochure with covering letter inviting her to attend next performance in nearby town', 'call back in September' and so on. As you progress, you create a file of contacts so that, as time goes by, you can telephone people easily, in a relaxed manner. Do not telephone anyone unless you have something specific to tell them and have a specific commitment in mind for them.

Development

As I have said before, the whole process takes time. Your work in generating an awareness of yourself through PR activities, your self-advertising, your engagements, all contribute to the growth of your career. With determination and a level of common sense the talented musician can carve out a career. Many before you have been successful; good luck with it!

Public Relations
in Music
and the Arts.

◆

Promotions • Presentation • Image Consultancy • Press & Public Relations
Prestige Arts Events • Concert Management • Entertainments • Sponsorship

◆

Laurence Jenkins M.A., B. Mus.
23 Pepys Road London SE14 5SA
Telephone: 01-639 1052

CONCERT MANAGEMENT AND PROMOTION
JEFFREY LONG

Jeffrey Long was formerly a theatre stage manager, assistant to Nicholas Snowman at the London Sinfonietta, promotion manager of Universal Edition and public relations manager of the London Symphony Orchestra. He is manager of the Ambache Chamber Ensemble and general manager of Tiger Promotion and Productions Limited.

Promoting your own concert is an expensive business. It consumes far more time than you imagine and is virtually always a loss-making activity. Before you begin, be sure that you can afford to lose everything you spend, unless you have a guarantee against loss.

Booking a hall

With your projected programme in mind, you need to book a hall. The factors governing your choice include its availability, cost, seating capacity, location, acoustic, interior suitability and its status in the public mind as a place of entertainment. These factors may affect what you can play. You may be asked to support your request with written evidence of financial or artistic credibility. There will probably be a non-returnable deposit.

How do you choose a hall? One of the best ways is to find an event similar to one you would like to promote and to attend it; this should give you a good idea of existing potential in a few seconds. Note if you were able to see and hear properly, if the players had any practical difficulties, if programme sales, box office, bar and ushering were efficient. Try to count the audience, bearing in mind that your estimate may exaggerate the numbers. Disadvantages, such as uncomfortable seating or poor local infrastructure, may cost you attendance.

Concept

With the hall in mind, you must now look at the whole concert concept, matching art against budget. Be realistic: you will get neither audience nor critics for a Reger programme on a Maundy Thursday evening at a church hall in Wolverhampton. You will get both if you discover Mozart's 42nd symphony and première it in the Royal Festival Hall on a November weekday. Your concert is an entertainment, in competition with other activities which might occupy people's leisure time. Ask yourself, would *you* make an effort to go? If you feel that nobody will come, however well you publicise it, you might as well have a rehearsal instead.

Having established a suitable programme, you need to check for clashes with similar concerts and the availability of artists.

Practical problems

You may have chosen a hall with what appears to be a suitable piano or organ, but you should check the tuning arrangements. A=440 is normal in Britain but, if you are managing a concert abroad, you will find that concert pitch is frequently higher. This can cause major problems if you are touring other keyboards or tuned percussion, and baroque music groups playing at lower pitches may find they must tour everything. Access should be measured: a doorway wide enough for a piano on its side may be too narrow for 32-inch pedal timpani. If you need to remove a door, I recommend a hefty screwdriver, penetrating oil and a pointed knife to scrape out the paint. Major orchestral tours to purpose-built halls have had to be changed on the concert day through failure to ascertain the amount of stage space. Some halls have their own music stands, and I discuss this aspect below.

Adequate heating is essential and very rare outside recognised halls, but lighting may be your worst problem. Concert lighting is quite different from that employed in the theatre – you need plain white light from overhead and plenty of it. Use *Contacts*, the theatrical directory (Spotlight Publications), to find your nearest lighting hire, but be advised that it may be costly. If you tour a lot to strange venues, it may be worth investing in quartz halogen lamps on long stands. If you are putting on anything staged or semi-staged, you will need lit music stands, as well as properly designed spotlighting for the performers. Make notes about how you want to organise the house lighting during the concert. Reduced house lighting helps audience concentration, but they may need to be able to read words in the programme.

In all cases, establish that the venue has an adequate power source from which cables may be run without causing a fire or a safety hazard. Do not forget that this applies to vibraphones, live electronics, amplifiers and any other electrical equipment.

Check to see if you need public liability insurance – you will require this if you are not covered automatically by the hall's insurers.

Budget

The budget for the concert should be written as a simple income and expenditure account. The income side will look a bit short: probably only projected gross ticket sales, subsidy and a deficit to make the thing balance. It is appropriate to keep separate accounts for activities associated with, but isolated from, the actual performance: programme sales, bar takings and so on.

The expenditure side can be a catalogue of woe but, unless you are realistic, your artistic success will be tempered. Expenses should be considered under two headings – those which relate to ticket sales, including all advertising and marketing (indirect expenses) and those upon which the performance itself depends, including players' fees (direct expenses). Begin with the hall hire fee and the commission charged on ticket sales, with VAT on top. If your ensemble is VAT registered, you will be reclaiming some or all of the latter. All promotional expenditure is incurred for the purpose of selling tickets, as are the costs of box office staff, ticket printing and ushers. You can divide your promotion budget into advertising and publicity. Advertising includes all media costs from design to space bookings, all printed material, including design, artwork, typesetting, layout, printing, delivery and distribution. Publicity embraces all public and media relations activities from press conferences and news releases right down to extra commission you might need to pay on complimentary tickets, or the car your conductor takes to a local radio interview.

Next come the players fees. Conductors, soloists and chamber groups usually receive a flat fee, with or without expenses. Contracts are advisable. Orchestral fees begin with the leader, followed by sub-leader, principals, sub-principals and rank-and-file. Each receives a concert fee to include a three-hour rehearsal on the day. Extra rehearsals are charged at half the concert fee plus a small supplement if you are having a single rehearsal on a day other than the concert day. For professional players, you will need a schedule of rules from the Musicians' Union, which establishes minima for different kinds of performance. Certain players, including 'cello, double bass, harp, timpani and percussion, also receive established rates of porterage to contribute towards their transport costs. Some players are registered for VAT, which they will charge you. All payments must be made within a month of the concert date, just as all players booked within a month beforehand must be paid, irrespective of any changes you make. There may be a need to make special payments for learning a new instrument or undertaking a particularly difficult part. Broadcasting fees will appear in both income and expenditure accounts.

Your fixer will normally charge you 10% of the players' remuneration, excluding broadcasting fees and certain expenses, for booking the personnel.

Players travelling further than 15 miles from their centre of employment will be paid distance money, in addition to the costs incurred by moving the entire group to the venue. If return to base by rail, or by the transport you are providing, is not possible before 2 a.m., you need to budget for a hotel and a subsistence payment for each player. The Musicians' Union or your fixer will provide full details. Your travel costs should be calculated on the basis of second class rail fares, or scheduled economy flights if abroad. If you fly, you will need an additional seat for each 'cello, something to remember if you are bringing a piano trio into the UK, for example.

Instrument hire, transport and tuning is your next consideration. Percussion hire is a matter of negotiation: some players run their own hire businesses. Music hire or purchase, composer's commission fees and performing rights fees (frequently included in hall hire, but check) come next. You will also need music stands, chairs, stools, tables for percussion sticks or electronics, rostra, heat and light.

Librarians, stage staff, flowers and gratuities complete a long list. You should calculate your administration costs (time, office, schedule distribution, telephone, post, etc) realistically. They won't go away.

It is normal to add a contingency figure to the expenditure account: somewhere between 5% and 10% of the total so far.

It is better to budget for programme books separately, including the cost of notes, design, typesetting, layout, printing, finishing, delivery and programme sellers. This can be balanced by income from programme sales and advertising and, quite possibly, another little deficit.

Organisation

Once you have booked the hall, you are committed, so you had better make a plan of action. You will already know how many rehearsals you need so, if your ensemble is anything more than domestic, tell your fixer and book a rehearsal hall immediately. The concert hall itself is ideal and, even on the busy South Bank, there are times when you can hire rehearsal periods. Otherwise, you will need somewhere with a reasonable acoustic and the same facilities as the concert venue.

You are now in a position to write a provisional schedule, available to anyone who needs it other than your competitors. The final version will include dates, times, venues with exact addresses and contact numbers, maps where necessary, recommended sources of sustenance, your address and contact numbers, telex, programme, artists, orchestration, notification of broadcasts, rehearsal order, dress, travel and hotel arrangements and special instructions or reminders concerning visas, passports, instrument transport and so on. A word about dress: all professional musicians are equipped with dinner suits and short black dresses or tails and long black dresses. Choose anything else, and you will be subjected to a wide variation of tastes so that, to establish uniformity, you will need more money and time.

Promotion

Marketing strategy is discussed elsewhere in this book, and Keith Diggle's *Guide to Arts Marketing* is *de rigeur*. Appropriate ticket pricing is a crucial matter. If you need to print tickets, do not delay; your price structure is unlikely to be better tomorrow. Many recognised concert halls request a reduction policy for parties, youth or the disadvantaged. Remember that disabled people go to concerts too! If there is no seating plan, make one. You may need to offer bulk deals to your own contacts, club or orchestra members. There are several specialist firms producing numbered tickets quickly and cheaply. Book them direct, unless you can afford to pay your regular printer an extra 10%. Consult the box office staff on the format – they may want a system with several stubs. Estimate the number of complimentary tickets you need, not forgetting your sponsors, board of management and critics, draw them and list them for reference. You must know where your chairman is sitting. Always keep two pairs of house seats for emergencies.

Once these matters are under way, you can turn your attention to the main business of filling the hall with people. Selling the arts is qualitatively different from selling soap. In the first place, there are no funds for individual market research. However, they are hardly necessary because much has been done for you. We know that audiences for classical music show remarkable consistency. They are mostly people who are, or will become, educated decision-makers. Classical record sales, as a proportion of total record sales, are a low single-figure percentage. Classical music reaches less than 5% of the total population. Over 90% of *Gramophone* readers are men. It is unlikely in the extreme that you have the funds to make an impact outside the established target market, however much we all wish you could. And the more you spend beyond a certain figure, the more money you will lose. Such is the nature of deficit finance.

Second, the possibility of changing your product as a result of research is restricted. If a manufacturer finds that the customer will not buy his rough, purple soap, he goes back to the lab to make a smooth, white product. Your position is less flexible. And your product talks. I have never known it possible to advertise a conductor as *New, Improved, and with Added Rostrum Style*. Promotion of classical music is product-oriented, so you had better live with it. That we would prefer not to, is obviated by the enormous range of diatonic music now being rediscovered. Can you image the rush if someone discovered a Mozart opera written between *Figaro* and *The Magic Flute?*

Your concert tickets have a shelf life. Consider this: as a supermarket manager, you are asked to sell some yogurt. You are told that it will be kiwi-fruit flavour and nothing else, all to be sold in one store. Five hundred pots only are available. Few people have heard of kiwi-fruit and even fewer are known to like it. It will be delivered on 23rd October. It has a sell-by date of 23rd November, but your customers can eat it only on the sell-by date. You might feel you had a problem. But when your group manager tells you that each pot costs £1.50 to produce and that you have only £50 to spend on promotion, you might feel in need of an idea or two.

Do not be disheartened. Several people have been actively seeking kiwi-fruit yogurt all their lives. All you have to do is find them.

Advertising is the obvious method, but by no means the only one. Nevertheless, it is a method over which you have some kind of control, so the secret is cost effectiveness. Your first priority is to decide what will attract the audience. The late Eric Bravington, a very successful managing director of the LPO, had a useful rule of thumb for programme planning. He said that to fill a hall, two out of the following three factors should be box office certainties: content, conductor, soloist. I recommend you to decide which are the most attractive parts of your offering and use them as the basis of the message. Then use that message consistently in all your promotion.

Space booking in newspapers is often done in association with the hall, resulting in savings from bulk buying. You should always take advantage of these schemes. You can also use an agent. Their experience, especially with wording, will more than pay for their fee. They will advise you on the merits of lineage, semi-display and display, as well as position and the correlation of readership and target market. With specialist music, entertainment or tourist magazines, it is probably simpler to deal direct, linking display advertisements with the graphic design of your leaflets. You should also place listings in area entertainments or concert guides.

Leaflets and posters can be the best way to spend your money, but only, and I stress only, if you pay as much attention to distribution as production. Print nothing you cannot distribute. Be warned that, like some press advertising, posters and their sites are often expensive for the effect you get. This is because your advertising is competing against multi-million pound campaigns, and reaching many who will never attend a concert. There are agencies available to place leaflets and posters where they will be seen, but I regard that as the beginning of a task which will consume large quantities of your time, imagination and dedication. Use your friends, clubs and business acquaintances. Copywriting, design and printing are specialist skills of sophistication. Mistakes are costly, so be prepared to accept advice and make changes. Calculate lead times carefully. Ideally, you need your printed material delivered about two months before the concert. My best advice is to use people experienced in music promotion: they know what you can afford and have seen most of the problems before. As with many other things, you can use your talents to break the rules successfully only when you know why they are there.

For small, one-off concerts, use of TV, radio and cinema advertising is prohibitively costly, but should be considered for series and festivals.

As the most useful adjunct to advertising, but by no means a replacement for it, is a dedicated media relations campaign. Sometimes you will hear the phrase 'free advertising' used to describe successful public relations activity. Nothing could be further from the truth. There are many pamphlets and books available for consultation, as well as skilled practitioners who will give value for money. Organising press conferences, writing news releases and distributing them, and placing stories, are once again highly specialised skills. It would be more than a hint to say that there are people who can do these jobs effectively for you.

Briefly, if you have to write your own news release, it should be set out with meticulous accuracy on your A4 letterhead, one and a half- or double-spaced, with wide margins. One hundred words of crisp copy should begin by answering who, what, where, when, how and why, the last being a cue for you to write a story which demonstrates why your concert is so worthy of the attention of sub-editors, who pride themselves on their world-weariness! There should be a short, unambiguous heading, with a date and a contact name and number at the foot. If you have photographs or cassettes to offer, say so. The Arts Council publishes a reasonable press list, but PR practitioners should include more contacts. Enclose your leaflet. Send review tickets to arts editors or chief music critics with their copy of the release. In the case of new music, invite critics to the general rehearsal. Do not forget the free events listings.

The monthlies will have to be informed separately three months in advance, otherwise six weeks is about right. If you can find a second, different story as you go along, there is no harm in having another go. Follow up with telephone calls, so that you can arrange interviews, photo-calls or lengthier articles.

Programmes

You will need a programme book or leaflet, unless details are included on the promotional leaflet. If you are commissioning notes, you will need to know how long they can be. Writing good programme notes is difficult. In my opinion they are often unnecessarily analytical, sometimes over the heads even of the musicians. Take care not to alienate the audience before the concert begins. Make a dummy programme to calculate how much copy can occupy each page. List the credits you need. Try to make the biographies more than a list of achievements. Include the selling price and the fire regulations. Use photographs which your designer advises you will make reproducible half-tones. When you send copy to the designer/printer, it must be accurate and legible; you cannot expect him to read your mind as well as your words, let alone have your musical knowledge. Author's corrections will be charged to you. Keep an eye on the lead times: the printer owes you nothing. Tell the programme sellers the price of the programme so they can organise their floats.

Programme advertising needs a special sort of salesman – there are few good commercial reasons for taking space. Remember that big companies move much slower than the music business, and that you will pay for setting and layout if anyone does not send camera-ready artwork.

As the day approaches

During the run up to the concert, monitor ticket sales on a graph. They may be slow. Only experience will tell you if there is a problem, but there may be some action you can take if there is. One such is judicious gifts of free tickets, known as 'papering the house'. Of course, blanket papering can give the impression that your concert is not worth attending, but the right amount can create interest which may even stimulate a few sales. It is best to choose people who would not normally come to a concert, but who might have friends who would. Papering works only well ahead of time, and is itself time-consuming.

As the rehearsals approach, attend to the little details. Write desk numbers on the string parts and give them to the leader for bowing, or to individual players. If you are having flowers in the hall, check that your soloists do not suffer from hay fever.

Rehearsals

If you are responsible for setting up at the hall, you must make certain you are there early. An hour is not too long to give you time to check out everything you need. You will know if the heating and lighting are acceptable, but there's always a chance that something will have been switched off – boilers after 1st March, for example, irrespective of awful weather conditions. And check that noisy air-conditioning will not be turned on automatically as soon as the audience's temperature begins to rise. You may find that someone has removed the chairs or music stands you thought were there, or that an item of percussion has not been delivered.

Set the stage out according to a written plan – it should summarise the number of music stands, chairs, low and high stools. Don't forget that the conductor and some players may need something very substantial for contemporary scores. 'Cello players like to have their bottoms on something firm, and frequently prefer piano stools. Lute and guitar players usually need music stands lowered further than those in many halls will go. Bass and 'cello spikes wreck parquet flooring – the usual solution is a triangular piece of hardboard or plywood with a hole in one corner to fit round a chairleg. Has the piano survived its move into position, and did you put the brakes back on?

Now find the toilets and, if you need dressing rooms, check they are unlocked. Touring? Take toilet paper and soap, towels if possible. Check that the interval coffee will be available when you want it, and find the nearest working telephone. You need coins, a phonecard or other tokens. Check that a latecomer can actually 'phone through to the rehearsal to let you know – the number is on the schedule. Check that instruments and other valuables are secure during the break or between rehearsal and concert. Find a place where the musicians can rest or warm up.

If there are pieces where the visual relationship between players is crucial, take some chalk or plastic gaffer tape of different colours. Mark out the stands or instruments on the floor during the rehearsal, when the players have decided on the format. Note the marks on the stage plan.

If you are the fixer as well, you will have a list of the players, the times they were called and their telephone numbers. If they all arrive on time and the rehearsal begins with no problems, find the location of the nearest photocopier, in case there are part problems. With new or difficult music, it is advisable to pack manuscript paper, plain paper and a stock of pens, Tippex, pencils, erasers, paper clips, sellotape, Pritt, masking tape, magic tape, scissors, knife. These are essential if you are doubling as librarian. Playing out of doors? Four clothes pegs with springs per music stand, and an umbrella to hand. If you are using electrical equipment, straight and cross-head electrical screwdrivers, a fit-all plug, an assortment of fuses and a pair of pliers would probably help you to kick-start a reluctant vibraphone, but don't tackle anything like that unless you are sure of your ground.

Think about how much of a nursemaid you need to be. A friend of mine left Heathrow on a fine warm February morning without a coat. He was flying to Helsinki. A car rug and big sweater should complement the jump leads in your boot.

During the rehearsal you need to be silent but available. Tell the leader or director where you will be. Give the director and stage staff reference copies of your stage plans. You also need to ensure that extraneous noise is kept to a minimum, and to keep a weather eye on unexpected guests. It does no harm to be suspicious in a friendly way – you can prevent theft and bootleg recordings. If things go wrong, try to remain unruffled. Most problems have a quick solution and you are not flying an aeroplane. Ask yourself – if I were playing, what would be annoying me most at the moment? If you can think of something you can act on (and we all know those you can't!) you need to take care of it straight away. Your function is to create a safe space in which musical risks may be taken.

Be firm about breaks, because they are essential to everyone, even if they don't think so. You must have fifteen minutes in three hours. Make sure you know where your players have gone: there is nothing more embarrassing than a misunderstanding about letting the trumpets go just before the conductor decides to go over a piece again.

If you need to make announcements, make sure that they occur at a convenient time and that the director is aware of their imminence. Musicians who have absorbed the input of a rehearsal have their attention elsewhere, so keep what have to say short, simple and unambiguous. You will find that the acoustic of a good concert hall is cruel to the spoken word, so project your voice to the front of the mouth and speak slowly, without fading away at the ends of words or sentences. Good use can be made of the fact that people remember anything funny, especially if sex is involved!

Be clear about requests and suggestions made to you. Act stupid, rather than assume you have understood someone. You need certainty.

Rehearsals are useful for administrative procedures, such as paying out, presentations or photocalls. Plan in advance: nobody likes waiting around. Suppose you want photographs of the ensemble. A new set of considerations arise: lighting, reflections, use of flash, colour, access, dress, interruptions to valuable rehearsal time and camera noise, besides questions like – can you photograph the whole band when the trombones have already been sent home? Consultation is the key. Ask the photographer what is necessary. Check with the hall to see if you need a pass for him.

Are you undertaking any radio interviews at the rehearsal? If so, you will need a soundproof environment away from the music.

Bear in mind that everything takes longer than you think, and you cannot be in two places at once. I have a theory that, if it takes half a minute for two people to sit down, twenty people will take five minutes.

Accidents are rare, but if you know where the first aid kit is kept, you are forearmed. The biggest problem in the UK is sustenance, especially on Sundays in the provinces. A box of fruit and convenience food can take the edge off a cause for upset.

143

At the end of every rehearsal or concert you should check the whole area for items left behind. If you are acting as librarian, you need certainty in your relationship with players who keep their music.

During the rehearsal, you should prepare for its end and deal with the problems to be encountered at the next one or at the concert. One will be curtain calls. Some musicians have a natural presence which makes their interaction with the audience an integral part of their performance. The rest need rehearsing. The players should be quite clear about the way they enter and leave the stage. Sloppiness here can wreck a concert.

At the general rehearsal, time the pieces as they are run through, and inform the stage and front-of-house staff so they know when to prepare for the interval or the end. Tell them if you are playing encores, and also the names of the publishers of the copyright works. Check that piano retuning will take place as arranged and that time is available for soloists to warm up in the hall before the house is let in.

If you are selling records in the foyer, you will need staff, stock, a float of change, safe storage, a display, and instructions or facilities for taking cheques and credit cards. Mention the opportunity in the programme, if possible.

The time has now arrived to ask yourself if you have that special feeling – the one where you feel you have done everything you could possibly have done.

The concert

Be at the concert hall an hour and a half in advance. Check that the programmes have been delivered to the hands of the sellers, draw the complimentary copies you need for your guests, soloists, orchestra and so on. Leave envelopes of complimentary tickets to be collected from the arranged place. Establish that the stage is set up correctly, clear of extraneous articles and with music in the correct order on stands. Find the person who will present flowers to the soloists to be certain of the arrangements. Make sure your players arrive, change and are aware of the time. In the theatre, it is normal to call the half

(35 minutes), quarter (20 minutes), five (10 minutes) and beginners (5 minutes) before the show. You may not need this formality.

If you are paying out on the night, have the cheques prepared in advance; there will be no time at the concert. You may be arranging a party afterwards; now is the time to make sure that everything is in order.

Dealing with VIPs needs special consideration, depending on how 'I' they are. A further schedule may be necessary, and is indispensable for royalty. In any event, you should be available from the quarter to greet arrivals, hand them a programme, find them a drink or take them to their seats.

When you are satisfied that all is well, and not before, you can set the concert in motion.

By now, it should run pretty smoothly. But your work is not over. You must use the interval to set the stage and music for the second half, to check that there are no problems and to entertain your guests. At the end of the concert, see that the stage and backstage areas are properly cleared. Few musicians leave without their instruments, but a trail of wallets and clothes is not so uncommon. You may be needed to help some players with the get-out. You should have sufficient money to tip helpful stage staff. Thank the musicians and anyone else who needs acknowledgement. Make arrangements to collect spare programmes for future promotional use. Now go for a drink.

Follow-up

Next morning, buy all the papers and scan for reviews. Send copies to the relevant people. In the old days of primitive technology, concert reviews appeared on the following day. Not so today. You may have to wait – six days is the maximum in my experience! A press-cuttings agency will make sure you get them all, but you will have to wait a month.

Invoice the programme advertisers and bulk ticket purchasers. Pay the participants and invoiced services and prepare the accounts. Thrill to the reviews, groan over the deficit and take a holiday. You deserve it.

SPONSORSHIP: THE RIGHT APPROACH

TIM STOCKIL

Tim Stockil was educated at Oxford and trained as a director at the Bristol Old Vic Theatre School. In 1981, after a variety of jobs in the theatre, he joined Merseyside Young People's Theatre Company as administrator, where he became interested in, and successful at, raising sponsorship. He joined the Association for Business Sponsorship of the Arts in October 1984 as one of the administrators of the Business Sponsorship Incentive Scheme.

Sponsorship is the payment of monies by a business to an arts organisation for the purpose of promoting its business name, its products or its services. It is not charity, and neither is it public subsidy. Many statutory bodies – the Arts Council, the Regional Arts Associations, local authorities – have an obligation to fund the arts. Businesses do not. It follows that it is a great deal easier to get subsidy from a public funding body than it is to get sponsorship from a business.

A business will use sponsorship for increasing name awareness, client, customer and VIP entertaining, reaching a specific target market, enhancing corporate image and community relations, improving relations with staff, and associating its name with quality. Increasingly, there may also be an element of philanthropy or corporate responsibility in a business's sponsorship policy. If you can't offer some or all of these, you probably shouldn't look for sponsorship. If you can, the following guidelines should be helpful.

147

Self-analysis

First, examine your own operation. How are you established? What do you do? Why do you do it? Why is it important? Are you successful at it? How do you wish to develop? The last two questions are particularly important – if you consistently play to 40% houses, you would do better to improve your marketing, partly because selling more seats is the easiest way for you to increase your earnings, and also because a business is unlikely to sponsor an organisation which is not successful in audience terms. Development is also crucial; business sponsorship should be a supplement to public subsidy, not a substitute for it, not least because available business funds depend on market conditions outside your control and may be withdrawn at any time. It is prudent, therefore, to search for sponsorship for the extras – those things you would really like to do but for which you have never had the money. This may seem like wishful thinking, but a successful sponsorship of a special project should provide benefits, financial and otherwise, for your core operations.

The deeper your self-analysis, the better armed you will be. Is your board of directors going to be useful? Perhaps you ought to consider establishing a sponsorship sub-committee made up of businessmen sympathetic to your aims, and prepared to work to raise sponsorship for you. Do you really know your audience? You might consider doing an audience survey. Try attaching a survey to a prize draw – the returns are better.

Such self-analysis takes time – but sponsorship is a time-consuming business. Most businesses with sponsorship budgets commit themselves to their expenditure for one financial year in the middle of the previous year. For example, if you approach a business with a financial year which runs to 31st December to sponsor your gala concert in December 1988, you should be talking to them in early summer 1987, eighteen months before.

You may publish a brochure about yourselves, covering your history, constitution, *modus operandi*, catchment areas and audiences, and past successes, and such brochures are very useful in making approaches to businesses who may never have heard of you. An orchestra's promotional brochure, for example, can be an excellent sponsorship package in itself.

Packaging

If your self-analysis has led you to believe that you can, and should, search for sponsorship, the next step is to develop sponsorship packages. It is rare for a business to sponsor the whole of an arts organisation's operations as it is usually more effective in terms of name awareness to associate a company's name with a specific project – a tour, a special series of concerts, or a gala, for example. Each of these is a potential package, and each offers something different; a tour may reach towns where a sponsor wishes to be seen, a series of concerts might get high media coverage, a gala might be a particularly good entertaining opportunity. Each may reach a different audience.

Every package should be written up separately – type neatly, give each paragraph a number and a heading, and do not ramble (two pages is ample). A proposal should cover:

(a) *What the project is*
(b) *Who you are*
(c) *What you do*
(d) *The dates of the project*
(e) *The places you will be performing*
(f) *The number and make-up of your likely audience*
(g) *The publicity* Be specific: give print runs, size of posters, where they will be displayed, newspapers in which you will advertise, etc.
(h) *The benefits to the sponsor* Be specific but flexible: will you incorporate the sponsor's name into the title of the project – 'The Fred Smith Orchestra/Jo Bloggs & Co Tour'? Are there opportunities for entertaining? Will you offer the sponsor tickets at reduced prices? Will you have their logo displayed prominently on all publicity material? Will your sponsor have a free page in the programme?
(i) *The cost* (and don't forget the VAT) This should relate to the value of the promotional opportunity, and not to the

actual cost to you. It is perfectly possible for a concert to cost you £2,000 but be worth £30,000 to a sponsor. A range of costings can be sensible – obviously, if a sponsor wants you to have a bus shelter poster campaign, for example, it will cost more.

The purpose of this brief proposal is not to give a comprehensive breakdown of the whole project, but is to get to meet your potential sponsor. The neater, the more succinct and the more professional it is, the more likely you are to achieve that aim, not least because some of the big sponsors get upwards of 300 proposals a week. Include some background material (this is where your brochure comes in) but not vast reams which may well be filed in the waste-paper basket.

A valuable addition to any sponsorship proposal is the Business Sponsorship Incentive Scheme which is administered by the Association for Business Sponsorship of the Arts (ABSA) on behalf of the Minister for the Arts. The Scheme is intended as an incentive to businesses either to sponsor the arts for the first time, or to increase their commitment to the arts. It offers both government endorsement and financial support. BSIS funds can match new business money – money that has never been allocated to the arts before – either pound for pound or one pound for every three pounds of new sponsorship, depending on circumstances. Full details of the Scheme are available from ABSA.

The next stage is to determine which companies you will approach.

Research

You cannot research too much. Find out what a business has sponsored before and what its policy is now. It is pointless to send a proposal for sponsorship of a high-profile gala performance to a firm that only sponsors projects involving the arts and education: this is why you create separate packages. Is the business making a profit? Are they keen on corporate, as opposed to product, advertising? What is their target market? Where do they operate? Write and ask a business for its annual report – public companies are obliged to send you one on request. Read the financial papers and the PR and marketing magazines. Use some common-sense – a company that is the object of a takeover bid is unlikely to be increasing its sponsorship portfolio.

This process should determine which business to approach – try starting with a short list of six.

The approach

Once you have decided on your short list, ring up and ask who deals with sponsorship. If the switchboard doesn't know, ask for the PR department. Once you have the name (check the spelling) and the correct title, ring him up and ask what the company's sponsorship policy is. Do not try to sell your proposal over the telephone. Be brief, and specific – 'Are you still interested in sponsorships in Leicester and Milton Keynes? You haven't sponsored any jazz for three years – is this a policy decision? Will you be celebrating your 150th anniversary in any special way?' If it is clear that you are not wasting your time and his, say 'Thank you very much, I'll be writing to you'.

The letter you send to accompany your proposal should start 'Further to our telephone conversation . . .' which means that he has to read it. The rest of the letter consists of a two-line paragraph saying who you are, another two-line paragraph saying what the proposal is, and a final paragraph saying that you would like to discuss your proposal further and to that end you will ring his office in a few days' time to arrange a mutually convenient date to meet. If you get an immediate reply saying no, you will at least waste no more time and money. If you hear nothing, you have a tacit agreement to meet, so ring up again and arrange a meeting through his secretary.

Your short list may have to grow significantly before you can get someone to agree to meet you. Do not despair – polite persistence is the key to successful sponsorship raising.

Negotiation

Once you have an agreement to meet, go prepared. Dress smartly and arm yourself with back-up material. Be flexible. Begin by asking questions – it will allow you to see if you need to change your tack at all. You should have the authority to make immediate decisions as to whether your organisation can or cannot do something they suggest.

Make sure that, at the end of the meeting, you know what the next step is. Do they want further information? Do they want to come and hear your work? Will your proposal be put to the committee? Write and confirm what you understand to be the outcome of the meeting, and thank them for their time.

Management

Your proposal has been approved. Write a thank-you letter and specify exactly what the benefits will be, which of you is responsible for what, when you expect payment, and so on. Alternatively, they may send you a contract or a letter of agreement. One of these is essential – a 'reasonable number' of free seats may be ten to you but forty to them. Do they want to see proofs of artwork? Who is going to send out invitations to a press launch? You will need further meetings – you must keep in touch. If one of your venues burns down, tell them. If the opportunity arises for TV coverage of a concert, tell them. This is common courtesy, but it is also essential if you are to retain your sponsor. If you have kept in touch, if everything has gone smoothly, if you have both got out of the deal what you wanted and expected, if you have developed a relationship of mutual trust and understanding, your chances of retaining the sponsor for next time are good. Work at it – you never know what a goldmine you might have unearthed.

Some last points

Individuals Sponsors very rarely support individuals. If you are a soloist looking for your big break in a London concert hall, a sponsor is much more likely to sponsor the venue than you.

Joint sponsorships Don't – they are much more trouble than they are worth.

Touring abroad It is a great deal more difficult to raise sponsorship for touring abroad. Plan well ahead.

Sponsorship consultants If you are looking for a great deal of money, it may be worth a consultant's while to take you on. But, increasingly, sponsors wish to deal directly with the artists themselves, as their commitment and enthusiasm is far greater than a consultant's will ever be.

Bibliography

For general research, read *Campaign, Marketing, Marketing Week, PR Week, The Times 1000, Who's Who, Who Owns Whom,* the *Stock Exchange Yearbook* and *Key British Enterprises,* most of which should be available at a public library; so should the *Directory of Grant Making Trusts,* which is useful if you are looking for charitable donations, as is *A Guide to Company Giving,* available from the Arts Council Bookshop.

Final note

Please, as your experience in raising sponsorship grows, share it with other arts organisations – you won't lose a sponsor as a result, and the concept and practice of sponsorship will be more widely understood to the benefit of all.

TACKLING THE AGENCY WORLD
ANDREW GREEN

Andrew Green was, for several years, a director of one of the oldest-established London concert agencies, Ibbs and Tillett Limited, and is also a former general manager of the City of London Sinfonia. Having left Ibbs and Tillett in 1983, he now devotes his time to writing and broadcasting. He contributes a regular column, The Agency Angle, to Classical Music *magazine.*

It's been a fairly typical day at the All-Star Amalgamated Artists Agency. The managing director's desperately searching out a replacement for a sick bassoonist who should have arrived on the Isle of Skye two hours ago; his secretary's just brought in the glad tidings that the visa for the Peruvian percussionist isn't going to be ready in time; and, no, he didn't need reminding that his latest star attraction – that Hungarian horn quartet – is still double-booked on the second Thursday in March two years hence. And you? Already you're the fifth out-of-work 'cellist who's come banging on his door this month.

Why *should* he stop for five minutes to let you say your piece? And, if he's not that busy, *why* isn't he that busy – there aren't that many effective agents in the classical music field who can afford to take their hands off the tiller for very long. A tiny proportion of available untapped talent counts as hot property guaranteed to rivet an agent's attention – and this chapter is hardly going to be especially relevant to those in such exceptional demand anyway. Their's, as likely as not, will be an uncomplicated route to prominence.

You can only expect that established agents of any stature

start discussions with prospective clients with a deep-seated bias towards polite rebuttal – and you shouldn't be surprised at that. The current trend seems to be for many agents to cut their lists of exclusive artists rather than to expand, concentrating on building the careers of a few rather than dissipating energy on merely chasing individual engagements for the many.

What are agents looking for? Like the rest of us, they're after not only a decent income, but also a secure one in an industry based on commission proceeds. Security rests ultimately in the degree to which their artists are established in the public and professional eye – and if they're truly recognised as such, then there's a good chance of a steady groundswell of demand for their services at reasonable fees. You can hardly blame a hard-pressed manager for having eyes for competition winners, for those with record contracts and for media attractions generally.

'But I'm a serious artist', I hear you say. Well, an agent has to be a serious businessman to survive in a highly competitive field. In any case, simply by wanting to perform in public for a fee, you state an intention to join the whole music-marketing business. Of course artistic standards matter (though many will argue that their importance has gone out of the window in the current commercial environment) but it remains a simple fact that, barring a small elite, professional soloists or ensembles have to be clued up on the means by which careers are built.

What, then, is a career? At the risk of gross simplification, two very rough definitions can be attempted. Artists A's career is very much the agent's ideal outlined above – a good public profile combined with professional esteem producing a regular demand for engagements. Management, in this case, becomes a matter more of steering the ship than ceaselessly constructing it. However, demand for the artist may turn out to be short-lived in real terms, in which case category B may be more appropriate. Artist B's career experiences no consistent level of demand, for whatever reason, with the result that the agent may feel that each separate date is being carved out of solid granite and, even when they are fashioned, the exercise may well not be cost-effective. If that state of affairs persists, there are going to be strains on the artist-manager relationship which, shall we say, can lead to only a limited number of outcomes. One thing is sure. If artists in category B are intent on pursuing a performing career at any level, then their own input into the exercise is going to have to be significant. Granted, you cannot expect all agents to be saints or of the same level of competence but, time and again, one hears the complaint of artists that this or that agent 'hasn't come up with anything recently' when so often there seems to have been little contribution to the working relationship from the artist's side. His or her contacts and artistic ideas can be as important as the agent's in a situation where work is scarce.

I hope, then, that this at least modifies two misapprehensions that can bedevil relationships between artists and managers – the idea that all the latter are stinking rich and, hence, have time on their hands, and the assumption that, once you're on an agent's books, you can sit back and let the work roll in. This is not to paint all agents as whiter than white – but anyone seeking management should be aware of the nature of the world they're entering. What sort of career are you after? Can you assess your own abilities well enough at least to relate them broadly to the market place? What can you place before an agent that will be of positive, practical benefit to his work? I repeat, why *should* an agent take any notice of you?

If all this is not too discouraging, what can the promising young artist do in practical terms to give himself the best chance of getting on? Well, without trying to give the impression that 'all you have to do is . . .', let's try and piece together a general strategy.

Be well-informed. It should be no arduous task to get hold of artist lists from a range of agencies (the *British Association of Concert Agents' Directory of Artists* published by Rhinegold will point the way). Develop a feel for agency specialities, their strengths and weaknesses and, of course, their stature. An obvious weakness may indicate that your particular talent might be needed, or equally it may mean the agent concerned has no interest in that area. Likewise, an obvious speciality such as a bulging list of string quartets can mean it's *either* a good *or* a bad thing to approach that manager. An agent may be new or well-established, but what matters is his effectiveness. In all this you can but explore further.

If at all possible, talk with your own contacts about their knowledge of particular agents – how successful they are, how they work (unfathomable though that may be on some occasions), how long they've been around, and so on. It may not be accurate information, but it can at least get your antennae operating more effectively. Try and relate your own interests and standing to those of artists on the lists in front of you. Don't let that prevent you from aiming high but, if you do, it goes without saying that the all-round presentation of your case is really going to have to stand up.

Be aware that nothing is straightforward. A large list may mean that a given manager is hopelessly over-worked – but again, if that list is solid gold throughout, then it may be that that office's kudos and contacts are so exceptional that a new artist can be launched alongside the others very effectively (but can you get a foot in *that* door?). In the same way, a small agency list may indicate surplus capacity or it may not.

What if an agent approaches you? Well, plenty of people still buy double-glazing from the first door-to-door salesman who comes along – but unless you've already mapped out the territory, don't you think you owe it to yourself to get informed before making any sort of agreement? OK, maybe you'll emerge from a premature and ill-judged misalliance unscathed, but managers can be suspicious of agent-hopping artists – especially if things aren't going well (the 'no smoke without fire' syndrome ...). You may find nailing a new manager all the more difficult than it would otherwise have been.

Getting to see an agent could well be tricky – you can at least try, on some good pretext or with an introduction. But agents will display normal human curiosity when it comes to flipping through the morning mail. Here's where you have at least a few brief seconds to impress – and yet so often this is where artists give themselves no chance at all. Why waste money on a brochure that looks as if it was designed by committee, especially if it's filled with the unabridged version of your career history, supported by endless reviews from (no offence intended) merely local newspapers? Spend time, trouble and, yes, more money rather than less on putting together something that focuses on the *best* of you: it's going to be useful in finding concerts whether you attract an agent or not. It will be the greatest help to an agent if he can see immediately what threads he may be able to pick up and exploit: significant publicity you've received or generated, conductors you've worked with, important reviews, attractive and original ways of presenting repertoire and so on.

With a bit of luck, the agent you've approached is one of those who listens to demo-tapes at home in the evenings, gin and tonic in hand. Are you *really* happy with the quality (peformance and recording) of what you've submitted. If you're not, why did you send it? Yet dozens rush in in that fashion where harp-embracing angels would fear to strum. Then, if you're more fortunate still, an agent may be prepared to give up his gin and tonic and come to hear you in the flesh somewhere or other, hopefully in congenial and conducive surroundings. And then – well, all sorts of strange things can happen in the heady excitement of a concert atmosphere (provided there is one . . .).

If short-term tactics like these aren't getting you anywhere with any of your chosen targets, keep them informed of each significant event in your career – always presenting the information well – and hope that you'll work your way into that manager's subconscious. Meanwhile, pursue your career as your own manager. Fight for auditions whether you're an instrumentalist or a singer; develop your own contacts with music clubs and choral societies, orchestras and opera houses; make use of any opportunities for broadcasting; teach yourself to be your own publicist. Keep performing; keep meeting people. Think of the future. Give yourself a chance.

There are alternatives for the enterprising and able. Having your husband/wife/friend working flat out for you, fulfilling the function of an agent, may be useful up to a point, though it's unlikely to cut much ice with the more important promoters: it can be all too easy to see through the device of headed notepaper bearing your wife's maiden name. But, if a decent level of expertise and organisation are applied, this can set a ball rolling, and there are no legal requirements preventing you adopting this approach, provided no fee is offered for the work and as long as not more than one artist or ensemble is involved.

There are one or two instances where artists have successfully set up their own agencies to manage other artists while still looking after their own interests. But this is certainly going to require commitment, energy and expertise, as well as a Department of Employment Licence (obtainable for a fee at the regional Department of Employment Agency Licensing Offices in Stanmore, Birmingham and Leeds). Not for the faint-hearted.

The other option is, of course, to go freelance with a number of agencies. Representation by just one (competent) manager – *sole* or *exclusive* representation – will almost invariably be the correct course for the obvious high-flier insofar as there then exists one focus of responsibility for overall planning. But, if it's approached in the right way, a freelance career can provide regular work if, among other things, you're willing to get involved. The relatively few agencies that deal with freelances tend to have large numbers of them on their books, and you will probably have no option but to vie for the agent's attention on a regular basis – from the bottle of whisky at Christmas to frequent 'courtesy' phone calls, and to the consistent production of new and saleable ideas, new publicity material and so on. Keep your profile high.

But let's now assume that somebody is willing to take you on exclusively. Remember that you have every right to ask questions before making such a commitment. Be sure that there's a reasonable chance of you and your manager getting on (it can, after all, have a psychological effect on his work), and seek to understand just *how*, in broad terms, the job of marketing you is going to be done. Put your concerns on the table at the *beginning* (you must have some . . .). It's comparatively rare, in this country, that you'll be asked to sign a contract – 'letters of agreement' on basic working details and 'understandings' tend to predominate – but, if you're unsure about anything, speak up or seek legal advice.

You'll be expecting to pay commission, of course, and this varies from agent to agent in terms of a percentage of your fee. (Take VAT into account as well). Arguments over commission are a continual bugbear, so understand *your* agent's procedure from the start. Will commission be charged on the gross fee or on a net amount after the deduction of expenses? Most managers will want world representation for their British-based exclusive artists so, if an overseas manager is involved in raising a contract abroad, who takes what commission and what will that amount to overall? Unless otherwise informed, assume that an 'exclusive' manager will expect commission on every engagement in your diary, however that engagement came about – indeed, your manager will expect to hold the definitive version of that diary. Over and above commission, one or two agents may ask for a retainer, one reason being that they may have to wait some time before any financial reward accrues from their efforts – which may involve them in considerable expense. Again, a manager may look for a contribution to the cost of publicity material. Don't automatically assume that the aim is to fiddle you, but just keep your wits about you – it's one thing to ask how far you should trust someone with your money and another to be straightforward and honest with yourself over how far you're willing to invest in your career. There's no easy guideline.

Reaching an agreement over exclusive management is just the start of what should be a working relationship with input (let me reiterate once again) from both sides. As with freelance artists, you're almost certainly competing with others for your manager's time – so . . . compete! Your ideas and information matter. If you hear nothing from your manager for weeks on end, there may be a whole variety of explanations. Yes, he or she may not be up to the job but, in the same way, you may be proving difficult to sell (not something agents like having to pass on). It can take some time for genuine headway to be made, especially if an unknown artist comes on to the books at a flat time in the year for bookings generally. Just a few managers who specialise in touring orchestras or who run concert series may instantly be able to place new artists in engagements and tours, but somehow it's easily forgotten that an agent is usually distinct from a promoter, and relies on his clout and/or powers of persuasion to bend the relevant ears – abilities which may take a while to have an effect.

There can be no easy way to remedy the situation if work is not flowing in. In the long run, it will be obvious whether your career is under way – but, in the meantime, develop a feel for how the job that's being undertaken is being and should be done. How long do you think it *should* take to build a career?

One last word of advice: publicity is nothing new in relation to music and musicians, but competition for it gets ever fiercer. Distasteful it may be to some, but polishing the public profile whenever possible is a task that cannot be ignored these days. Few agents themselves specialise in PR work, so it may be necessary to seek advice on where to go for help. Venture capital may be required and, of course, may not be readily available – but there may be a point at which you have to decide whether you can afford *not* to invest in such assistance.

That, then, is a good part of the theory. Armed with a few ideas you can but throw yourself into the fray. A tiny proportion of those who read this will actually break through into anything like important careers. This is a rough, uncompromising profession and any kindly uncle would warn you to have something to fall back on if it doesn't work out – not least some self-esteem. Whatever the standby may be, I can only hope that anyone setting out manages to avoid the cynicism of the hard-bitten pro . . . and that he or she hangs on to a love of music in the process. That helps.

APPROACHING A RECORD COMPANY
CHRISTOPHER BISHOP

Christopher Bishop was, for fifteen years, a recording producer with EMI and was responsible for many of the best-known recordings of the 1970s. Since 1979, he has been managing director of the Philharmonia Orchestra, an organisation whose activities are closely linked with all the major, and many smaller, recording companies.

The appearance of an artist's name on a record is seen by the public as a sign that he has 'arrived'. He must have made his mark if his performance is worth laying down for posterity, and if a company is prepared to invest its money in him. All artists know this, and so the competition to record is intense. Records should thus be a reflection of an artist's concert career, and not a promotional aid – at least in the world of classical music.

It goes without saying that if an artist is a genius the record companies will all fight over him and his problem will be to decide on which company to choose. If, however, he is not one of the very few who spring to fame overnight, not an Ashkenazy, a Sinopoli or a Barenboim, he may have to work very hard for recognition. For him, the best possible course is to find a good agent who will then take on the job for him.

The career of the conductor Esa-Pekka Salonen is fascinating in this respect. He had made a good reputation in Scandinavia, and I first heard him praised by members of the Swedish Radio Choir when the Philharmonia performed with them in Rome under Muti in August 1983. When illness prevented Michael Tilson-Thomas from conducting a performance of Mahler's Third Symphony at the Royal Festival Hall a couple of months later, we tried all the conductors we could think of to replace him, but without success. Joeske van Walsum, Salonen's London agent, suggested to me that we might try Salonen.

Even though I vaguely remembered the Swedish choir's remarks, I was very dubious about engaging a 25-year-old unknown conductor in such a monumental work as Mahler's Third. Then van Walsum played a brilliant card – he gave me a video of Salonen conducting the Swedish Radio Orchestra. My years in the recording studio have made me very sceptical about auditioning from records, particularly in the case of conductors. A good editor can make a hotch-potch of takes sound presentable, and it is even possible to trim a ragged chord to appear as if the conductor has a wonderfully precise baton. But a *film* of a live performance cannot lie in this respect. I could *see* that the orchestra responded precisely to Salonen's very clear and authoritative beat, and I was pretty sure we had found a winner. And so it proved: Salonen made his debut with the Philharmonia a week later with huge success. So impressed was the orchestra that, soon afterwards, he was appointed Principal Guest Conductor. Then came approaches from three major record companies, of which CBS seemed to offer the best opportunities, and so he signed with them.

Salonen's big chance came in the concert hall and records followed, but recording can often give a dramatic thrust forward to an already successful artist's career. It is not necessarily a big company which gives this thrust, and Janet Baker's early recordings illustrate this. She had begun to make an impact on stage when, in 1961, her agent Emmie Tillett suggested her to EMI for the small duet part (with Heather Harper) in Mendelssohn's *Midsummer Night's Dream,* to be conducted by Klemperer. She then sang in Purcell's *Dido and Aeneas* for L'Oiseau-Lyre, and subsequently made a hugely successful record called *An Anthology of English Song* for the small company, Saga. *This* was her real breakthrough to the record-buying public. Her success was sealed when Barbirolli invited her to sing the Angel in his 1964 recording of *The Dream of Gerontius* for EMI.

Both Salonen and Dame Janet had embarked on successful careers *before* recording companies showed any interest, and both had astute agents. Van Walsum helped Salonen by clever and opportune action, while Mrs Tillett used her very considerable persuasive powers to progress the young Janet Baker's recording career gently, in a much more orthodox way.

There is no doubt that luck plays a great part in any artist's life and, while persistence and the judicious use of contacts can make a tremendous difference, a good agent is invaluable. A bad one, on the other hand, can be worse than useless since, if an artist thinks he can rely on his agent and that agent is doing nothing for him, he is wasting valuable time. If an agent *is* useless, the only sensible solution is to move to another one – fast.

Not everyone is lucky enough to find an agent, good or otherwise, and so I feel I should give some advice here to those thick-skinned enough to try the direct approach. In the world of pop music, I suspect that a demonstration tape may well be one of the best ways for a group to present itself to a record company but, in the classical field, it is one of the least likely to succeed. However, it is worth mentioning a few dos and don'ts which would apply to most artists.

If you wish to impress a recording producer with a tape of your performance, make sure that the quality of the recording is as good as you can possibly afford. A producer is used to listening to the very highest of high-fidelity on professional equipment and is very unlikely to make allowances for poor recording quality when judging a singer's voice or an instrumentalist's tone. Why should he? When your audition tape is one of hundreds, any defect will put you at a disadvantage. Therefore, if you send tapes to be auditioned, note the following points:

1 Make sure the tape is cleary marked with your name and address. The chances are that it will become separated from your accompanying letter. How sad if the producer thinks you are the new Fischer-Dieskau, but cannot get in touch with you!

2 Make sure it is clearly indicated whether or not Dolby noise-reduction has been used; it distorts a tape badly to play it in the wrong Dolby mode.

3 Your performance should start at the beginning of the

tape. Don't expect the listener to follow instructions such as a 'wind on to about half way for the aria, just after the chorus. Then go to side two, three-quarters of the way in'. Your tape will end up being given to the producer's children to dub their pop music, if not in the waste bin.

4 Make sure that the recording is of professional standard. Do *not* make excuses about the quality of the performance. If the tape is not good, don't sent it in the first place. It is depressing how often recordings are accompanied by such nonsense as: 'I'm sorry the recording isn't very good, but my dog Offenbach sat on the microphone just as we were doing it, and my regular accompanist was ill, so the lady next door (Mrs Smith, who says she knows you, by the way) did her best, although she has difficulty with flat keys. Anyway, I'm sure you'll be able to hear how wonderfully I sing – or would have done if I hadn't just got a frightful cold.'

5 If you do write to a producer, make sure you get his name and address right. Never address him as 'Dear John Smith', but as 'Dear Mr Smith' – or, of course, 'Dear John' if you know him personally. If writing to a woman, do not use the abomination 'Ms'. Take the trouble to find out if she is married or not. If in doubt use 'Miss'.

6 Letters should be personally addressed. A duplicated letter starting 'Dear Sir or Madam' will not impress. Remember that you need the record company more than it needs you at this stage in your career. The addressee does not need to be flattered, but he must see the writer as an informed professional rather than an amateur. It is amazing how often I get applications from people who don't take the trouble to spell 'Philharmonia' properly. A brief resumé of your achievements is worthwhile, but keep the letter as short as possible. You have no right to expect an unsolicited (or even solicited) tape to be returned, but you might be lucky, and your chances of getting a reply are increased by the inclusion of a stamped addressed envelope.

7 The people likely to engage a new artist in a record company are the producers rather than the administrative staff. If you can, try to find out which producer is

interested in your particular sphere, and write to him. Use your contacts in the profession, such as more experienced performers and your teacher, to help you.

I can think of very few occasions when I have engaged an artist for a recording without the intervention of an agent and, when I have, it has been for rather unorthodox and personal reasons. For example, I once heard a young singer at a festival in Norfolk who so impressed me that I contracted her for a small part in an opera recording I was casting at the time. I wish I could say that she fulfilled my expectations and is now a household name, but alas that is not the case.

It was a different story with another personal contact. I conducted a programme of madrigals for the BBC and through this met David Munrow, who led the only recorder consort I had ever heard which played in tune. Munrow's irresistible personality persuaded me to listen to tapes of his other activities in mediaeval music, and the result was a contract with EMI and a wonderful collection of records, cut short by Munrow's tragic death in 1976.

A conductor who is well established in the recording world is one of the people most likely to secure recording work for an artist. This applies particularly to singers: when casting an opera or oratorio, the wishes of the conductor are paramount, and to be taken under the wing of a powerful conductor can ensure the singer's success.

Nowadays, there is one certain way for a soloist or a conductor to interest a recording company, and that is by providing funds for a recording himself. This can be done either by using his own money, or by finding a sponsor who is prepared to back him. There is nothing at all new in the concept of an artist putting on concerts at his own expense; even the careers of such giants as Beecham and Boult were launched with the help of family money. However, the commercial sponsorship of records is relatively recent, dating back some fifteen years. A sponsored recording can be a very productive use of money and can put the artist before the public far more effectively than a concert. A record is permanent, and can be used as a 'visiting card' to show off the artist's talent.

Most record companies, short of cash at present, are only too ready to show interest in sponsored records, provided the artists and repertoire interest them. The independent company Chandos, for instance, has built up an excellent catalogue with a large proportion of sponsored records. There is nothing 'cut price' about them, and their sound quality is second to none. Most of EMI's Classics for Pleasure records are sponsored and, in 1985, one of them won the *Gramophone* critics award for the best record of the year.

Choice of repertoire is very important: it is better to find a gap in the company's catalogue than to suggest yet another over-recorded classic. No-one will buy an unknown conductor's Beethoven's fifth, but there are plenty of Havergal Brian's symphonies as yet unrecorded, and an enterprising record company might well take the risk if the orchestra's fees were paid. It costs about £4,500 to hire a symphony orchestra for a three-hour recording session, during which a permitted maximum of 20 minutes music can be recorded. (In practice, it is not usually possible to achieve more than 15 minutes.) Orchestras are paid twice as much for a recording session as for a rehearsal and concert and it is consequently not difficult for a conductor with funds to persuade a symphony orchestra to record for him. It has been known for a conductor offering a number of records to persuade the orchestra to 'play in' the music at concerts, and this is a double benefit for the conductor. Nevertheless, unless an artist has so much financial backing that he can bribe his way into the catalogues with a large number of records, the time will come when his ability and selling power must be the real criteria upon which the record company will base its decision as to whether or not it will invest its own money in him.

Finally, do not write to a record company for advice; you are most unlikely to get a reply. Record companies, like most commercial arts organisations, do not regard themselves as altruistic or educational bodies: they are at the top of the pyramid and can behave very grandly. How much greater the pleasure, then, when you become a success, to see a host of rival record company executives queuing up after your concerts panting with the desire to sign a lucrative contract with you.

172

GONE ABROAD...
MICHAEL LEECH

Michael Leech has been a travel writer for the last 20 years. He is vice-chairman of the British Guild of Travel Writers, and regularly contributes articles to the Guardian, *the* Daily Telegraph, *and* Giroscope *(the magazine of National Giro). He is also theatre critic of* What's On and Where to Go in London.

Home may be where the heart hears the best music, but abroad is often where the money is. Even if the remuneration isn't quite as big as expected, travel is certainly an attraction, whether alone or with a group. Of course, once the invitation has arrived, or the idea starts to become fact, problems *do* arise. Your friends may be envious, but they won't see all the detailed planning you have put into a trip. I should have said 'a successful trip' because, without that vital planning and organisation before and during a visit, travel can develop more prickles than a hedgehog. It is especially important for an artist to plan travelling on business, with performances and appointments to be carefully scheduled.

The first step is to find out as much as you can about the country you plan to visit, both from a professional and from a social point of view. Presumably, you will want to do other things besides performing and, if you like the country you are visiting, the contacts you make the first time around can be invaluable for later trips. Hence, a knowledge of what the people are like, what they will want to ask you, what special events are likely to be planned, will assist you in organising everything from conversational tips to what to pack. We are fortunate in that our language is so widespread: few sophisticated people are now without a little English, and it is a blessing that on the airlines English is the first language in use after the local one. A haltingly spoken English announcement

173

after a babble of foreign tongues coming over the loudspeakers gives you the relief of understanding what is going on. Even in France, where the antipathy to universal domination by the English tongue is still strong, the young are enrolling for English lessons, and hotel and information desk staff will usually have a good knowledge of our language. Still, it is wise to take a phrasebook and a small dictionary, particularly if your tour is to take you beyond the major cities – in Spain, for example, very few people will understand English beyond the capital and a few spots popular with tourists. In some countries, such as the French part of Canada, you may still find an active dislike of speaking English, so bone up on your French, if only for politeness, if your concert or recital is to take place in Quebec City or Montreal.

The library is the first port of call, for books from the travel and geographical sections. Take out all you can find and cream off the information you need, whether it is how to acclimatise to Mexico City's extreme height (a couple of days rest beforehand to get used to the thinner atmosphere) or necessary codes of practice in certain Middle Eastern states. Make notes – a small tape-recorder is useful – or, if you have a home computer, the facts you glean may well be recorded for future use, too. For information on currency exchange, it is better to go to a bank and see their daily rate displays for, like the cost of hotels, guides rapidly go out of date when quoting prices, however approximate. When you get to the point of needing foreign currency, go to a bank and, after checking how much currency you are allowed to take, compare rates: they can vary quite a bit, and a seasoned traveller never changes money at a hotel unless absolutely necessary: the rate will rarely be good.

Travellers' cheques offer a good way of insuring yourself against theft, and are negotiable everywhere. Exchange rates between cheques and currency can vary too. Don't change too much when you arrive (you will only have to pay another percentage to change it back again) but remember that in most countries it can be difficult to change money at weekends. Be careful how you carry your wallet, for pickpockets abound in some cities, and it is wise to take out only what you are likely to need, using the hotel safe to store valuables. It isn't wise to parade expensive 'extras' in poorer countries anyway.

Books will also tell you what to wear and what weather to expect – vital if your instrument is one that reacts adversely to humidity or hot, dry air. Most travellers go with far too much baggage; reflect carefully on what you will need when packing and, if you can keep it down to a cabin-sized bag, you will avoid long waits at the baggage areas at your destinations. Don't take clothes that will crease easily or, if you must, pack a small travelling iron and an adaptor plug, available from most shops stocking electric goods. An inexpensive, well-made bag is better than expensive and ostentatious luggage – I have a theory that such smart pieces are the ones that end with scratches and dents.

Bear in mind that you may acquire extra things on a trip, and so pack a light, folding, extra bag. On flights, you are allowed some small extras in addition to your carry-on bag, and women have the advantage of being allowed a handbag. If your instrument is your carry-on allowance, ensure that you pack with it such things as important papers, money, cheque-books and any medication you may need. Players of very large instruments have the dilemma of travelling with them and, perhaps, having to take an extra seat, or else putting that double bass in the hold with many 'fragile' labels and a comprehensive insurance policy. As a specialist traveller, you will need a specific policy, so check carefully with an agent to make sure you are properly covered and, if you make several trips a year, consider a policy that will cover you all the time – several good ones are available. With security in mind, choose baggage carefully: combination locks are a better bet than those with keys that may not be unique. Never part with items you cannot do without; carry them on and keep them close to your person. Remember that weight is not so much of a problem as bulk, so try to travel small if you can.

You will also want to have health insurance and this, of course, depends very much on where you are going – it is absolutely essential in countries such as the USA, where a spell in hospital can cost a small fortune and where it has been known for medical staff to make sure that you do have insurance before they will treat you. Most countries have some element of social concern when it comes to sudden illnesses, but you should check very carefully before you go. The EEC has a reciprocal arrangement between some member countries for urgent treatment, but find out which are operating the plan. Eligible citizens of the countries in the EEC get free or reduced cost treatment for emergencies, depending on the arrangements in a particular country. For full information and a leaflet that should explain all queries (SA 36, *How to get treatment in the other EEC countries*), write to the DHSS at Newcastle upon Tyne, NE98 1YX, marking the envelope 'Overseas Information'.

Your ability to claim may depend on your status within the national insurance scheme and this can be a problem for the self-employed. Apparently, and most unfairly, the scheme does not operate if you have been self-employed all your life, even if you have been sticking those little stamps on your contribution card every week. If you have been employed for any length of time during your working life, you should be eligible. It may be necessary to pay for your treatment and later claim back a percentage of the cost of it. If you consider taking out insurance, the DHSS leaflet should be of use. You will need a form to take abroad with you so, when your dates are fixed, inform the local branch of the DHSS and you will be given leaflet SA 28–30, *Medical treatment during visits abroad.* This you must complete (form included, on the back) and file with the DHSS office. They will then send you yet another form (don't despair!), the E 111, which you should insert in your passport. However, one or two EEC countries do not need this form.

For countries in Europe outside the EEC the situation varies, and you should ask the DHSS in Newcastle for information on specific countries. If you have to resort to the coverage offered by private schemes, then insist on a receipt when you pay. This is where a good travel agent is invaluable, for he or she should be able to provide you with all the information you need on insurance for the countries you are to visit. Ask questions before you go, when you are purchasing your tickets and making travel arrangements. This is particularly important if you are visiting the USA, and you should make sure that your cover is adequate. You may also have to pay at the time of application for treatment and, even if the insurance company later re-imburses you, this can mean a crippling bill when you least expect it. The whole business of travel insurance is a critical one, and you may also want to take out specific insurance to cover parts of the body that are vital to your profession – after all, your fingers, your eyes, even your feet, can be indispensable to your livelihood. For life insurance, your personal situation is obviously the issue, and you should consider taking out cover that is adequate if you have a family or dependent spouse or relatives.

Another aspect of health is immunisation against the diseases with which you may come into contact in certain parts of the globe. The list of diseases is much less long than it used to be, but certain precautions are still insisted on for a number of countries. For complete information you can check with an organisation such as Thomas Cook, which maintains a centre in London where all necessary injections may be obtained for all countries of the world. Not all are compulsory: some are suggested; but, if they are mandatory, you may well be refused entry if you do not have the necessary certificates in your possession. India and other Asian countries can be hard on the digestive tract, so take the kind of medications your doctor suggests to guard against stomach disorders whch could, after all, prevent you from performing.

It isn't necessary to be careful of drinking water in most countries unless you are of a delicate sensibility, in which case you will need to consider taking special food. In parts of Africa, however, and in certain other countries, it is wise not to drink tap water or ice made from tap water in drinks. In Mexico, it is sensible to wash fruit and vegetables if you intend to eat them uncooked. Sometimes, pills for purifying water are suggested – it might be an idea to take them with you if you anticipate problems.

Your NHS doctor should be able to provide you with all the immunisation and medical attention you may need before your trip, but you will need to ask of the country you are visiting what is required (usually a simple request to the consulate or business affairs section of the respective embassy). Let your doctor know in plenty of time. The service is normally free for residents of the UK and several injections can usually be given in one visit. Allow time to recover from possible after-effects, so don't plan to leave on your visit immediately – some courses of treatment can take several weeks. The principal problems are still cholera and typhoid, with yellow fever in parts of Africa and Central America; tetanus boosters should be taken for some tropical countries. In addition, it is always wise to include a small first-aid kit in your carry-on bag – if only to be used for the occasional sticking plaster or dose of aspirin.

Visas and special permission may be necessary as well as your valid and up-to-date passport. (It is amazing how many people forget to check, and then find that their passport is about to run out, necessitating a quick trip to the Passport Office.) Most countries do not require visas, but with some you will not get far without one. The USA is a prime case: it is not difficult to obtain a multi-entrance visa (the stamped page in your passport will then allow you in for a period of years) but it takes some organisation. If you are going to get visas yourself, then allow lots of time since you are in the hands of a bureaucrat behind a desk (or a screen) who can sometimes turn you down for what seems like no reason at all, especially if you are going to certain 'difficult' countries in the Middle East and Africa, notably Nigeria, Libya and Gabon.

You will also have the problem that you are going there to work – in which case you may well need a letter or documentation from the organisation sponsoring you. They should be able to inform you of this, but it would be maddening to go to an embassy visa office with the filled-in forms, the photographs, the passports and, last but not least, the money (cash usually, cheques aren't recognised), only to find that you have no guarantee to cover your appearance there. Again, the first thing to do when you receive your request to perform is to write to the embassy of the country concerned asking *all* the questions you need answered. It would probably be wise to enclose a stamped addressed envelope, too! In general, while crossing borders has become easier in Europe (they don't even check your passport as you drive between Holland and Belgium now), it has become more difficult to travel in the Third World. Remember that, if you are officially working in a country, you will usually not be applying for a regular tourist visa, but for a special one to cover your particular case. Again, allow plenty of time to obtain such permission, especially by post. Most countries are represented in London, but not all, and you may have to communicate with offices in Paris or elsewhere. It is also necessary to take a certain amount of cash into some countries in hard currency, and not to export any local money on your way out. So, if you are tempted to buy some black-market currency in Tanzania – don't: you will have to provide bank slips on leaving to show just how much you used up. This can be trying if you are staying for an extended tour of concerts or appearances. Usually you will need to be quite specific in stating how many days you intend to stay – and some countries can levy fines if you overstay the period. It is hard, and sometimes impossible, for women to obtain visas to certain extremist Muslim countries. If countries do not require visas, they will usually demand that you have a ticket valid for the next leg of your journey onwards. Visas can sometimes be extended once you have arrived.

For shorter journeys closer to home, transport is often your own car. There are several ways to cross to continental Europe – by boat, by hovercraft or by train which will carry your car to a city near your destination. There are all sorts of lures offered by the ferry people to get you to take short breaks, and these can be a boon if several people are going to perform in France or Belgium and return in a couple of days. Go to a travel agent and arm yourself with the brochures of Sally Line, Sealink, Hoverspeed and Townsend Thoresen, not to mention Brittany Ferries, which operates a useful service to Santander and saves a great deal of boring motorway driving for the price of 24 hours at sea.

This quick way to northern Spain isn't the only distance saver – check the ports of France for closeness to your destination. The short sea crossing from Dover to Calais may not end up being economical if your visit is to Paris, for example, which happens to be a lot nearer to Le Havre or Dieppe. Some time spent with up-to-date maps before you plonk down money for expensive ferry journeys is wise. To drive to Europe, you will need your driving licence, current car insurance and, usually, a certificate of international motor insurance (a *green card*), proof of ownership and, in some cases, an international driving permit. Information on what you need, and the various documentation, is available from the principal motoring organisations. Your car must be road-worthy, and a pack of tools and spare parts is necessary – I've more than once been saved by those useful puncture kits when suffering sagging tyres in quiet, garage-less roads.

This information is, of necessity, brief. As I said at the beginning, find out as much as you can before you cement your plans, with visits to libraries, bookshops and professional organisations. Publications I have found useful in the past are books distributed by Vacation Work of Oxford, who issue annual guides aimed at those wanting to work abroad. *The Traveller's Handbook* published by Heinemann with WEXAS International, is also recommended. And your local travel agent, if he or she is a good one, is invaluable, and will want to see you come in again – so make as much use of them as possible.

SECTION 3:
ADVICE FINANCIAL
AND MATTERS OF LAW

THE LAW OF CONTRACT
LAURENCE WATT

Since 1974, Laurence Watt has been a partner in the firm of Charles Russell & Co. in Lincoln's Inn. He acts for a number of professional musicians, including two of London's best known self-governed symphony orchestras, and was responsible for conducting the litigation which confirmed the freelance status of the members of such orchestras. He is secretary of the Council of the London Philharmonic Orchestra and is also an amateur french horn player.

The law of contract is such that encyclopaedias are barely sufficient to encompass in-depth analysis of its all embracing principles. None can escape its tentacles; the musician who wants nothing more out of life than to make music, still needs to eat and sleep and, accordingly, will need cash to pay for it. He, therefore, has to persuade an audience to pay him money in return for his ability to transport them into his own particular harmonious brand of heaven.

OFFER, CONSIDERATION AND ACCEPTANCE

At the simplest level, the musician makes his services available and the public offers money for him to play. The essence of the contract which is thus formed is the *offer*, the mutual *consideration*, (this being the performance in return for either an agreed sum of money or an equivalent benefit) and its *acceptance*. Without these three elements in some form, a contract cannot exist. However, life is never as simple as it appears and, if the law of contract were as straightforward as this, there would be no need for this chapter.

The regulation of the complex web of legal relationships that exists between the musician and his audience devolves down to these three fundamentals, and an understanding of them is, therefore, of prime importance.

Offer

The advertising of a musician's services, in whatever form, is a simple indication to the profession and the world at large of his availability to perform. The first stage in the contractual process is when an offer is made to engage that musician's services. The offer can be in writing, it can be verbal, directly or over the telephone, or it can be inferred from conduct. It must, however, be more than an indication of intent. 'I am planning a performance of *The Pines of Rome,* and I intend to offer you the part of the nightingale' will not, by itself, consititute an offer by a promoter which is capable of acceptance, even though that musician may hold himself available for the performance.

Consideration

Consideration is basically the legal requirement for something of value, not necessarily money, to pass between one person giving and another receiving a 'promise', to make that promise legally enforceable. It is essential that it is reciprocal, but it must also be understood that the law does not require that thing of value necessarily be adequate. One might make a good deal or a bad one, and the fact that the apparent benefit derived by one party might be hugely greater than that enjoyed by the other is not, in the absence of fraud or misrepresentation, something in which the courts will usually be interested. A member of the public who decided to purchase a ticket to hear Florence Foster Jenkins, expecting an enlightening operatic experience, would have been in for a rude shock, but would not have been able to claim back the price of the ticket.

Acceptance

The offer having been made, and the terms of that offer having been ascertained, the contract is concluded by its unqualified and final acceptance. As with the offer, an expression of intent to accept is not sufficient. A response to the *Pines* invitation above, along the lines 'I intend to accept if my dentist agrees' would not bind the promoter to engage him if the dentist gave him the all clear. Unless the person making an offer has stipulated that acceptance must be in a particular form, it can be verbal (including by telephone), in writing, by post, telex or otherwise. It can also be by conduct: if our colleague turns up for the first rehearsal of *The Pines* (the offer not having been withdrawn) but misses the performance, it will not usually suffice for him to say 'I could not find my teeth but, in any event, you never confirmed acceptance' (but see *frustration* below).

Postal acceptance can be tricky. A decision to use the post must be reasonable according to the circumstances, but if it *is* reasonable, then the acceptance operates from the moment of posting. Furthermore, if that postal acceptance is not received, the contract will still be complete, such that if the date is then offered by the promoter or engager to someone else, then that promoter or engager will still be bound by his contract with the first person. In practice, it would always be sensible in such situations to keep proof of postage, even though 'post' means in the ordinary course of the post. It should be noted that, whilst this rule applies to telegrams, it does not apply to telexes, where actual communication must be proved.

An offer can be withdrawn at any time prior to its final and unqualified acceptance, although such withdrawal must be communicated to the person to whom the offer was made. This seems an obvious statement perhaps; but a note of caution where acceptance has been by post: in view of the rule that acceptance takes place at the moment of posting, a withdrawal of an offer which is posted *before* the acceptance was posted, but which arrives afterwards, will be too late and the contract will be binding, regardless of that withdrawal.

Finally, in whatever manner they are made, both offer and acceptance must be clear enough to be capable of enforcement.

RULES CONCERNING CONTRACTS IN WRITING

There is a common misapprehension that, to be enforceable, a contact needs to be in writing. As can be seen from the above, a contract, subject to the exceptions mentioned later, can be in any form which will satisfy the basic rules described.

However, there are a number of legal exceptions. The important ones are as follows, where the contracts must be in writing, or evidenced in writing, signed by both parties and where, in some cases, special rules are rigorously applied:

1. *Contracts relating to the disposition of land or an interest in land*
2. *Employment contracts under the employment legislation* Where there exists an employer/employee relationship, it is a requirement of that legislation that a written statement of the terms of employment be given to an employee within 13 weeks of employment being taken up. Such a statement does not of itself form the contract; it simply records, and is evidence of, the contract terms.
3. *Consumer credit agreements* There are very strict rules imposed by the consumer credit legislation which regulate comprehensively the supply of credit to individuals. The all-embracing Consumer Credit Act was passed in 1974, covering the ground previously occupied by a jumble of legislation, including the 1965 Hire Purchase Act. Consumer credit agreements are very strictly controlled and have to be in writing. There is, normally, a ceiling of £5,000, but one section of the Act specifically deals with extortionate credit bargains where there is no upper limit on the amounts involved. The rules, insofar as they relate to the lender/hirer, are extraordinarily complicated, very strict and cover such things as –
   (a) cash loans and any form of financial accommodation, which will range from a standard bank overdraft to a mortgage,
   (b) credit sales in relation to goods,
   (c) the supply of services on credit, including cheque cards and credit cards, and
   (d) consumer hire agreements, which could include the

hire of anything from a bombardon to a video recorder.

The important facts in relation to these rules as they apply to the musician are:

(i) such agreements must conform to the particular type of agreement they purport to be and which are defined in the Act,

(ii) they must be signed in the manner prescribed in the Act,

(iii) they must set out all the terms of the agreement and, as such, be legible. Furthermore,

(iv) there are detailed provisions for withdrawal and cancellation under particular circumstances – a defined cooling-off period is provided for, within which a hirer or buyer under a hire purchase, credit sale or conditional sale agreement can cancel that agreement.

4. *Contracts for insurance*

5. *Assignments of copyright* on whatever grounds, and whether in whole or in part, must be in writing and signed by the person doing the assigning.

PARTICULAR TYPES OF CONTRACT

Agency contracts

An agency contract is one where the musician or ensemble (the principal) requests or authorises another (the agent) to act on his behalf, and that other person agrees and acts accordingly. The agent is thereby empowered, within the ambit of his instructions, to enter into a contract on behalf of his principal, and to perform, to compose or to conduct as if he were the principal. It is particularly important to delineate very carefully the actual authority being given to the agent, the type of work to be undertaken, the fee scales to be applied, the agent's own commission, and the limits of authority within which the agent can operate.

There is implied in any general agency agreement (where not dealt with expressly) a power for the agent to incur reasonable expenses to carry out his duties. In the absence of any contrary agreement, there is a duty on the agent to keep a separate account of all money received and expenses disbursed on behalf of his principal (the performer) and to make payment promptly, and there is a duty on the principal to make prompt payment of any commissions due to the agent.

Agents come in various shapes and sizes, ranging from those catering for many musicians, to telephone or diary agents, who keep a diary for orchestral and other musicians and who are thus always available for consultation. Their authority will depend upon what is agreed but, within that authority, a date made for a musician will be binding.

Since the very nature of the agency relationship is a personal one, the performer will always be dealing with an individual, whatever the size of the company. The agent's authority will be governed by contractual principles; any arrangements made by an agent on behalf of his principal can be subject to confirmation by the principal only if that is what is agreed at the outset.

Often, an agent will issue a note of confirmation of a date arranged between the agent on behalf of his artist (the principal) and a promoter or engager. There is occasionally argument as to the contractual status of such notes. Unless it is signed by both parties (unlikely), it will simply serve as evidence of a fixture already verbally agreed between the agent and the promoter which, depending on the agent's authority, will bind his client.

An agent will not be liable to the musician in respect of any problems arising between the musician and the engager providing:

(a) he has used proper care and skill in arranging the contract. Any breach of such a duty of care will potentially render him liable to the musician for any pecuniary loss suffered, and

(b) that it is clear to the promoter that he is contracting with the agent as an agent and not as a principal.

The operations of agencies are restricted by virtue of the provisions of the Employment Agencies Act of 1973 which, whilst not altering the basic agency law, made obligatory as from the 1st July 1976:

(a) the registration of employment agencies and businesses, together with detailed particulars of their operation and affairs. The relevant class of employment listed in relation to musicians is for *performers and other occupations in the entertainment industry,*

(b) the provision by the agency to its clients of a written statement of the current terms under which the business is conducted.

Auctions

Musical instruments, particularly ones of high value, frequently change hands as a result of an auction sale. The contractual principles governing an auction sale are as already set out above. It is important to note that the auctioneer's request for bids is only the 'invitation to treat', and it is the actual bid which constitutes the offer. The formality of acceptance is specifically provided for by statute (Sale of Goods Act 1979 Section 57), which states that a sale by auction is complete on the fall of the hammer – assuming it has not been dropped accidentally. Up to that point, a bid may be withdrawn. A seller at an auction is entitled to fix a reserve price which, if not met, will terminate the sale. It should be noted that, if the auctioneer makes a mistake and purports to accept a bid below the reserved price, he can still withdraw the item from sale. The auctioneer is also entitled to bid himself, providing the right to do so has been expressly reserved; otherwise, any sale where this happens may be treated as fraudulent by the buyer, entitling him to repudiate his acceptance of the bid and thus his contract.

Freelance contracts and contracts of service

The real distinction is between a contract *for services* and a contract *of service*. The former category governs the relationship that exists between players and, for example, the four self-governed symphony orchestras in London, and *ad hoc* orchestras and smaller ensembles across the country. The fact that such players are not employed in the statutory sense of the word, does not mean that they are not working under a contract. An engagement for a single session is as binding as for a series of engagements. A common practice is to present a schedule of firm dates to the players for a forthcoming period. This constitutes the offer for those dates which apply to the particular player. The acceptance of all, or (with the agreement of the promoter) a proportion of, the dates for the relevant fee and conditions will represent the conclusion of the contract. If a player, having confirmed his availability, fails or refuses to turn up to a particular session in such a list, he will be in breach of contract.

Contracts with persons under a disability

English law defines four groups which come within this heading:
1. Minors
2. Drunken persons
3. Married women
4. Mentally disordered persons

Since married women are now largely emancipated from their traditional restrictions, their position is not of concern in relation to the subject matter of this article. Furthermore, whilst mental disorder may well be a matter of subjective and strongly-held opinion from person to person, the clinical state to which this category refers again takes us away from practical realities for our purposes. This leaves us with categories 1 and 2.

Drunken persons It cannot be a frequent occurrence that a contract is purported to be concluded when one or both parties are in a state of complete intoxication. If it is, the courts will say of the affected party that he is 'of no agreeing mind' and that the contract is void accordingly – unless later ratified when sober.

Minors In view of the prodigious musical talents of mere babes in arms that one from time to time comes across, it is necessary to consider the validity of contracts sought and made with persons under the age of 18. The general rule is that no contract made with a minor is absolutely binding, except a contract for what are termed *necessaries*. Necessaries are defined as being things 'necessary and suitable for the condition and life of the infant'. For example, contracts for the repayment of money by a minor and contracts for goods supplied are regarded as absolutely void unless they are necessaries. Necessaries can, under certain circumstances, include legal or medical services.

A logical extension of this principle is that a minor can bind himself to contracts of apprenticeship, education and instruction which must be beneficial to him. Whilst some, especially the minor, might dispute what a court would regard as being fair and beneficial, such a contract has to be so regarded in relation to the minor when he enters into it. For a musician, the purchase of an instrument, subject only to the reasonableness of the terms of that purchase, would probably be regarded as coming within the category of necessaries.

There are categories of contract which a minor can enter into which, whilst strictly invalid, can be ratified and confirmed within a reasonable time of the minor achieving majority. These relate to land, marriage, partnership and share purchase.

PERFORMANCE, VARIATION, TERMINATION AND REMEDIES

Performance and breach

A contract having been entered into, all the parties concerned must perform that which they have undertaken to do at the appropriate time and in the manner intended. Frequently, a contract may provide for flexibility in performance. A promoter engaging an orchestra to perform *The Pines of Rome* may reserve the right to substitute an alternative work of equivalent orchestration (difficult!). If he substitutes a Haydn symphony, he will be in breach of his contract and will be liable to pay for any loss and expenses incurred by the orchestra as a result of the change. The orchestra will have included the larger work in its schedule and, assuming all those regular players and any extras have accepted the date, would in turn be bound by those individual contracts – our nightingale's peculiar talents make him quite unsuitable for anything else other than Leopold Mozart's Toy Symphony, and he would have to be compensated accordingly.

Contract terms are either fundamental (as above) or of less significance in relation to the whole performance of a contract. In a contract to perform, clearly the time of attendance for rehearsal and performance is vital. Failure by a player to attend a rehearsal would entitle the promoter, be he the orchestra itself or an independent entrepreneur, to treat the contract as at an end and to employ a substitute player. An alteration of the dress requirements or the venue for a performance is unlikely to be fundamental, and would only entitle a performer, inconvenienced by such change, to compensation for any extra costs he might incur as a result of the change.

Variation

A contract can always be varied in its terms (whether such a variation is fundamental or otherwise) by agreement between all parties. If there is a unilateral variation, such as a change of date by a promoter or the cancellation by a record company of a recording session, this will represent a breach of contract with the performer. A lawful variation can only be by mutual agreement within the contract.

If a performer or ensemble refuses or fails to perform a contract, thus repudiating it or being in fundamental breach, the courts in this country will not insist that the contract is carried out. They will only compensate the aggrieved party with damages for any loss and expense arising since, as a matter of principle, the courts will only enforce a contract for services under the most exceptional circumstances. It is arguable whether this would be extended to forcing an orchestra to comply with its contractual obligations to play at a particular place and time. The resolution of that argument may well depend on the make-up of the orchestra itself; the position with one of the freelance self-governed orchestras may be very different to that of an employed orchestra, such as those coming under the auspices of the BBC. So far as I know, the position of an orchestra in such a situation has never been tested.

Frustration and force majeure

This might, under different circumstances, be regarded as a definition of a subject more appropriate to a criminal text book. However, a contract may be terminated by fundamental circumstances beyond the control of either the musician or the promoter or agent. Strike, civil war, riot, tempest, flood, sickness are all typical conditions referred to by lawyers as *force majeure*, or simply *frustration*. In 1956, the following legal test was formulated by the House of Lords: 'frustration occurs whenever the law recognises that, without default of either party, a contractual obligation has become incapable of being performed because the circumstances in which performance is called for would render it a thing radically different from that which was undertaken by the contract'.

The contract itself terminates on the occurrence of the frustrating event. The legal consequence of such a situation used to be that the loss lay where it fell; payments advanced were irrecoverable, as were payments due. In 1943, a law was passed to remedy the patent unfairness of this situation. Although a contract can, and frequently does, provide for what is to happen upon frustration, the law now requires that, unless otherwise provided for, all sums paid or payable shall respectively be repayable or cease otherwise to be payable. There is an exception, however, that where just expenses have been incurred, a contracting party can keep or recover compensation accordingly. It is worth noting that, if a contract is frustrated at a point (and for different reasons) *after* a breach has already taken place, the party responsible for the breach may still be liable in damages.

The importance of this aspect of law to the musical profession comes into particular prominence

    (a) where a performer is sick or otherwise incapacitated from performing for reasons demonstrably beyond his control, and

(b) when considering some of the overwhelming problems that can occur with foreign tours by artists and orchestras. It is, however, important to ensure that any contract for such a tour is governed by English law, otherwise the statute referred above will not apply. This is fine if all fees and expenses have been paid in advance, but potentially disastrous otherwise.

MISTAKE, MISREPRESENTATION AND FRAUD

Mistake

A contract entered into as a result of a mistake will be void. Such a situation is very rare, since the word 'mistake' is so narrowly defined. A mistake must be mutual and go to the very root of a contract and, in any event, must be one of fact rather than law. It must be much more fundamental than a situation where, for example, our nightingale discovers that it is not intended that he should use his peculiar personal talents, but simply press the button on a tape recorder. The only circumstance where this would not be correct would be where the performer of the nightingale had become so famous, or notorious as the case may be, for his talents that the audience were coming to hear *him* as opposed to *The Pines of Rome*. In that event, the following two headings could have some relevance.

Misrepresentation

This is a subject governed by the common law and statute, and basically means what it says. If a person is induced to enter into contract as a result of a misrepresentation of fact by the other party, whether fraudulent or innocent, express or implied, then he will be entitled to reject the contract. To that extent it will be void. He may, however, affirm it after discovery of the true facts and, if he does so, the contract will be valid and enforceable. As with most other areas of contract law, it has convolutions (convulsions even) and intricacies of interpretation which are beyond the scope of this chapter.

Fraud

A contract induced by the fraud of one party will, as with misrepresentation, be voidable. In other words, it can be rejected by the aggrieved party unless he chooses to affirm it. If the audience turning up to hear Florence Foster Jenkins had been induced to attend by extravagant comments concerning her prowess as a coloratura soprano, there will certainly have been a misrepresentation, possibly even a fraud – but I don't think anyone would have minded . . .

A PRACTICAL GUIDE TO COPYRIGHT LAW
RUTH BELTRAM

Ruth Beltram qualified as a solicitor in private practice in 1977. After a period of general experience in the law, she began to specialise in commercial litigation and became a partner in a firm in Chancery Lane. She joined the Performing Right Society in October 1983 and now holds the position of Solicitor (Membership) and Registrar with responsibility for the overall protection of members' interests.

It is intended that this chapter should be of use to those who need to have a working knowledge of copyright law, both as creators and as users of music, and should offer guidance through the minefield of legislation. It will also explain some of the main points to be considered by anyone who wishes to perform or otherwise use musical works, or to offer his own works to others for publication, performance, recording or broadcasting.

In practice, there are problems for copyright owners in trying to enforce their rights, and for music users in ensuring that these rights are respected. Unlike a manufacturer of goods, a composer of music cannot withhold supply of his work as a way of negotiating better terms once it has been made available to the public and, indeed, his livelihood depends upon the widest possible exposure. Music is particularly difficult to protect, both by its very nature, and also given the technological advances which have provided sophisticated methods for its widespread reproduction and dissemination. There is an ever-increasing risk of piracy, such as recordings of high quality being made of a live concert which are then readily marketable without payment of royalties to the composers and/or publishers of the music, out of whose talent and investment the profit will be made. The *Live Aid* piracy problem is but one example. However, many ordinary people may also inadvertently break the law through ignorance, and deprive composers of income, for example, by making photocopies of musical scores for the church choir, or by taping from the radio for use as background music to a theatrical production. No actual profit may be made in such circumstances, and the unauthorised use of the music in each case may not be widespread, but eventually such consistent lack of reward for those whose works are being freely used would have consequences no music-lover would wish to see. With little or no incentive, new works would cease to be created, concert promoters, publishers, broacasters and record companies would go out of business for lack of musical talent and, in the long term, the nation's culture would suffer. It is, therefore, very much in the interests of everyone involved in the music world to be aware of his own legal rights, and to respect the rights of his fellows.

THE NATURE OF COPYRIGHT

First, a word of warning: copyright is a complex area of law, and legal advice should be sought if there are any doubts about rights or obligations in a particular situation. The legal principles discussed here are embodied in the Copyright Act 1956 and subsequent amending legislation (for example, the Cable and Broadcasting Act 1984). The Act governs copyright law in the United Kingdom, and has evolved during a period which, significantly for the musician or composer, has seen the invention of the gramophone record, radio and television, cable and satellite transmissions, tape recorders, computers and photocoping machines. Historically, the first right which was recognised by law for a creator was the right to prevent others from copying his work without his permission, hence the term *copyright*. However, given all the developments which have occurred since that right was first legally recognised, the copyright in a work now embraces several different rights, including the exclusive right to perform the work in public, to broadcast it, or to publish it. In effect, the owner of the copyright, usually at first the creator of the work, has the right to prevent anyone else from doing those things without seeking and obtaining his permission, for which, in turn, the copyright owner is entitled to negotiate terms as to payment.

DURATION OF COPYRIGHT

Copyright protection in the United Kingdom lasts for the lifetime of the composer and for 50 years after the end of the calendar year in which he dies. There are various additional provisions which introduce complications to this simple rule – for example, for works of joint authorship, anonymous works and posthumous works (i.e. those unpublished or unperformed until after the composer's death). If a work was in copyright before the 1956 Act came into force, there are also various transitional provisions which apply to the copyright period. Even if the work itself is no longer protected by copyright, a publisher may still own the copyright in the typography and layout. This protection lasts for 25 years from the date of first publication. Therefore, it is always important to check this aspect thoroughly when planning to perform or otherwise exploit a musical work.

COPYRIGHT PROTECTION

Copyright arises automatically when a musical work is put into a *material form* such as a manuscript score or a recording. There is no copyright in an idea, or in a tune which someone whistles in the street. However, no actual formalities are required in order for copyright to subsist once a work is reduced to writing or some other material form, and fulfils the other conditions in the Act to qualify for copyright protection (see below). It is common practice, however, to use the symbol © with the name of the copyright owner beside it, for example on printed scores of the work, which will indicate the person (or company) from whom permission must be sought.

The Act does not define a musical work; although it is not

expressly provided in the Act, the words and music in a song would each be protected, but as two separate entities, the lyrics being a literary or dramatic work, and the music being a musical work.

In order to be protected, the work must also be produced by a *qualifying person,* someone who is a citizen of, or resident in, the United Kingdom or another appropriate country, or it must have been first published in such a country. In practice, 'appropriate country' means one which, like the United Kingdom, is a party to one or both of the multilateral treaties governing international copyright protection, namely, the *Berne Convention* and the *Universal Copyright Convention.* Of all the major powers, only China belongs to neither.

The work must also be *original,* which is not defined in the Act, but it has been established in practice that the work must not be derived from the efforts of others, and must involve some skill and labour. This means that a new arrangement of an existing musical work can, in certain circumstances, acquire its own separate copyright in law, and the arranger is then in the position of original composer as regards the arrangement, with the exclusive rights mentioned above (and detailed later in this chapter). This is so, even if the existing musical work is no longer protected by copyright at the time of the arrangement; for example, a piano arrangement of a Beethoven orchestral work. If the existing work is in copyright, however, permission must be sought of the copyright owner before the arrangement is made, otherwise it will infringe that copyright, and the arrangement must be of considerable originality before it would qualify for separate copyright (though this is a matter of fact in each case).

OWNERSHIP OF COPYRIGHT, ASSIGNMENTS AND LICENCES

The Act uses the term *first owner* of the copyright, and this is normally the composer, in the case of musical works. It is only by express agreement to the contrary that someone other than the composer can claim first ownership; for example, his employer, by a contract of service under which the composer is creating musical works in the course of his employment. This, in turn, is strictly interpreted in law, with a distinction between *contract of service* and *contract for services;* as an example of the latter, when a composer is commissioned to write a specific work by the BBC, it would be the composer who is the first owner unless otherwise agreed in writing.

An *assignment* of copyright, which passes ownership of the copyright, similarly takes effect only by express agreement in writing, and must be distinguished from a *licence,* which is the term used to describe the form of permission given by the copyright owner to others to perform, publish or broadcast the work in return for payment. As we have already seen, copyright is a collection of different, separate rights and it is possible in theory to assign or licence each right individually to separate persons. In practice, however, the copyright in a musical work is usually assigned by the composer as first owner to his publisher in return for a share of royalties on sales of sheet music, performances and so on. The publisher is then the copyright owner, and permission must be sought from him by anyone else wishing to use the music (the composer will still benefit by receiving royalties under the terms of the assignment). As usual, there is a complication here, because many composers are members of the *Performing Right Society* (PRS) and will already have assigned certain rights to the Society under their terms of membership. This enables the PRS to administer these rights on their behalf by granting licences giving the necessary permission to music users, (for example, to the BBC) to broadcast its members' music, and collecting royalties paid in return for such use, which are then distributed to those members whose works are used in this way. The assignment of copyright to a publisher by a composer who is already a PRS member at the time of the assignment is always subject to the rights already assigned to the PRS.

ELEMENTS OF COPYRIGHT

As stated above, copyright embraces different and separate rights. The effect of vesting these rights in the composer as first owner is to enable him to restrict others by imposing terms for giving his permission for exercising those rights, or doing specified acts. The elements of copyright are accordingly known as *restricted acts* and are as follows:

(a) reproducing the work in any material form
(b) publishing the work
(c) performing the work in public
(d) broadcasting the work
(e) including the work in a cable programme
(f) making an adaptation of the work
(g) doing, in relation to an adaptation of the work, any of the acts specified in (a) to (e) above

Items (c), (d) and (e) together make up the *performing right* which is controlled by the Performing Right Society on behalf of its members. Those rights, together with the reproduction right, are likely to be of most interest to the readers of this article, and will be discussed in some detail below. At this stage, however, it may be helpful first to explain that *secondary* or *ancilliary* copyright also arises, for example, where a musical work is broadcast by the BBC. The copyright in the music itself may be owned by the composer or publisher, but a separate copyright also arises in the broadcast, of which the music is only a part, and the BBC owns that copyright. Similarly, there is separate copyright in a sound recording which, when first embodied in a gramophone record or cassette tape, gives rise to rights for the company or persons first producing the record or cassette. The broadcast use of such a record or cassette must be authorised by the copyright owner. Thus, although a broadcast or recording is really serving as a medium for conveying the music to the public, the law has nevertheless conferred separate copyright protection which is additional to and independent of the copyright in the music, even though without it the recording or broadcast would not exist. The 1956 Act effectively divides copyright into two categories; Part I of it is concerned with the musical works themselves and Part II with the technical means of broadcasting and recording.

In general, failure to obtain the necessary permissions from all copyright owners involved would infringe the copyright in the musical work, in the recording or in the broadcast (and sometimes in all three) and would give rise to remedies for the copyright owner in each case (for example, a claim for damages). It is, therefore, important for readers to appreciate the implications of these technicalities, and the practical consequences of failing to observe them.

REPRODUCING THE WORK IN ANY MATERIAL FORM

For musical works, the commonest means of reproduction are (a) photocopying the score and (b) making a recording from a live performance or taping from a broadcast record.

Photocopying

In theory, permission for taking even one copy of the score of a copyright musical work, or any substantial extract from it, must be obtained from the copyright owner, who is usually the publisher. There are exceptions to this requirement, including copying for research or private study, criticism or review, provided that it is accompanied by sufficient acknowledgement which identifies the work by its title or other description and names the composer. Copying for the purpose of judicial proceedings also does not require permission. Section 41 of the Act also provides a number of exceptions for educational purposes. Copying by certain libraries and museums for specified purposes is also exempt.

Recently, steps were taken to regularise the situation for the user and copyright owner alike with the establishing of a Code of Fair Practice for copying musical works, which Code has been agreed between representative organisations for the composer and publisher and a wide range of bodies which use music, including schools and amateur orchestras. The extent of copying is still limited to specific circumstances in which the copyright owners have agreed that they will not claim for infringement, and does not include the taking of copies to avoid the cost of hiring or buying the score. Copies of the code are available from the Music Publishers Association, the Incorporated Society of Musicians, the National Federation of Music Societies and the Amateur Music Association.

Recording a musical work

The first aspect to consider here is when a musical work is performed live and a recording is made of that performance. The recording right is controlled by the owner of the copyright in the musical work and is known as the mechanical right. This right is administered on behalf of its members by the *Mechanical-Copyright Protection Society* (MCPS), and their licence must be sought before a recording of any kind is made of a live performance. The performer of the music could not give the required permission, and should never attempt to do so.

A second or *ancilliary* right arises in any recording of a musical work. If, for example, a private individual tapes a friend's gramophone record to save the cost of buying the record himself, he is infringing the copyright of the person or company which first made the record, as well as the copyright of the composer and/or publisher of the music. The right to perform or broadcast recordings is controlled on behalf of the record industry by *Phonographic Performance Limited* (PPL). A broadcaster or dance hall which uses a gramophone record must therefore obtain PPL's permission before doing so.

If it is purely for private and domestic use, a tape of a radio or television broadcast does not infringe the copyright of the broadcaster in that broadcast. However, it would still infringe the record company's copyright if a record was being broadcast, and also the copyright in the musical work itself.

It is important to note that, even if the music itself is no longer protected by copyright, the gramophone record will probably still be protected, the duration of copyright protection for recordings being 50 years from the end of the year in which the first recording was made. Broadcasts are similarly protected.

Statutory licence to record musical works

Where a recording of a musical work has already been made with the permission of the copyright owner, record makers wishing to make further recordings of the work for the purpose of retail sale need only pay a licence fee or royalties of 6.25% of the retail sale price. The procedure still involves seeking out the owner of the copyright in the musical work and making standard enquiries; special forms for enquiries and for payment of the royalty are available from Her Majesty's Stationery Office. In practice, if the music has not been recorded before, the copyright owner is unlikely to refuse permission and will probably have to accept a royalty rate of 6.25%. The record maker will know that succeeding makers will only have to pay that rate in order to produce further recordings once he has made the first. This rather long-winded procedure is usually simplified in practice by agreements between the major record companies and the publishers or licensing societies (in this country, the MCPS).

Private recording

The MCPS also used to operate a scheme whereby, for a modest fee, the individual user could obtain a licence to make private recordings for domestic use. However, audio and video taping has reached such proportions that it has become impossible to administer such a scheme. Instead, copyright interests have been pressing for legislation which would impose a levy on blank tapes at the point of sale. A royalty is already payable as a percentage of the sale price of pre-recorded gramophone records and cassettes, which is passed on to the owner of the copyright in the music and in the recordings; sheet music sales also contain an element of reward for the copyright owner. The blank tape levy is intended to extend this principle, to compensate for the loss of income caused by the effect of home taping on record sales. It would reward copyright owners for the use of their works by the millions of domestic users of taping equipment. Such a system is already operating in West Germany, Austria, Hungary and Australia, and is still under consideration in the USA and France. The European Commission has recommended a levy as part of the drive to harmonise copyright legislation in the Community. Until adequate legislation is passed, music users must continue to obtain the necessary permissions from the owners of all copyrights involved which, as we have seen, can mean approaching several different persons or companies.

PERFORMING THE WORK IN PUBLIC

A public performance is not defined in the Act, but the concept has been considered often by the courts, and various decisions have established that even a performance in a private club, or the playing of a radio in a garage for employees' benefit, constitutes public performance. It can be confusing to realise that a television set can also give a public performance if it is situated in a hotel lobby and that the hotel premises must obtain a licence for that use, even though the hotel is not responsible for the broadcast itself.

The public performance, broadcasting and cable rights in paragraphs (c), (d) and (e) of Section 2(5) of the Act (as set out above) are all administered on behalf of its composer and publisher members by the PRS; the effect is worldwide, through the international network of similar societies in most other countries, so that an American work performed here will be credited in the same way as a British work, and the American Society to which the composer/publisher belongs will be paid the appropriate royalty for onward remission to its member.

For the live public performance of musical works, blanket licences are issued by the PRS to premises where such performances take place, giving permission for the performance of all or any works in the PRS repertoire. Performers or concert promoters should always first approach the PRS to establish whether a licence is already in force which will cover the performance in question. Concerts promoted by music societies or clubs affiliated to the National Federation of Music Societies are automatically covered by a special agreement with the PRS, even if the premises do not have a blanket licence. However, care should be taken to ensure that details of works performed are still sent to the PRS so that the composers and publishers can be paid royalties to which they are entitled.

There are several kinds of public performance which are

commonly and mistakenly believed to be exempt from the licensing requirements; for example, in a church, for charity, where an unpublished manuscript is used and where the composer has already been paid a commissioning fee. There are also certain kinds of performance not covered by the PRS blanket licence, for which an individual licence would have to be negotiated; for example, choral works, or excerpts therefrom, lasting more than 20 minutes. It can easily be ascertained from the PRS whether a blanket licence is in force and, if so, whether it excludes any kinds of music or performances for that particular premises. The licence fees are fixed by reference to standard tariffs agreed between the Society and representative bodies of music users. The PRS does not set its own licence fees and, if a music user considers a fee unreasonable, the matter can be referred to a special arbitration tribunal set up under the Act called the *Performing Right Tribunal,* which is empowered to hear both sides of the case and to make an order setting the terms and level of tariff for the particular category of use.

The Society does not administer the performing right in dramatic performances of musical plays, operas, operettas or ballets, for which a licence must be obtained direct from the copyright owner (usually the publisher). It is relatively simple for the parties concerned to identify and to negotiate with each other, hence the Society's non-involvement. However, the PRS does control *excerpts* from such works in many cases, and also controls concert performances.

For the sake of clarity, it should be emphasised that a PRS licence permitting public performance in a premises does not give anyone the right to make a recording of that performance, and the performers of the work are in no possition to give that separate permission: an MCPS licence is needed. Furthermore, a public performance which uses a gramophone record requires two permissions: from the PRS for the performance of the music itself, and from PPL for the performance of the recording.

PERFORMERS' RIGHTS

Not to be confused with the right of public performance of a musical work, the rights of singers, musicians, actors or dancers are protected by separate legislation, the Performers Protection Acts. Written permission must be obtained from the performers before a recording or film can be made of their performance, otherwise a criminal offence is committed. Thus, if a member of the audience tapes a concert without the orchestra's written permission, that person is guilty of an offence, quite apart from the question of infringement of the copyright in the material being performed. It is also a separate offence to use the recording to manufacture 'bootleg' gramophone records or tape cassettes for sale to the public, or to broadcast the live performance without the consent of the performers concerned. These offences under the Performers Protection Acts are committed whether or not the works performed are protected by copyright law. There is, however, no personal remedy available for the performer by way of monetary compensation or otherwise, and there is no copyright for him to own in his performance as such.

BROADCASTING THE WORK OR INCLUDING IT IN A CABLE PROGRAMME

These rights are administered by the PRS by issuing blanket licences to the BBC, or to the Independent Broadcasting Authority and Cable Television Authority as the representative bodies for commercial broadcasting and cable companies respectively. The terms for these licences are either negotiated or, failing agreement, are determined by the Performing Right Tribunal. A composer who is a member of the PRS does not, therefore, have to negotiate the terms on which his works are to be broadcast or cabled, but he is still in a position to require a commissioning fee if the work is to be specially written, for example, as the theme for a television series or for an advertisement. Payment of the commissioning fee accordingly does not relieve the broadcaster or cabler of his obligations to the PRS, as is often mistakenly supposed, nor can the broadcaster or cabler purchase the performing right from the composer under such an agreement if he is already a PRS member, as he will have assigned the performing right to the PRS on his admission to membership.

MUSIC IN FILMS

A film, as defined in the Act, includes 'the sounds embodied on any soundtrack associated with the film'. The maker of the film is thus the first owner of the copyright in the recording of music on the soundtrack, unless expressly agreed to the contrary. Where a recording of a musical work already protected by copyright is subsequently used in a film soundtrack, the owner of the copyright in the soundtrack does not acquire the copyright in the original recording, but he does have the right to prevent anyone else from using the soundtrack incorporating that gramophone record.

It is common nowadays for records and tapes to be issued of a film soundtrack to promote the film and to provide an additional source of income. The owner of the copyright in the film must give permission before anyone else can issue such a record or tape which is directly derived from the soundtrack itself. Separate copyright in the gramophone record or tape then arises; if a broadcast or public performance takes place of the recording, it will not infringe the copyright in the *film*, provided the permission of the copyright owner of the record or tape has been obtained.

Commissioning agreements

When music is specially written for a film soundtrack, the terms of the agreement will depend first upon the type of music to be commissioned, from background links to full score. Although such agreements tend to be in fairly standard form, care must be taken in defining the extent of the composer's services, who will own the copyright in the music, and the terms of payment. For example, the composer often does not simply write the music; he can be involved throughout the making of the film, re-writing, advising generally, and participating in the recording. The basic rule as regards copyright ownership is that the composer is first owner of the copyright in the music, but it is not unusual for the film company to take an assignment of that copyright in return for royalty payments to the composer, or to agree that the composer's publisher takes the copyright. However, the right to the soundtrack as a whole (of which the music forms part) will belong to the film company, as we have seen above, as part of the copyright in the film. This is an area in which the composer must take separate legal advice; often a substantial lump sum is offered, as well as future royalties, but where, for example, the music is of fundamental importance (as in a film of an opera), the composer should negotiate for a share of the profits as well. The composer may also conduct the performance of the music for the soundtrack and be paid an additional fee for that, together with an increased share of royalties on the sale of the gramophone record of the soundtrack (if one is made) to acknowledge his services both as conductor and as performer.

CONCLUSION

To summarise the most important practical points, here are two checklists for the copyright owner and for the music user respectively, to ensure that the owner protects his rights and the user does not infringe them.

The Composer as Copyright Owner

(a) The work must be in material form, and it is important to sign and date the manuscript or tape which first embodies the work.

(b) *Duration of Copyright* To establish the date when protection commences, send the manuscript or tape to yourself by recorded delivery post, or deposit a copy, signed and dated, in a bank vault. This could be important if an infringing work subsequently appears. If the work remains in manuscript or on tape, but is not performed or published in your lifetime, copyright will last for 50 years after the date on which the work is first performed or published.

(c) *Arrangements* Always be sure to trace the copyright owner of the music to be arranged, and obtain permission before making the arrangement. Even if the copyright period has expired on the original work, there may be another arrangement already in existence and you may risk infringing that copyright.

(d) *Assignment* This should always be in writing, dated and signed. Legal advice should be sought for entering into an agreement with a publisher, but the standard form usually assigns the whole copyright to the publisher (subject to PRS rights) in return for a share of royalties and a percentage on the sales of sheet music and records. The *British Academy of Songwriters, Composers and Authors* (BASCA) can offer some guidance here, and can also recommend expert lawyers.

The Music User

(a) *Photocopying* Consult the Code of Fair Practice if in doubt, depending upon the purpose for which the copying is made. If it is not covered, seek the permission of the copyright owner as indicated on the document to be copied.

(b) *Recording*
  (i) From a record or tape: consult the MCPS
  (ii) From a broadcast: no permission is needed from the broadcaster if it is purely for private domestic use, but you will infringe the copyright in the music itself, and in the recording if it is a gramophone record, unless permission is obtained. However, it may be that, depending on the purpose of the copying of recording, a free or nominal licence will be granted by the copyright owner or by the appropriate organisation on his behalf.

(c) *Public Performance*
  (i) For live performances, always check with the PRS regarding the licence for premises, type of performance, etc.

(ii) Always check with the PRS for performances of records and tapes, and with PPL, as their licence is also required.

(d) *Broadcast/Cable* A PRS licence is required. If you wish to record before broadcasting, a licence from the MCPS is also required. If broadcasting a gramophone record, a PPL licence is needed as well.

216

FORMING A REGISTERED CHARITY
RUTH MIDDLEMASS

Ruth Middlemass is a solicitor working in London. She has been responsible for the charity registration of various arts organisations, including the National Youth Wind Orchestra.

There are three advantages in registering your organisation as a charity. First, it ensures a degree of permanence for the organisation and its work. Second, it is very much easier for charities to attract outside funding and support than it is for non-charitable organisations. Third, there are considerable tax advantages, which I shall discuss in greater detail later in this chapter.

Many arts organisations are already registered charities, and many more could become charities with only minor changes to their structure and administration. To become a registered charity, a body must be established for purposes which are exclusively charitable. There is no statutory definition of 'charitable', the law being interpreted by the judges and, to a lesser extent, by the Charity Commissioners. However, it is possible to outline four areas of charity, as follows:

(a) the relief of poverty,

(b) the advancement of religion,

(c) the advancement of education, and

(d) purposes 'beneficial to the community', which has been held to include recreation and leisure.

In addition, except in the case of the relief of poverty, an element of public benefit must also be shown. For instance, a fund to provide music lessons for the children of one family would not be charitable, but a fund to advance the musical education of young people in general would be. Most arts organisations will find that their objects are considered charitable, being classed both as for the advancement of education, and also for other purposes beneficial to the community. Care will have to be taken, however, to ensure that the objects are limited to purposes which are *exclusively* charitable, as any non-charitable object will prevent the registration of the body being accepted by the Charity Commissioners.

Having decided that it would be advantageous to establish a charity to undertake some or all of the activities of an existing organisation, or to establish a completely new body, the organisers are faced with the question of how the charity should be structured so as to best meet their needs. There are three alternatives. The *unincorporated association* has the advantage of simplicity and flexibility but, in most cases, this is far outweighed by the fact that the liability of those running the charity is unlimited. In addition, the unincorporated association has the practical disadvantage of not being liked by the Charity Commissioners. The *charitable trust* is both simple and cheap to establish, is flexible and its objectives can easily be amended where necessary. However, the trust also suffers from the disadvantage that the trustees must take on responsibilities in their own names rather than in the name of the charity. Their liability, therefore, is again unlimited. In general, the charitable trust is more suitable for smaller, less commercial bodies, whereas larger organisations often establish a *charitable company limited by guarantee*. This is generally more time consuming and more expensive to set up, and the structure of a company is more unwieldy than that of a trust. Also, a charitable company, like any other limited company, must fulfil strict requirements for holding meetings and submitting audited accounts (although all charities are required to submit an annual statement of account to the Charity Commission). However, where one is dealing with a charity which is primarily a business, the protection offered by limited liability usually outweighs the disadvantages: the company is a continuing legal entity separate from the persons running it, and this is a particular advantage where the charity is acting as an employer or as a lessor or lessee.

Those who control and administer a charity, whether they

are the members of an unincorporated association, the trustees of a charitable trust, or the directors of a company, are called *charity trustees* and they have certain obligations. The primary duty of a charity trustee is to use and manage the charity's property so as to give effect to the charitable objects as set out in the trust deed or, in the case of a company, the memorandum and articles. In carrying out this duty, the trustee must exercise the same degree of care as if the trust property were his own. This, however, requires qualification: although a charity trustee is personally liable for his actions, he will not be held responsible, even if he has acted in breach of trust, where he has acted honestly and reasonably and, in the words of the Trustee Act 1925, 'ought fairly to be excused'. Also, while a charity trustee must look after the trust investments with the same care with which he would look after his own, he is always under an obligation to carry out the charitable objectives in the *long-term* interests of the charity. Thus, he may not invest trust funds speculatively or against proper advice, even though he might conceivably risk doing so with his own investments.

A charity trustee has a duty of loyalty to the general public, and he must never put himself in a position where there is any possibility of his own interests conflicting with that duty. There are two aspects to this duty of loyalty. First, a trustee may not profit from his position, so that he cannot lend or sell his own property to the charity, neither should he have any business dealings with it. The duty not to profit from his trusteeship extends to the acquisition of information as a result of his trusteeship: this information cannot later be used for personal gain. Second, a trustee must act gratuitously and, while he is entitled to be repaid any expenses he incurs, he may not receive any other remuneration for his trusteeship.

This second area can cause problems where the promoters of a charity wish to be involved in its management, but are unable to do this on a voluntary basis. This difficulty can often be overcome by appointing a salaried officer, such as a musical director or artistic adviser, who is not himself a charity trustee, but who can still be involved in the day-to-day administration.

Having decided on what sort of structure is most suitable for the particular organisation, the next step is to register with the

Charity Commission and obtain a registration number, registration being compulsory with very few exceptions (principally, places of worship and charities with an income of less than £15 a year). This is best done by sending a draft of the governing instrument to the Charity Commissioners before the deed is executed, asking them to confirm that the document will be acceptable to them. Negotiation with the Commission prior to receiving this confirmation can take six months or more, even though the problems may involve only minor drafting points in the administration clauses of the document.

Once they have satisfied themselves that the document is acceptable, the Charity Commissioners will usually send the draft to the Inland Revenue for comment before registration. Although this further adds to the delay, it does mean that there will ultimately be no difficulty in obtaining the favourable tax treatment granted to charities. These special tax rules benefit charities both directly through relief and exemptions from taxes, and also indirectly by encouraging donations. A charity's investment income is exempt from income tax. However, trading income (that is, profits from the sale of goods, or fees for providing services) is not generally exempted from income tax (or from corporation tax, in the case of a charitable company) even if the charity applies its profits for charitable purposes. In practice, this difficulty can usually be resolved by separating the charity's trading activities and having them run by a separate, non-charitable body, which can then covenant all its profits to the charity, thus effectively obtaining full tax relief. However, it is importatnt to ensure that the trading company pays an amount to the charity which is not less than its total profits for each accounting period (often, the exact profit is not known until some time after the end of the period). Even if it makes up the shortfall later, that shortfall will not qualify as part of the covenanted donation and will not be eligible for tax relief. It is, therefore, better to make an overpayment (which can later be repaid, if the covenant is properly worded) than to pay too little.

Charities are exempt from capital gains tax on any capital profits which they make; an individual does not pay inheritance tax in respect of gifts to charities; and there is no stamp duty on the transfer of property to a charity. However, charities are not exempt from VAT, although there are a number of specific reliefs, including what is known as *live aid relief*. For example, if tickets for a performance are advertised at a basic minimum rate (this being not less than the usual price of a ticket in similar circumstances), and the public is then invited to make donations in addition to the minimum ticket price, only the basic minimum, and not the additional voluntary payment, will be liable to VAT.

Charities also benefit considerably from tax laws specifically designed to encourage charitable giving. Payments to charities under *deeds of covenant* now amount to about £400m per year, with a further £130m being paid by the Inland Revenue to charities in respect of these covenanted donations.

In order to obtain tax relief and to enable the charity to reclaim tax, a covenant by an individual has to be capable of lasting for more than three years. The individual pays an amount to the charity out of his taxed income, and the charity is entitled to reclaim the tax paid by the donor on this amount from the Inland Revenue. One useful variation is the *deposited covenant* scheme. The donor signs a covenant in the usual way, at the same time making an interest-free loan to the charity of an amount equal to the payments over the whole period of the covenant. Each year, as payments are due under the deed of covenant, a part of the loan is waived. For example, an individual who covenanted to pay a net sum of £50 each year for five years could deposit £250 with the charity as soon as the deed had been signed. It is also worth considering deposited covenants as a method of obtaining tax relief on lump-sum donations, if the donor is prepared for the amount given to be spread in theory over a number of years.

Similar provisions apply to covenants made by companies, the covenanted sum being deductible from the company's profits in computing its liability to corporation tax. Following the 1986 budget, a company can claim tax relief in respect of one-off gifts to charities, up to a maximum equivalent to 3% of the ordinary dividends paid by the company.

Finally, a leaflet is produced by the Charity Commission giving basic information on how to register a charity. Copies may be obtained from the Charity Commission, 14 Ryder Street, London SW1.

British Association of
Concert Agents

DIRECTORY
of
ARTISTS

A composite list of artists showing sole representation by agents
in membership of the British Association of Concert Agents

*Contains the names, addresses, telephone and telex
numbers of the concert agents in membership of BACA
and the names of the artists they represent - some 2000
eminent concert artists from Britian and abroad are listed.*

*This invaluable guide for promoters in Britain and
abroad is available at £3.00 postfree in the UK and £4.50
for airmail posting abroad.*

*Book Sales Dept., Rhinegold Publishing Ltd.
241 Shaftesbury Avenue, London WC2H 8EH*

NUISANCE – CIVIL DEFENCES

ANDREW BRITTON

Andrew Britton studied law at King's College London and is a partner in the city firm of Davies, Arnold & Cooper. Formerly a member of the British Youth Symphony Orchestra, he now sings with one of the major London choirs.

The first person to complain about a musician practising was probably a parent; after all, even the early endeavours of a budding Menuhin are less than entertaining. However, many musicians will have had some experience of their neighbours complaining about the level of sound they are creating. In almost every case, common-sense will have prevailed and an amicable arrangement will have resulted. However, what is your position when this (or something like it) drops through your letter box:

Dear Musician,

We act for A. Pleb, Esq., who has the misfortune to live next door to you.

Much as our client enjoys classical music (he has an extensive collection of Mantovani) he can no longer put up with the constant nuisance and annoyance you are causing. He informs us that you play your trumpet every day for at least three hours, sometimes for as much as ten hours, and frequently very late at night. Despite repeated complaints, you continue to play incessantly.

Unless you cease playing, we are instructed to take proceedings against you for nuisance, both at common law and under the Control of Pollution Act, and to seek substantial damages.

We also act for your landlord, E. Screwem, Esq., and must further inform you that by giving music lessons you are in breach of your lease which permits the premises to be used only as a private residence. You are also in breach of the covenant forbidding you to commit a nuisance.

Proceedings will be taken to terminate your lease and evict you unless you cease these activities forthwith.

Yours faithfully,

HUGE FEES & CO.
Solicitors

What do you do? What does the law say? The first rule is: *Don't panic.* Your neighbour and landlord do have rights, but these can only be exercised in limited circumstances. In this chapter, we look briefly at the problems raised by our hypothetical solicitors' letter.

Nuisance

Nuisance can take two forms; public nuisance – where the wrong affects the rights of a person as a member of the public (for example, obstruction of the highway), or a private nuisance – where the wrong directly affects a person's enjoyment of his own property. It has long been established that excessive noise can be a nuisance.

Despite, no doubt, many musicians' protestations that their music could not possibly be considered a legal nuisance, the fact is that it can be. In a nineteenth-century case, a neighbour was so infuriated by the musician giving piano lessons next door that he took to banging plates to annoy the musician, and was himself found liable in nuisance, although (as the judge observed) the position may have been different had the neighbour acted reasonably and brought an action himself.

The character of the neighbourhood is also relevant. In

another nineteenth-century case concerning noise from a trade, the judge commented 'what would be a nuisance in Belgrave Square would not necessarily be so in Bermondsey'. Does this mean that playing Mozart in Mayfair may not be nuisance, but that rock music would be? The answer is no: it is the level of noise, and not the type, which is considered in relation to the neighbourhood and the general level of noise normally found there. Duration of the alleged nuisance is also important, and far fewer problems will occur when it is a one-off or a very occasional event. Short but regular practice sessions can, however, constitute a nuisance. There are other technical ingredients in establishing a nuisance, but these need not trouble us here.

With this background, let us examine our imaginary solicitors' letter. The solicitors have threatened action under the Control of Pollution Act 1974, which largely regulates public nuisance. This enables an individual (or, more usually, a local authority) to apply to a magistrates court for an order preventing the person committing the nuisance from doing so. In practice, although it is very alarming for a musician to be informed that he is committing a pollution, it is highly unlikely that any steps would be taken under this Act. Most cases involve clubs or pubs using juke boxes or live bands, rather than individuals practising in their own homes. Besides the difficulty of establishing a claim under the Act, it does, in any event, not provide for an award of damages and is thus not very popular with Mr Pleb and his like.

It is far more probable that – if he has a case at all – Mr Pleb would bring an action for private nuisance. This would enable him to apply not only for an injunction to stop the nuisance occurring again, but also for damages in respect of past occurrences. Mr Pleb has stated that our trumpeter plays for as long as ten hours a day and also at nights. The musician might reply that he was living there long before Mr Pleb arrived and Mr Pleb must, therefore, accept the situation. Unfortunately, the law does not accept this as a defence: a new occupier is entitled to complain about excessive noise which may not have bothered his half-deaf predecessor. However, the fact that the neighbour is hypersensitive, or has just suffered a nervous breakdown, does not entitle him to special consideration.

What about the amount of practice? Are the claims accurate? Has a diary been kept showing the hours played each day? Can the musician prove that Mr Pleb is exaggerating?

Regular late-night practice is likely to constitute a nuisance, and so may lengthy practice during the day. However, the musician has a much better chance of being allowed to continue without the threat of action if a sensible approach is adopted.

The musician must act reasonably. In our example, Mr Pleb would probably succeed in his claim if his facts were accurate.

The landlord's complaint

If you are renting your accommodation, your landlord's rights depend on exactly what arrangements you have with him. If he lives on the premises or next door, he will have the same remedies as Mr Pleb. In addition, the terms of the lease will be very important: you must find out if you are a real tenant, just a lodger, or a licensee. As a lessee (i.e. a tenant) you are in a far stronger position than the others.

The distinction between a lease and a licence is one frequently agonised over by lawyers and the courts. Two points can be made. First, if a written agreement states that it is either a lease or a licence, this is *not* conclusive proof that it is what it claims to be. Second, if the tenant has what is known as 'exclusive possession', (that is to say, the tenant has the property to him or herself) this tends towards a lease rather than a licence.

Assuming our troubled musician is a tenant, he has probably signed an agreement containing terms (called *covenants*), one of which is likely to cover the situation where a tenant is creating too much noise. For example, a typical covenant may provide that

> The tenant shall not do or suffer to be done any act or thing which may be a nuisance to the landlord and the other occupiers or users of the building or of any adjoining premises.

Nuisance would then be interpreted along the lines discussed above. However, each agreement must be looked at individually and no general rules can be laid down.

Most tenants will have some protection under the Rent Acts against harrassment and eviction, and it is thus very unlikely that a musician would be evicted in these circumstances. However, committing a nuisance *is* a ground for possession, even under the Rent Acts. The breach can be remedied by modifying hours of practice, as discussed above. Strictly speaking, this might mean little or no real playing but, for a musician, this is not a practical proposition. A degree of moderation, together with an acceptance of some risk of further action, is likely to be the sensible solution.

Where the musician is only a licensee, his protection is much less and the landlord is in a stronger position as regards regaining possession. Finally, as a lodger, the musician must bow to the inevitable, the courts being sympathetic to the view that a house-owner need not be forced to share his house with someone else.

Our musician has also been threatened with action because of a breach of another covenant – using the place for business purposes. There is little doubt that taking paying pupils is a business use and this action could, therefore, seriously prejudice the musician's position. Again, the breach is capable of remedy, but only with a serious impact on earnings. Nonetheless, the musician has an obligation to honour the terms of his lease.

The most likely outcome of most possession actions is that a *suspended order* would be made. This is where the court refuses to give the landlord immediate possession, but rather suspends the possession order for a period of time. If the tenant does not breach the covenant again, he will be able to remain in the property.

Tips for the musician

What practical steps, can you take to try and ensure that you do not fall foul of any of the legal provisions mentioned above. The following advice should be of assistance:

1 If you are living in rented accommodation, read the agreement which allows you the use of the premises. Is it a

    lease or a licence? Does it prevent you from taking private pupils? Clarify these points with the landlord; if he is aware of your profession, he is less likely to complain later on.

2 Try and obtain agreement with your immediate neighbours as to hours of practice: respect their right to enjoyment of their premises.

3 Do not practise very early in the morning or very late at night.

4 Keep a diary of the hours you play. This is very important: a neighbour will look very foolish in court if he complains about your incessant playing on a day when you can prove you were playing for the LSO.

5 Ensure the room you play in has *some* soundproofing – even if this is only a matter of keeping the door shut and having carpets laid. If you have a piano, don't put it against a party wall.

6 If legal action is threatened, seek guidance from your local Citizens' Advice Bureau in the first instance. It may also be wise to consult a solicitor or other suitable adviser, and you may qualify for legal aid.

7 Once proceedings have been issued, ensure that (if you haven't before) you follow the advice given above. The ideal course of action would be to stop the alleged nuisance entirely, although this may well not be practical.

8 Remember that very few cases ever reach court; most are settled by an amicable arrangement. There has been no reported case on the law of nuisance within the last ten years concerning a musician playing in private accommodation.

Finally, you can of course be *too* concerned with your neighbour's rights. A tale is told of an undergraduate listening to *La Forza del Destino* for the first time. With his record player at full volume, entranced by Verdi's music, a loud knocking on the wall prompted him to turn it down. It was only on the fourth hearing, when he noticed that the knocking always occurred at the same moment, that our intrepid student realised it was part of the score! I know the story is true, by the way: I was the undergraduate ...

Galaxy 7 for all your musical equipment insurance

ARRANGE YOUR COVER NOW

Exclusively through your local broker with

or direct to:- Insurance Chambers
21 Market Place, Abbey Gate
Nuneaton CV11 5UH
Tel: (0203) 386022, 3 lines

INTERNATIONAL UNDERWRITING AGENTS

INSURANCE – A VITAL CONSIDERATION
ALAN CLARKSON

Alan Clarkson is a Fellow of the Chartered Insurance Institute. In 1979, he joined the staff of a firm specialising in musical instrument insurance and spends much of his time trying to persuade musicians of the need to be adequately insured. He is an amateur trumpet player and is second cornet in his local brass band.

I am usually disappointed to find that, when insurance men write on their subject, they fall into the error of assuming that everyone understands the technicalities and the 'lingo' we use amongst ourselves. I will try to avoid this pitfall by beginning this chapter with a brief outline of one or two of the basic principles on which the practice of insurance is founded, without recourse to everyday insurance jargon.

How often have you heard someone ask 'what's the use of insurance? I have paid premiums on my household policy for years and never got anything out of it'? They can only say this because they have not had the misfortune to suffer loss or damage to their property by fire, storm, burst pipes, theft, or one of the other perils which would have been covered by their policy. They have failed to understand that, when they enter into a contract of insurance of this type, they undertake to share in the losses of those other policyholders who have not been so fortunate.

Insurance is a matter of the losses of the minority of policyholders being paid for by the contributions *(premiums)* of the majority. The task of the insurer is to accumulate sufficient funds from the premiums paid to be able to pay for the insured losses or damage incurred, and to meet the cost of administration, together with setting up reserves for the very bad years. A reasonable return on the shareholders' capital must also be provided. The policyholder, for his part, undertakes to share in the loss or damage suffered by the other policyholders, secure in the knowledge that they will likewise share in his misfortune should the need arise. In a nutshell, everyone loses a little by paying premiums, but no-one suffers catastrophically as would be the case if, for example, they had to bear the entire cost of rebuilding their home following a fire.

Data collected over many years enables insurers to assess, with a reasonable degree of accuracy, the cost of claims for a future period. If unusual events occur, such as extremes of weather or an industrial disaster, the reserves referred to above, which have been built up over the years, help to even out unexpected demands on the fund.

Premiums are calculated by dividing the estimated cost of claims plus administration expenses, reserves and profit, by the number of units of risk. The most common unit of risk is the sum insured. Insurers can only get their arithmetic right, therefore, if sums insured represent the full cost of replacing the damaged property. This is why some policyholders find themselves penalised when they have not taken the trouble to ensure that the amounts for which they have asked to be insured are adequate. An inadequate sum insured means that the policyholder does not make a full contribution to the fund and, consequently, is not entitled to a full reimbursement of the loss.

A full sum insured is essential if a policyholder is to be fully indemnified. To *indemnify* means to place the policyholder in the same financial position after loss or damage has occurred as he was in immediately before it happened. This would normally mean that you could not replace new for old but, in recent years, this principal has been modified in some cases. It has, for example, become the practice to offer the alternative of household contents insurance on a new for old basis. Perhaps it has something to do with the fact that many items seem to have built-in obsolescense these days that makes it easier to replace old with new. It does make the financial burden on the claimant less onerous: it would be very difficult, in many instances, to find a secondhand item in similar condition, thus necessitating laying out extra money for a new item were the claim settlement limited to the value of the item at the time the loss occurred. Where new for old cover is available, it is even more essential that the sum insured represents the full replacement cost as new, and that it is regularly updated to keep abreast of inflation.

We will now look at the particular insurance requirements of the professional performer, the private teacher and the administrator in turn.

The professional performer

The professional performer will be concerned with insurance under two main headings. First, the insurance of *property* and, second, the insurance of *income*. I have already made a brief mention of household insurance with which, together with motor insurance, most individuals are already familiar, and I will not take up valuable space by discussing them in detail.

Under the heading of property, I will restrict my remarks to the insurance of musical instruments. When considering this subject, the professional performer requires an insurance policy which will

    (a) offer cover in the most straightforward terms possible,

    (b) provide the widest cover available, and

    (c) apply anywhere in the world.

In order to meet the requirement in (a), the policy should be specifically designed to apply to musical instruments. Insurance policies are legal documents and must be capable of interpretation in a court of law should the need arise. This is why many insurers are reluctant to meet the demand for 'plain English' policies. If the policy has been specifically designed to apply to musical instruments, it will not contain unnecessary clauses which will make it more complicated than necessary. I have seen some attempts at adapting commercial policies containing pages of exclusions and additions which are totally irrelevant and only serve to obscure those with which the policyholder is really concerned.

The best type of policy will usually be referred to as an *all risks* policy. The term 'all risks', however, only means all *insurable* risks, as some risks are simply not insurable. The cover should, therefore, be against accidental loss or damage to the property insured. The insurer should undertake at his own option to pay cash or to repair, replace or reinstate the lost or damaged instrument in the event of a claim.

You should make sure that the policy will apply whilst you are playing professionally anywhere in the world. Some policies only provide limited cover overseas. One policy I have in front of me, for example, only applies in the United Kingdom, Isle of Man, Channel Islands and Eire plus fourteen days in the year anywhere in Europe. Another quotes different rates for various geographical limits. Professional musicians travel extensively nowadays, and it would be a nuisance to have to arrange for the policy to be extended each time you travel outside the limits, even if you always remembered to do so. In addition, you may end up paying a considerable amount of extra money by way of minimum additional premiums for these extensions of cover because of the extra administration costs incurred by the insurer. It is by far the best course to go for the widest cover at the outset.

Pay attention to the conditions and exclusions (sometimes called *exceptions*) printed in the policy, together with any additional clauses added by way of an endorsement slip. Read them carefully and make sure they do not have an adverse effect on the cover so far as you are concerned. If you do not understand anything in the policy, ask your broker or insurer to explain its meaning to you.

There is not enough space available here to discuss all the terms likely to be found in various policies, but you will usually find that losses from unattended motor vehicles are not covered by the basic policy. This cover can normally be added to the policy after payment of an extra premium and subject to certain conditions. In the case of orchestral instruments, it may only be necessary for all the doors and the boot to be locked and the windows securely closed. With electronic instruments, however, the terms may be more onerous and include the fitting of burglar alarms to the vehicle.

I must return now to the subject of sums insured. Professional valuations, or a recent purchase receipt, are normally required for instruments worth £500 and over. The sum insured should represent the full cost of replacement.

With new instruments this is straightforward enough but, where antique instruments are concerned, other factors come into play. Such instruments cannot normally be replaced by new ones and the cost of a similar antique instrument will be affected by supply and demand at the time. It is in the owner's interest to have instruments (especially stringed instruments) revalued every three or four years at the very least.

It is becoming common practice to *index-link* sums insured on house buildings and contents so that they are automatically increased with inflation. It is not possible to do this with musical instruments because of the various factors which affect the values of different types of instruments. Stringed instruments usually improve with age and their values increase, whereas brass instruments usually deteriorate.

It is important that the insurer understands the needs of the professional musician when loss or damage occurs. If your car is stolen, you will normally be required to wait six weeks or so before the claim is settled, to give the police a chance of finding it. If you have a series of concerts arranged and your instrument goes missing, you may need a replacement straight away. Your insurer should be prepared to pay for an immediate replacement and, if the instrument is subsequently recovered in good condition, should offer you the first option to buy it back if you wish. Immediate replacement of lost instruments is particularly important to the student or young musician who may not be able to afford a good second instrument, and to whom continuity of practice and performance is essential. It is also important that the insurer understands the complexities of instrument repair and has a good relationship with dealers and repairers based on mutual trust.

Members of the Musicians' Union have a limited amount of cover for instruments which are registered with the Union, as part of their membership benefits. This is an 'all risks' cover, limited to a total of £400 in all. It is on an indemnity basis (not new for old) and excludes losses of instruments left in unattended motor vehicles for more than thirty minutes during the hours of darkness. If subscriptions are not paid on time, however, this cover is forfeited. Supplementary covers are available if the basic limits are inadequate. These limits change from time to time, so you should refer to the Union for up-to-date details.

I will turn now to the insurance of income which may be lost for various reasons. You may be unable to earn income as a result of temporary or permanent disability resulting from accident or illness. There is a class of insurance available known as *personal accident* and/or *sickness* insurance. These policies pay either a fixed sum in the event of death or permanent disability resulting from an accident, or weekly payments for temporary disablement resulting from accident or sickness. The weekly payments are normally only made for up to two years in the event of accidental injury and one year as a result of sickness. You are able to choose the amount of the payments subject to certain limitations, one of which is, obviously, the amount of premium you can afford to pay. Within the definition of permanent disability is included the loss of use of eyes, hands and feet, and there is a limited availability of cover where the loss of use is restricted to fingers – an important consideration for most musicians.

Nowadays, however, *permanent health* insurance is a far better form of protection. This type of policy does not make any payment in the event of death, but the payments for total disability will continue to be made for as long as the disability lasts, up to normal retirement age. If, after a period of total disability, a claimant is able to earn a limited income, the policy will make up the difference between the reduced income and the earnings prior to commencement of the disability.

Income might also be lost if you were to be sued for damages as a result of an accident caused by your negligence. Your motor policy will protect you in respect of accidents involving a car, but what would happen if you were accidentally to knock over a fellow musician's valuable violin or 'cello? Some years ago, a motor cyclist was awarded damages against a pedestrian who carelessly stepped off the kerb into his path with disastrous results. The pedestrian ended up paying about £2 a week for twenty or so years because she had no *personal liability* insurance. Nowadays, most household contents insurance policies include personal liability cover, but this excludes liability incurred in connection with the policyholder's business or profession. Various insurers place different interpretations on what constitutes 'business or profession' and, in the case of an orchestral musician, some might regard the accident described above as covered by the household policy extension. If your insurers would not, however, they might be prepared to extend the household policy for an additional premium, and this would normally be the cheapest way of obtaining cover. Otherwise, a separate public liability insurance will be required.

The private teacher

The subjects covered above will also apply to the private teacher. I would, however, emphasize the need for liability insurance. The household contents policy would apply to accidents happening to friends coming in for a musical evening (provided they could prove negligence) but not to accidents happening to fee-paying pupils. Here again, however, the household contents insurer may be prepared to extend the policy for an additional premium. If not, a separate public liability insurance is essential.

The administrator

The tasks of the administrator in the world of music are many and varied, and range from those of the college administrator to the duties of the concert promoter. I will concentrate on the needs of those involved with organising musical events.

First, it will be necessary to hire a venue in which the event can take place. This will involve signing a contract which will impose certain liabilities on the hirer. The terms of such contracts can be extremely onerous and not all of the liabilities imposed can be insured against. If the contract makes you responsible for damage to the venue resulting from your negligence, it is usually possible to extend an existing public liability policy if you have one, or to arrange a short-term policy for the period of the hiring. If you are responsible for fire damage, you should try to arrange for the owner's fire insurers to note your interest by endorsement of the existing policy, in order to keep your costs to the minimum. These extensions of cover are necessary because standard public liability policies exclude damage to property in the policyholder's custody or control.

Public liability insurance has already been discussed, and this is essential for any business or other type of organisation, such as a voluntary or charitable body. If, however, you employ someone, then the law imposes very strict liabilities upon you in connection with accidental injury or illness associated with their employment. You are required to take out *employers' liability* insurance, and must display a certificate at each place of employment to show that you are correctly insured. Employers' liability policies provide an indemnity which is unlimited in amount.

You will incur considerable expense in arranging any event, most of which would be lost if the event were to be cancelled for any reason. You will, therefore, require *cancellation and abandonment* insurance. Such policies can provide insurance against (a) accident or sickness of the performer or (b) any cause beyond the control of the policyholder or the performer. Such causes might include death of the monarch, war, strikes, destruction of the venue, bomb scares and epidemics.

The insurance will not apply to cancellation due to any pre-existing illness or condition of the performer. In some cases, medical evidence of good health may be required at the policyholder's expense. There will be a warranty as to the fitness of the performer at the time the insurance commences. It will also be a condition of the insurance that all financial arrangements will have been concluded prior to its commencement. Losses due to financial failures or lack of support will not be covered.

For open-air venues, insurance against cancellation due to heavy rainfall can be arranged. *Pluvious* insurance, as it is called, is arranged on the basis of an agreed sum insured being paid in the event of rainfall reaching an agreed level during set times on the day or days of the event.

In conclusion, a word or two concerning the best way to go about buying insurance. In the case of a simple musical instrument policy, it is possible to go direct to an insurance company. Many musical instrument dealers and repairers are able to recommend a suitable insurer; they know from experience in dealing with the replacement or repair of lost or damaged instruments which insurers provide the best and most sympathetic service when it comes to making a claim.

For the other classes of insurance, I would strongly recommend that you seek the services of an insurance broker. If you do not already know one in your area, the British Insurance Brokers' Association will be able to put you in touch with one. The Musicians' Union have their own adviser on insurance matters. I give this advice because the insurance requirements of each individual differ. Also, the attitudes and specialities of insurers vary, as do costs and availability of cover. The professional insurance broker knows the market, and should be able to find the insurer who can most economically meet your particular needs.

I know of two insurance brokers who are also professional musicians and, if you can find someone such as this who is experienced in both the world of music and the world of insurance, you will not do better.

It has not been possible to mention every aspect of insurance in this chapter or, indeed, to deal in very great detail with the subjects covered. I hope, however, that these few remarks will guide you in the right direction and enable you to seek out the protection you need.

LIFE ASSURANCE, INCOME PROTECTION AND PENSION PLANS

PETER EDWARDS

Peter Edwards was a performing musician and record producer for over 15 years. He subsequently obtained a degree in business studies, specialising in marketing and finance, and is presently an associate of Allied Dunbar, advising professional musicians on all aspects of financial planning.

When the hard-working, professional musician eventually stops to think about his personal finances, he will often wonder if he is being paid enough for the work he does. Possibly, he may be in a position to ask if there are ways for him to earn even more. However, it it not very often that he will consider if he has arranged his financial affairs in the best possible manner. Three particular topics should merit his special attention:

1. *Life assurance* which is used to protect an individual's dependants against the possibility of premature death.
2. *Income protection* which is a means of guaranteeing a regular income to an individual should he become physically incapacitated.
3. *Pension plans* which ensure that, at a date in the future when he is no longer earning, the musician will still have sufficient income to live comfortably.

Each of these financial vehicles costs money. The precise amounts spent, and the choice of the policies which are used, depend upon
(a) disposable income,

(b) domestic circumstances,
(c) age/sex/state of health, and
(d) expected career pattern.

The rest of this chapter will discuss the range of options available to the reader in order to help him ascertain his own requirements.

LIFE ASSURANCE

Originally, life assurance was pure risk assurance. It provided for the payment of a given sum on the death of an insured person within a specific time. Modern life assurance contracts can be 100% protection orientated, or may have both a death benefit and an investment content. The professional musician should use life assurance policies to cater for

(a) family protection,
(b) loan protection,
(c) medium-term savings,
(d) payment of inheritance tax.

Family protection

This is the most obvious use of life assurance. There are two ways of effecting this cover. The cheapest is to use a *term assurance* policy. This is rented life cover: the policy holder chooses a period of time and pays the premiums. If he dies before the term is up, then his dependants will receive a lump sum. If the policy holder is still alive at the end of his chosen term, his cover merely expires and no cash is paid out. Term contracts are rather inflexible as no provision is made for inflation or for changes in circumstances. The best way to overcome these inflexibilities is to buy, rather than rent, life cover. In fact, the ideal way to protect a family from the premature death of the breadwinner is to use a *whole of life* policy. This offers basic life assurance, plus the right to increase cover at regular intervals or to index the cover to a measure of inflation, such as the Retail Price Index or the Average Earnings Index. It may also include a facility whereby, if the policy holder falls ill and cannot work, the insurance company will pay the premiums until either the policy holder returns to work or until his selected retirement date if the disability is permanent.

Whole life policies can be cashed in once the need for life cover has disappeared, and thus they have both an investment value and also offer life assurance protection. Roughly, whole of life cover costs three times as much as term cover. The earlier a plan is started the better, as the cost of life assurance tends to double every ten years. Life assurance companies require that potential clients are 'looked at from the inside'. In practice, this means that the medical track record of a potential client is checked, and that he must undergo a medical examination paid for by the company. Once the individual is accepted, the company cannot subsequently withdraw cover, nor can he have his rights to increase cover tampered with.

If money is short, then it is possible for both husband and wife to be assured on the same plan. Life companies will accept *joint life first death* contracts on both a term and a whole life basis. Here, the death benefits are paid to the surviving spouse.

One last point on family protection policies: any sizeable policy should be *written in trust* for the beneficiaries at no extra cost to the policy holder. This is a means of

(a) putting the right money (all of it, with no tax deductions)
(b) in the right hands (the named beneficiaries)
(c) at the right time (soon after the receipt of a death certificate).

Loan protection

This is most often used as mortgage protection. There is a possibility that the borrower may die before the mortgage has been repaid, and life assurance ensures that the mortgage debt is cancelled and that the deceased borrower's dependants or beneficiaries can keep the property.

There are two common types of mortgage, and each has a form of life assurance associated with it. A *repayment* mortgage pays off both the borrowed capital and the interest at the same time. A single or joint life term policy is often used here, the amount of cover equating to the capital borrowed and the term of the policy being restricted to the term of the mortgage. In real life, very few people stay in one property for the full duration of the mortgage term. It makes sense to use a whole of life policy to cover not just the first mortgage, but all future mortgages as well.

Endowment mortgages are those whereby interest only is paid on the borrowed capital. The capital repayments are postponed until the mortgage is redeemed. Besides paying interest, the borrower also pays premiums into an investment policy, the value of which will eventually be worth at least the borrowed capital. Any excess value of the policy is returned to the policy holder as tax-free cash. Mortgage endowment policies have built-in life cover. This is to pay off the lender in case of the premature death of the policy holder. The property is then owned by his beneficiaries.

The reader may also encounter *pension-based* mortgages. A pension plan which is eligible for tax relief is used instead of an endowment policy. Interest is paid to the bank or building society by the borrower and the capital is repaid when either (a) the individual resells the property and redeems the mortgage or (b) when he retires, the capital being part of the tax-free lump sum associated with pension funds.

Medium-term savings

Investment policies are useful because they can convert small monthly premiums into sizeable amounts of tax free capital. To qualify for full tax relief, these policies must be kept for at least ten years. They have very little life cover and a high investment content, and offer the small saver a gateway to the world's investment markets. The insurance companies have the expertise and resources to manage large portfolios of shares, commercial properties and fixed interest securities on behalf of considerable numbers of small investors. The rate of return is determined by the type of fund chosen by the investor, by market conditions, and by the skill of the fund managers. In general, such policies give greater returns than building societies. If the reader has any policies that were in force before 12th March 1984, he should keep them as long as possible. Tax relief is still available on the premiums, and the policy holder pays only 85p for every pound's worth of investment. New policies do not enjoy this government subsidy.

There are two different ways of allocating profits to policies. The original *with profit* method requires the life company's actuary and accountant to work out each year how well the investment portfolios have performed, then to

(a) subtract all the company's expenses and salaries from this profit,

(b) decide an appropriate amount to pay the shareholders,

(c) decide on how much to retain for cash reserves and, finally,

(d) give the remainder to the policyholders in the form of a bonus.

This tends to give the policy holder a less than optimum return. In order to sweeten this, a *terminal bonus* is offered. This is the promise of a large sum taken out of the company's cash reserves if the policy is kept for the full term. Eight out of ten policies are, in fact, surrendered prematurely, and thus no terminal bonus, which may be as much as 40% of the value of the policy, is paid out in most cases.

The alternative is to use a *unit linked* contract, in which profits are allocated according to the number of units or shares a policy holder has bought. The value of these units may rise and fall as market conditions change, but the greatest advantage is that the savings plan can be open-ended, in that it is up to the policy holder to decide when he wishes to take his profits. He need only wait the ten years that the Inland Revenue decrees, and then may take his contributions, plus all his profit, at any time thereafter in the form of tax-free cash.

Investment policies vary in form from quite simple plans linked to the performance of a single fund to complex maximum investment plans which enable the policy holder to switch between more than one investment fund and thus to take advantage of market conditions. It is even possible to draw any profits as income from these plans after ten years, and still leave the capital intact until needed. These modern plans are first-class medium-term investments.

Payment of inheritance tax

Inheritance tax is a tax on capital. The capital in question is the total value of any assets anywhere in the world at the time of death. If the individual is married, then the tax is payable on the death of the surviving spouse, i.e. it is merely postponed. Inheritance tax is not just the province of the very rich and, if the musician owns a property or a valuable instrument, he may well find that his estate will eventually be liable for assessment.

It is possible to use a special life assurance policy to meet a liability for inheritance tax. A 'single life whole of life' policy will apply for an individual, and a 'joint life second death' policy will suit a married couple.

The procedure is as follows:

(a) A policy is taken out for the estimated current tax liability and is index-linked to account for inflation.
(b) The policy is written in trust for the beneficiaries of the policy holder.
(c) On the death of the policy holder, the cash benefit goes to the beneficiaries on production of the appropriate death certificate.
(d) The estate passes through probate, and its value is assessed.
(e) The appropriate amount of inheritance tax is levied.
(f) The beneficiaries pay the tax out of the proceeds of the policy and/or by selling off assets from the estate.

This enables the policy holder to transfer his assets to whom he wishes. The decision to break up an estate thus becomes an option for the beneficiaries, and not a necessity.

INCOME PROTECTION

Income protection schemes have been in existence for about 100 years in the United Kingdom. Although most people can readily see the need for life assurance, they seem to ignore the possibility that serious illness and long term disability could be just as severe for their families and themselves as premature death. After good health, the greatest asset an individual can possess is the capacity to earn. Income protection plans are simply devices to protect potential earnings.

The premiums for such policies depend on
(a) age, sex and general health,
(b) strenuousness of occupation, and
(c) deferment period, this being the interval between the disability occuring and the commencement of the benefit payments.

Almost all of the music-related professions are classified as A-grade occupations and the premium rates are, therefore, cheap.

It is possible to insure for up to 75% of the applicant's gross income, less the state disability allowance. A deferment period of one, three, six or twelve months may be chosen, and obviously the longer the deferment period, the cheaper the premium rate. It is also possible to index-link premiums to a measure of inflation.

As with modern whole of life policies, it is likely that medical evidence, and even a medical examination, will be required. This will again be at the expense of the life company and gives the policy holder the right never to be denied the insurance once he has been accepted, no matter how many times he claims.

Income protection schemes are worthy of serious attention. They are not expensive and, because long-term illness would financially cripple most people, should be considered a vital element of personal financial planning.

PENSION PLANS

Life assurance and income protection are often ignored because of a belief in the 'it will never happen to me' syndrome. However, it is highly likely that most readers of this chapter will one day wish to cease work. It is all too easy to earn and spend, but to be able to spend and not have to earn means that sufficient savings must have been accumulated to generate a decent income. The state provides a safety net, paid for out of national insurance contributions. This basic state pension would only provide the professional musician in real terms with the running costs of a small car. It is essential to build on top of this meagre sum.

The best solution to the problem of saving for retirement is to use what is known as a personal retirement plan, as approved by the Inland Revenue under the Income and Corporation Taxes Act 1970. Professional musicians may take advantage of these plans if they are either (a) self-employed, or (b) employed, provided that there is no group pension scheme associated with this income.

A personal pension fund is simply a pool of money which is accrued utilising an array of tax reliefs. From this is payable upon retirement a lump sum of tax-free cash and a private income for life. Benefits may start from age 60 onwards for both sexes, although professional singers and brass instrumentalists may take benefits at 55.

What is so good about saving for retirement with a personal pension plan? The answer lies in the tax advantages given to these schemes, and these are worth looking at in detail:

What happens to money as it is paid in to a plan? Contributions are deductible from earned income for tax purposes at the highest rate the individual pays. For most of us, this means that every pound invested reduces the tax bill by 29p, or whatever the current basic rate of income tax might be.

What happens to it while it is growing? Whilst the money is in the hands of the investment company (usually a life insurance company), it is linked to the investment funds of the individual's choice. These funds are allowed to grow completely free of all UK taxes.

What happens to it after retirement? Upon retirement, the musician may take about one-third of the fund as a tax-free lump sum, leaving the residue to pay for a private income for life.

These tax advantages are very generous and beat hands down any other method of saving for retirement. There is, however, a limit on the amount which can be saved in this way. This is usually 17.5% of the musician's *net relevant earnings*. For self-employed musicians, net relevant earnings are simply defined as gross income less business expenses and capital allowances. Net relevant earnings for employed musicians are

17.5% of gross income. Individuals born between 1916 and 1933 are allowed to contribute 20% of their net relevant earnings.

In fact, most people cannot afford to invest the maximum while they are bringing up families and repaying mortgages. There is an opportunity to boost the fund by going back for up to six years to make up missed contributions.

The benefits of personal pension plans are not confined to tax advantages. All plans have the following characteristics:

(a) They are represented by assets which are growing in a tax-shelted environment in the UK, over which the policy holder has complete control.

(b) Contributions can be paid from any source of earned income which is not already pensioned.

(c) The policy holder may choose to retire from 60 onwards.

(d) The policy holder decides the form of the benefits.

(e) The funds are held in trust for the policy holder's benefit. Whilst the money is in the hands of the insurance company, no creditors can touch it.

(f) If the policy holder dies before retirement, the whole of the value of the fund will go to the beneficiaries by writing the policy in trust.

(g) The pension plan can be used, in certain circumstances, as a substitute for a mortgage endowment policy, as explained above.

In addition to these general features, good pension schemes allow the policy holder to increase the premiums to counter inflation, or to reduce them in times of financial hardship. In addition, there will be a facility to insure the premium against the policy holder's inability to continue the premiums due to ill health or disability. Finally, there should be an *open market option*. This enables the policy holder, at no cost, to transfer the full value of the fund upon retirement to the institution offering the best annuity rates.

The reader must, by now, realise that the whole subject of life assurance, income protection and pension planning is complex. From whom can he receive advice relevant to his own unique personal situation? This is a very difficult question to answer; it is not easy to discern if first-class or impartial advice is being given. Even insurance brokers, accountants and solicitors can display appalling ignorance concerning the scope and application of insurance and pension products to individual needs. Ask friends who are happy with the service they have received for the name and telephone number of their financial adviser. Failing this, consult a licensed sales associate from a reputable life assurance company.

The reader may also wish to know how to protect himself from the practices of unscrupulous salesmen who still abound in the financial services sector. Here are some guidelines:

1 Ask about the salesman's qualifications. All reputable companies insist that their staff pass examinations on life and pension products.

2 Remember that there is a statutory 'cooling-off period' of ten days, during which any life assurance contract may be cancelled.

3 Ask the salesman some technical questions based on the information given in this chapter. If his replies are vague and ill-defined, your potential financial consultant is simply incompetent.

4 If any mention of loans or mortgages is made, ask to see the salesman's credit broker's licence.

251

Worldwide suppliers
offer a wide range
of new stringed instruments of quality at
reasonable prices.
Also a very good selection of bows, cases,
strings, & all accessories. Primarily
European manufacture including a few very
fine
hand-made master instruments & bows.

BEARE & SONS DISTRIBUTORS UK
Wholesalers of Musical Merchandise
Violin Specialists
Bingham's Park Farm, Water End,
Hemel Hempstead, Herts.
Telephone: 0442 48624

INCOME TAX AND NATIONAL INSURANCE
TREVOR FORD

As I write this chapter, I have beside me a book giving the basic rules for the calculation of income tax. The book has 2,000 pages. The British tax laws are complex in the extreme and there is no way that this chapter can attempt to set out in detail all the rules for the computation of income tax; neither is it intended to render the employment of a good accountant unnecessary. Rather, it aims to be a practical guide with the purpose of assisting the average musician to understand the basic tax and national insurance laws and also suggesting some ways in which his relationship with the Inland Revenue and DHSS may run its course with the minimum of trouble.

Schedule D or Schedule E?

Many musicians seem to be obsessed with the idea that 'being on Schedule D' is all that counts in life. A particular violinist, who was joining a contract orchestra after a period as a freelance, remarked to me that he would be 'alright' because he had a Schedule D number, as if this was the magic key which could lock the Inland Revenue, and particularly the PAYE system, out of his dressing room for ever. He was deeply hurt when his first payslip showed a large tax deduction, and gave the appearance of one who has been told that his Stradivarius is only worth £25. In fact, he had no idea of what the tax schedules are all about and wouldn't really believe me when I told him that his cherished Schedule D number was merely a reference used by the Inland Revenue for tracing (or, more often, losing) his personal tax papers. Some explanation of the general rules employed in the computation of income tax is, therefore, necessary before looking at their specific application to the music profession.

The computation of income tax

The rules for the computation of income tax are divided up into various classifications, known as *schedules,* according to the type of income being assessed. Thus, Schedule A deals with profits arising from rents under leases of land – not a source of income which many of us have to worry about. The schedules that the musician is most likely to encounter are (i) Schedule E, dealing with income from employment and (ii) Schedule D, dealing with income arising from self-employment. It is quite possible, and indeed common, to be assessed under both Schedules D and E simultaneously. A musician who is employed as a full-time instrumental teacher by a local authority will almost inevitably be subject to income tax under Schedule E. However, if he also undertakes a certain amount of freelance work and private teaching, this will be assessed separately under Schedule D.

There are many advantages in having one's income assessed under the rules of Schedule D, and a considerable amount of confusion exists as to which income may correctly be classed as arising from self-employment. Thus, a freelance musician who is engaged part-time as a professor at a music college may well find that his tax inspector will attempt to classify the fees received as income from employment and will instruct the college to deduct tax. However, it is often possible to have this decision reversed, and the intervention of a good accountant is invaluable here. The tendency at the moment is to treat musicians as employed persons wherever possible, as many of us have found to our cost in recent years.

The rules for the taxation of income from employment are less complicated than those for income assessable to Schedule D and so these will be dealt with first.

(i) *Schedule E* Under normal circumstances, the employer will operate the *Pay As You Earn* method of tax collection, whereby income tax is deducted at source and paid over to the Inland Revenue by the employer. Every tax-payer is entitled to certain statutory allowances which are deducted from his earnings before tax is calculated. The amount of the allowances to which an employee is entitled is computed by the employer after referring to the *code-number* allocated to the employee by the Inland Revenue. This is calculated by adding together all the allowances and expenses (see below) to which the tax-payer is entitled for the year, and removing the final digit. Thus, if the entitlement is to allowances of £2,795, the code number will be 279; the fate of the odd £5 is shrouded in mystery. The code number is usually followed by a letter, H or L for example, indicating whether the employee qualifies for the higher (married) or lower (single or married woman) rate of personal allowance. This facilitates alterations to code numbers in general should there be a change in allowances during the course of the tax year following a budget or other economic statement by the government.

On each pay day, the employer will deduct the appropriate proportion of the year's allowances from the employee's earnings (one-twelfth if the employee is paid monthly, or one-fifty-second if weekly) and tax will be calculated on the balance. At the end of the year, any necessary adjustment will be made by the Inland Revenue.

If the musician has more than one employer, allowances and expenses will usually be allocated to one of them, whilst the others will operate code BR, indicating that tax at the *basic rate* is to be deducted from all income, thereby avoiding the possibility of allowances being given twice.

(ii) *Schedule D* Self-employed musicians are assessed under the rules of Schedule D, Case II, which encompasses earnings arising from the following of a profession or vocation (it is fortunate that some musicians do not have to decide which). The musician will submit accounts once a year, and the tax due will be calculated with reference to the profit shown. These accounts may be made up to any date which the musician chooses (see below). Because there will inevitably be an interval between the dates on which the income is earned and the time that the accounts including that income are submitted, a method of computation known as *preceding year basis* is used. Unlike Schedule E, where it was seen that tax is charged on income during the year in which it is earned, preceding year basis looks to the income arising in the *preceding* year when calculating the tax due. For example, a musician may choose to make up his accounts to 30th November each year. His 1986 accounts (which will include all his earnings from 1st December 1985 to 30th November 1986) should be submitted with his 1987–88 tax return during the following April and will form the basis of assessment for that tax year. The tax thus computed is due in two equal instalments on 1st January in the year of assessment and on the following 1st July. In the example above, the tax due would be payable on 1st January and 1st July 1988.

The following table shows how to calculate the year of assessment and the due date for payment of tax from the musician's accounts date.

Accounts made up to any date between	Year of assessment will be	Tax due for payment 1st January & 1st July
6.4.85 and 5.4.86	1986–87	1987
6.4.86 and 5.4.87	1987–88	1988
6.4.87 and 5.4.88	1988–89	1989
6.4.88 and 5.4.89	1989–90	1990

There are special rules for computing tax due in the early and final years of self-employment. As can be seen from the table above, if a musician first started working on, say, 10th April 1986 and made his first accounts up to 30th April 1987, under preceding year basis he would have no tax to pay until January 1989. To compensate for this, three years' tax assessments are based on the first accounts submitted. The first covers the period from commencement to the following 5th April, the second covers the first full year's earnings, and the third establishes preceding year basis. In our example, the first accounts cover 55 weeks and assessments would be made as follows:

1986–87 51/55 x profit (period from 10.4.86 – 5.4.87)

1987–88 52/55 x profit (first 12 months)

1988–89 52/55 x profit (preceding year basis)

In future years, annual accounts will be prepared up to 30th April and the table above will apply. Similar rules apply in the final years of a business.

Accounts may be prepared up to any date, and so the first accounts may cover anything from 52 to 103 weeks. It is also possible to change the accounts date, and there are advantages in making one's accounts up to a date early in the tax year, as will be explained later.

The advantages of being assessed under Schedule D are obvious. First, the musician receives his fees in full and has the use of the money until the tax on it becomes due – this may be as much as three years later. Second, the tax rates may be more favourable after this period has elapsed; in times of inflation, what was considered to be a high annual income when the fees were being earned, with tax rates set accordingly, may well appear below average when the time to compute the tax comes round, and tax rates will (we hope) have been reduced in consequence. Third, the value of the money with which the tax is paid will depreciate in the period between earning it and paying the tax due. A £1,000 tax bill may seem a lot to pay in 1986 but may feel a little less like the end of the world by 1988. However, a word of warning is due at this point. It is vital to save a proportion of your fees in anticipation of the tax which will eventually have to be paid. A good year's work in 1986 may result in a heavy tax bill in 1988, and the Inland Revenue will not agree to delay payment even further because you have either spent the money or because you happen to have an empty diary at the time. In fact, they will charge you interest on all overdue tax.

Finally, the expenses which may be claimed under the rules of Schedule D are far more wide-ranging than those qualifying for relief under Schedule E. This is dealt with in full in the next section.

It was shown above how a musician's annual accounts are

used as the basis of assessment for the computation of tax due. However, it is often the case that the figure shown on the final tax assessment differs from that shown on the accounts which have been prepared. This is because certain adjustments are often necessary before the accounts will be fully acceptable to the Inland Revenue. For example, it is usual practice to include telephone bills as an allowable expense, but a proportion of the total amount claimed will probably refer to private usage and an agreed proportion will have to be 'added back' to the profit each year. A typical tax computation as submitted by a professional accountant may look something like this:

Profit per accounts to 30 Nov 1986	5,750
add Private use motor expenses, 10% × £950	95
Private use telephone, 15% × £350	52
Assessment 1987–88	£5,897

Once the computation has been agreed by the Inspector of Taxes, he will issue an assessment to the musician, showing how his tax liability has been computed and, of course, attaching a Notice to Pay. The assessment must be checked most carefully – an amazing proportion contain mistakes, usually in the Revenue's favour – and it is wise to let your accountant see it immediately, even though he should automatically have been sent a copy.

If, for whatever reason, the agreement of your tax liability is delayed, the Inland Revenue will issue an estimated assessment (easily identified by the letter E to the left of the figure shown for income). This will usually be for an excessive amount and acts as an incentive for you to get your affairs up to date. The tax assessed as due is payable in the normal way unless it can be shown that you are being overcharged. It is usual practice to appeal against the estimated assessment – you have thirty days from the date of the assessment to do this – and also to apply for postponement of the tax so charged. Under normal circumstances the appeal will be accepted, provided that it is followed up shortly after by your completed accounts.

Allowances and expenses

There tends to be some confusion about the difference between allowances and expenses. Briefly, expenses are deductions made from an individual's gross earnings to arrive at his net income. These will include, for example, travelling expenses and professional subscriptions. Allowances, on the other hand, are fixed by the Chancellor of the Exchequer and are applied in the tax year in which the income is assessed, be the income assessable under Schedule D or Schedule E. Thus, referring to the example given above, the self-employed musician making his accounts up to 30th November 1986 will have his profit assessed as income for the tax year 1987–88, and from this will be deducted the allowances for 1987–88. Under this heading are found such items as personal allowance, dependent relative relief and age allowance; that is, items relating to personal circumstances, rather than to business activities. Pension contributions are also treated in this way.

As was mentioned above, there are considerable differences in the range of expenses which may be claimed under Schedule D and Schedule E. The reason for this is to be found in the careful wording of the appropriate tax legislation. To qualify for relief, expenses claimed under Schedule E must be 'wholly, exclusively and necessarily incurred in the performance of his duties'. Expenses claimed under Schedule D, however, must be 'wholly and exclusively for the purposes of the profession'. The matter hinges on the word *necessarily*. Whereas a self-employed musician who spent £100 on sheet music, £150 on a tape recorder to record his practice sessions and £1 each fortnight on *Classical Music* would have little difficulty in claiming these items as business expenses, the musician who is deemed to be employed might well find that none of these items was considered to be necessary expenditure for the carrying on of his employment – in other words, he would still be able to perform his duties without them. His claim could, in consequence, be rejected by the Inland Revenue.

The employed musician finds that, as a result of the wording of the Taxes Act 1970, there are very few expenses that he may successfully claim. Those generally allowed include:

(a) *Instrument repairs and tuning* This includes reeds,

strings and all usual maintenance. See also the section on *capital allowances* for relief of the cost of instruments.

(b) *Special clothing* This will include dress suits, etc., but not ordinary clothing worn for professional work. (Strictly speaking, women should have more trouble claiming under this heading than men, although this is rarely the case.)

(c) *Travelling expenses* Only expenses incurred while work-ing are allowable – not expenses in getting to the place of work. For example, a musician employed by a local authority to give school demonstration recitals will be able to claim the cost of transport between schools, if this is not reimbursed, but not the cost of getting to the first venue from his home, nor the cost of returning home at the end of the day. It may, however, be possible to claim 'home to work' travelling if the musician has more than one source of income.

(d) *Subscriptions* to professional associations

(e) *Interest on bank loans* for purchase of instruments (but not on overdrafts).

Occasionally, fixed deductions are negotiated with the Inland Revenue for all members of a particular organisation (a contract orchestra or an opera chorus, for example). This makes life easier for all concerned and, as a concession, the deductions so negotiated tend to be on the generous side. Where no fixed deductions have been negotiated, and the individual musician is left to negotiate with the Inland Revenue, it will be necessary for him to submit an estimate of his expenses in advance at the beginning of the tax year. This estimate will then be used when calculating his code number (see above) and an adjustment will be made at the end of the year when his actual expenses are known.

The self-employed musician, governed by a more lenient wording, finds himself in a position where negotiation between himself and the tax inspector is more often necessary. The following expenses, however, are almost invariably found to be admissible, in addition to those mentioned above:

(a) *Travelling expenses* Expenses incurred in travelling to professional engagements will be allowed, although difficulty may be encountered if a regular journey to a particular venue is claimed. Expenses may be incurred on either public transport, or by use of a private vehicle. If a private car is used, it is accepted procedure to claim for all running expenses, including tax, insurance, repairs, petrol and parking fees, and to deduct an agreed percentage for private use.

(b) *Hotel expenses,* but not the cost of meals when away from home (although the Inland Revenue may be lenient here) and not the cost of entertaining, unless involving an overseas client or promoter

(c) *Office expenses,* including telephone charges (or a proportion thereof), printing, stationery, and postage. Fees paid to a diary service may also be claimed.

(d) *Advertising,* including brochures, publicity photographs and advertisements in magazines and newspapers

(e) *Sheet music*

(f) *Instrument insurance*

(g) *Agents' fees*

(h) *Professional research* A proportion of concert tickets, gramophone records and tapes may be claimed, as may theatre visits for musicians employed regularly in theatres and the cost of a television set for a TV performer. The comment made above concerning individual negotiation must be borne in mind here.

(i) *Accountant's fees*

(j) *Fees paid to other musicians,* including accompanists' fees and deputy fees

(k) *Hire charges* Hire of instruments, rehearsal rooms, recording studios and equipment

(l) *Professional magazines and newspapers*

(m) *Cleaning and laundry,* where this relates to special clothing for professional use

(n) *Use of home as studio or office* If part of a private house is used for business purposes, a proportion of household expenses (i.e. heating and lighting, rent and rates, insurance, decorations) may be claimed. However, if part of the house is used *exclusively* for business purposes, this may give rise to a liability for capital gains tax when the house is sold.

(o) *Salary paid to spouse* If a musician's wife or husband is either not working or does not have sufficient income to be liable for income tax, then it may be wise to pay them a salary for secretarial assistance. This may then be deducted from the profit in the normal way. However, certain important conditions must be observed: (i) the amount must actually be paid; (ii) the salary must be realistic for the work done; (iii) the annual total must be entered on the tax return as income of the recipient. Also, particularly where the spouse is a pianist, it may be possible to employ them in their professional capacity. For example, a clarinettist who taught privately at home was able to claim a salary paid to his wife as accompanist for his pupils during lessons and at examinations and competitions.

Contrary to common opinion, most medical fees may not be claimed. In *Prince v. Mapp*, a musician claimed £81 paid for an operation resulting from a cut finger. The expense was disallowed, the payment not being wholly and exclusively for the purpose of his profession. However, medical expenses which can be shown to be in connection with musical activities *only* may be well worth negotiating.

Capital allowances

The cost of purchasing instruments, equipment or motor vehicles is not liable for relief under any of the above headings, but is treated separately. *Capital allowances* are granted, and these allow for the expenditure to be relieved over a period, rather than solely in the year in which the expenditure is incurred.

In the year in which the item is purchased, a *first year allowance* may be claimed. Until the 1984 budget, this was up to 100% of the cost, but has been gradually reduced to 25%. Rates of first year allowance apply as follows:

Expenditure prior to 14th March 1984	100%
Expenditure on or after 14th March 1984	75%
Expenditure on or after 1st April 1985	50%
Expenditure on or after 1st April 1986	25%

If a full claim for first year allowance would result in a very low profit, or even in a loss, it is prudent to claim only part of the allowance, or even none at all, carrying the expenditure forward for future use. In subsequent years, a *writing down allowance* of up to 25% of the unclaimed cost may be claimed. When the item is sold, an adjustment is made so that the total allowances granted over the years equal the difference between the purchase and the sale prices. However, should the sale price exceed the purchase price, only the original cost need be declared; any profit is assessable separately under capital gains tax, and then only in the event that total gains in the current tax year exceed the lower level for assessment (£6,300 in 1986–87).

Expenditure on instruments and other equipment is pooled, and this simplifies matters considerably. For example, a musician buys a flute in 1985 for £3,200 and claims 50% first year allowance. In 1987 he sells it for £3,400 and buys a replacement for £4,500. In 1988 he buys a piccolo for £1,225. Allowances, assuming they are claimed in full, will be as follows:

			Allowances
1985	Purchase of flute 1	3,200	
	First year allowance	1,600	£1,600
		1,600	
1986	Writing down allowance	400	£400
		1,200	
1987	Purchase of flute 2	4,500	
		5,700	
	Sale of flute 1 (cost)	3,200	
		2,500	
	Writing down allowance	625	£625
		1,875	
1988	Purchase of piccolo	1,225	
		3,100	
	Writing down allowance	775	£775
	Carried forward	2,325	

Cars are subject to slightly different rules, the maximum claim for the first year always being restricted to 25% of the cost under normal circumstances.

If a musician has used an instrument for 'non-business' purposes (for example, as a student), and subsequently brings the instrument into use professionally, his is deemed to have incurred expenditure equal to the market value of the instrument on the day on which the instrument is first so used. This is of vital importance to students, who may thus claim the values of their instruments at the start of their professional careers against future tax liabilities. Valuations of all their instruments made by a recognised dealer when they leave college will prevent any dispute. Instruments received as gifts from generous friends or relatives may also be treated as though purchased by the musician on the day they are received.

Copyright royalties

Royalties received by composers and other musicians are normally treated as income under Schedule D Case II. If, however, the composer has spent more than 12 months in writing the composition, special rules apply to enable the tax to be spread over a number of years:

(a) *Lump sums received on assignment of copyright about time of first publication,* and

(b) *sums receivable within two years of first publication other than lump sums* If the period of work has not exceeded 24 months, one-half of the payment is treated as being received on the actual date of receipt, and the other half is treated as having been received 12 months earlier. If the period of work exceeded 24 months, one-third is treated as being received on the actual date of receipt, one-third as having been received 12 months earlier, and the remaining one-third has having been received 24 months earlier.

(c) *Lump sums received ten or more years after first publication* If the assignment is for a period of at least two, but less than six, years, the payment may be spread by equal annual instalments from the date on which the payment became due, the number of instalments being equal to the number of years of the period. If the assignment is for six years or more, the payment may be spread in a similar way over six years.

Overseas earnings

Special provisions relate to earnings from engagements overseas. These tend to be complicated, and only the broad details are given below.

If a musician who undertakes a foreign employment is absent from the UK for a continuous period of 365 days or more, no liability for UK income tax will arise on his earnings overseas. He is allowed to spend in the UK (a) up to 62 consecutive days or (b) up to one-sixth of the total number of days spent abroad without affecting his entitlement to this relief.

Until 1983–84, self-employed musicians who spent at least thirty days of the fiscal year (i.e. between 6th April and the following 5th April) working overseas were entitled to a reduction in their tax liability. The deduction was calculated by multiplying the assessable profits for the relevant year by the number of days absent from the UK, dividing by 365 and then dividing the result by four. This relief was halved for 1984–85 and abolished altogether for 1985–86 onwards.

Tax planning

The idea of tax planning has gained currency in recent years. For the average musician, however, there are few dramatic money-saving tips, apart from the obvious one of ensuring that all expenses and allowances to which one is entitled are claimed. Nevertheless, the points below should be borne in mind.

(a) *Accounting date* By choosing an accounting date that falls soon after the end of the tax year, the delay before tax becomes payable may be maximised. A musician making his accounts up to 30th April will pay his tax a year later than one making his accounts up to 31st March.

(b) *Separate assessment* If both husband and wife are working, it may be advisable to apply to have the earnings of each assessed separately. However, their joint income should be over £25,000 before considering this.

(c) *Date of purchase of equipment* The purchasing of instruments, equipment and cars near the beginning of the accounting period should be avoided. By incurring the expenditure a few days before, capital allowances may be claimed against an earlier year's earnings. For example, a musician who makes his accounts up to 30th September 1985 buys a new instrument on 3rd October 1985. He will be entitled to claim capital allowances in the tax year 1987–88. Had he purchased the instrument three days earlier, the expenditure would have fallen in an earlier accounting period, and the cost would have been available for relief in 1986–87.

(d) *Saving for tax* It is prudent to try to save a proportion of one's earnings regularly to be set against future tax liabilities. It can be disastrous to find oneself with a large tax demand for earnings received two years previously, during a year in which work is scarce.

Keeping records

Musicians are notoriously bad at keeping records, and this partly accounts for the fact that many members of the profession pay too much tax.

Well-kept records have three advantages. First, the preparation of accurate end-of-year accounts, either by an accountant or by the musician himself, will be greatly facilitated. The musician who has to rely on memory when listing his year's expenses will inevitably forget some items, and these may mount up over a period of years to a considerable sum. Second, should a dispute arise with the Inspector of Taxes, the musician who can produce documentary evidence in support of his figures is in a far better bargaining position than the person who only produces an untidy diary and a shoe-box full of payslips. Third, accountants do not enjoy sifting through heaps of screwed-up petrol bills, credit card vouchers and till receipts, and consequently charge high fees when obliged to do so. Musicians who are registered for VAT, and who have thus been forced to keep legible records, have often found that both their tax bill and their accountant's bill have been reduced.

In their simplest form, a musician's records may consist of a small book with receipts entered on the left hand pages and expenditure on the right, and a box in which payslips, receipts and bills are filed in date order. Suitable account books, known technically as *cash* or *single-cash* books, may be purchased from any stationer, and it is a good idea to buy two so that records can still be kept while the accountant is preparing the annual accounts. A typical account book might look like this:

1987		RECEIPTS				1987		PAYMENTS				
Feb	16	AB Orchestra	12		150	00	Feb	16	Petrol	10		17	50
	17	Teaching fees			15	00			Reeds	11		8	00
	18	BBC	16		25	50		17	Insurance	13		105	00
	21	XY School – fee	20		65	00			Taxi fare			5	50
		– expenses			5	50		18	Accountancy	14		126	50
	23	Sale of oboe			850	00			Dress shirt	15		15	25
	24	CD Orchestra	23		90	00			Concert ticket			4	50
									Bus fares				75
								19	Telephone	17		80	70
									Music	18		5	50
								21	Petrol	19		17	00
								22	Hotel Bill	21		35	00
								23	Brochure Printing	22		75	00
									Fares			1	30
									Postage				72
								25	Gas bill	24		89	50

The space next to the figures column is for reference numbers, and this may be used to cross-reference entries in the book to the relevant payslips and receipts.

Accountants

A good accountant is invaluable to any musician and the knowledge that one's tax affairs are in capable hands should be more than worth his fee. However, finding the right accountant is not always an easy matter. A recommendation from another musician can be valuable, but one is unable to tell if the accountant is being recommended for the right reasons. To assume that the best accountant is the one who reduces one's tax liability to the lowest figure seems an attractive idea, but is misleading. A better definition would be: the one who honestly attempts to ascertain the lowest amount of tax legally payable. It cannot be too strongly emphasized that the responsibility for the accuracy of the accounts submitted ultimately rests with the musician concerned, and not with the accountant. To assume that a false claim or an over-generous estimate has been 'got away with' because the figures have apparently been accepted by the tax inspector, or because the incorrect amount originated with the accountant, is totally wrong. The musician signs his own tax return, and the Inland Revenue can re-open inquiries into any past year; there is no time-limit to how far back the Inspector may go. Be wary, therefore, of accountants with a reputation for reducing tax liabilities to incredibly low figures.

Investigations and back duty

The Inland Revenue is currently using a system of checking the accuracy of submitted accounts which has caused not a little unnecessary panic in recent years. For many years previously, all accounts were thoroughly examined, any queries resolved and the figures then passed as accurate. Under the new system, the majority of accounts received by the tax inspectors are read through and, provided that there are no obvious discrepancies, passed without further ado. However, a small number of tax-payers are selected each year, more or less at random, and their accounts are subjected to exhaustive checking. This may involve asking to see books and receipts and, on occasions, the tax-payer himself. It must be explained that this procedure is quite routine and, assuming that accurate records have been kept and that all sources of income have been declared, the Inland Revenue will be easily satisfied.

This should not be confused with the investigations which take place when the Inland Revenue has reason to suspect tax evasion. These investigations, which can last for years and may go back to the commencement of business, can be extremely unpleasant and almost invariably result in the payment of unpaid tax, or *back duty*, interest, and a fine. Should a person find himself the subject of such an investigation, the only sensible thing is to be completely honest and to co-operate with the Inland Revenue as far as possible. Any further attempts at concealment will result in very heavy penalties.

National insurance contributions

No-one, not even the Department of Health & Social Security, seems to understand the national insurance rules as they apply to musicians. The problems arise because so many musicians are simultaneously employed and self-employed, while others, who are treated by the Inland Revenue as fully self-employed for tax purposes, still find national insurance deducted from their pay cheques. A brief description of the four types of national insurance contribution is necessary before any practical advice can be given.

Class 1 contributions These are calculated as a percentage of gross earnings and are deducted at source by employers under the PAYE scheme. As a general rule, Class 1 is only payable by employed people, but certain orchestras and opera and ballet companies, together with many educational establishments, deduct Class 1 contributions from everyone who works for them.

Class 2 contributions are payable weekly by the self-employed, either by purchasing a stamp from a post office, or by direct debit from a bank or National Giro account. Small earnings exemption is granted on production of a certificate obtainable from the DHSS when earnings are low.

Class 3 contributions are voluntary and may be paid by people who would not otherwise be making regular contributions, to enable them to qualify for certain Social Security benefits.

Class 4 contributions These are extra contributions payable by the self-employed and are assessed as a percentage of profits above a certain limit. For example, for 1986/87, Class 4 contributions are charged at 6.3% on earnings between £4,450 and £14,820. Half of the amount payable may be deducted from the musician's profits for the year for the purpose of calculating his income tax liability.

It is quite possible, and indeed common, to pay Class 1, Class 2 and Class 4 contributions all within the same year, and this is why so much confusion arises. The government, via the DHSS, sets maximum contribution levels and, if an individual's total contributions exceed this maximum, he will be entitled to a refund. This is usually dealt with automatically by the DHSS when only Class 1 contributions are involved. However, the situation is far more complex for the self-employed, and many musicians actually end up paying more than they should.

What, then, can the musician do to ensure that the DHSS does not end up with more money than it is entitled to? The following advice should be helpful:

1 Make sure that anyone who deducts national insurance from you has your correct national insurance number, otherwise the contributions will not be credited to your account.

2 If you are self-employed and do not qualify for small earnings exemption, pay your Class 2 contributions on time. If the price of a Class 2 stamp is increased, it is not possible to buy stamps at the old rate and your arrears will cost you more.

3 If Class 1 contributions have been deducted from occasional earnings which you have included in your self-employed accounts, *and* you have been assessed for Class 4 payments on those accounts, you can apply for a refund of Class 4 contributions to compensate for the fact that you have been charged on the same earnings twice.

4 If you regularly pay Class 1 contributions on Schedule D (self-employed) income, you should apply for *deferment*. To avoid the lengthy process of first paying too much and then having to apply for a refund, the DHSS will defer charging *any* Class 4 contributions until your correct liability has been ascertained. If your Class 1/Schedule D income is substantial, deferment may also be granted for Class 2 contributions. Should you be awarded Class 2 and Class 4 deferment, deduction of Class 1 contributions will continue as usual, but you will not be expected to purchase a weekly Class 2 stamp, neither will you be assessed for Class 4 payments. As before, the DHSS will wait until all Class 1 contributions have been credited to your account and will then calculate any additional amount due from you.

To apply for deferment, it is necessary to fill in a simple form, and the leaflet *Class 4 contributions and the self-employed,* obtainable from most post offices, includes this form. Alternatively, contact Class 4 Group, DHSS, Newcastle upon Tyne, NE98 1YZ, who will also deal with applications for the refund of overpayments in previous years.

THE MUSICIAN AND VAT
TREVOR FORD

The number of musicians registered for VAT has decreased quite considerably in recent years, registration now being compulsory only for persons with an annual 'taxable turnover' of over £20,500, following the 1986 budget. However, in many respects, being VAT-registered can have considerable advantages for the musician, and many who have deregistered as the registration limit has been increased are now finding themselves financially less well off. How, then, can HM Customs & Excise help a musician towards a rather healthier bank balance (or smaller overdraft) than he would otherwise have had? This chapter attempts to explain the workings of the VAT laws and to set out the benefits which may result from either compulsory or voluntary registration.

What is Value Added Tax?

Value Added Tax is, as the name suggests, a tax on the value of goods or services. However, the tax is value added in that the amount of the tax increases as the goods gain in value. This, coupled with the fact that registered persons or businesses are enabled to claim back the tax which they have paid, ensures that only the ultimate consumer actually pays any tax. Consider the following illustration:

Choppit & Co. (Timber Merchants) come across a piece of wood which they think would be suitable for making a violin. They value the wood at £100 and decide to sell it to Eric Guarneri & Co. (Violin Makers). However, being VAT-registered, Choppit's charge Guarneri's an extra 15%, and Guarneri's end up paying £115. Eventually, Choppit's will pay £15 to HM Customs & Excise.

Meanwhile, Mr Guarneri decides that the piece of wood is too good for him and arranges to sell it to his friend, Neville Stradivari, who has a reputation as a craftsman. Since Guarneri's have spent some time cleaning the wood up and investigating the beauty of the grain, they sell it for £150. Being VAT-registered, they have to charge an extra 15%, and so they receive a cheque from Mr Stradivari for £172.50. Guarneri & Co. must then pay over the £22.50 tax to HM Customs & Excise, after deducting the £15 paid to Choppit & Co.

Neville Stradivari, who is also VAT-registered, spends some weeks producing a rather splendid violin, and eventually decides to sell it to Fiddlers (Dealers in Fine Instruments). He feels that it is worth £1,000, charges 15% tax and collects his cheque for £1,150. Later, he will pay HM Customs & Excise the £150 VAT charged to Fiddlers, less the £22.50 paid to Guarneri & Co.

Fiddlers put the instrument in their shop window in Portobello Road with a price tag stating that the violin can be purchased for £2,875, this being £2,500 plus VAT at 15%. In walks Raymond O'Glickstein, cheque book at the ready, hands over his cheque and walks out of the shop. Fiddlers pay HM Customs & Excise the £375 which they collected from Mr O'Glickstein, less the £150 paid to Neville Stradivari, and there the story ends: O'Glickstein is not VAT-registered and, therefore, cannot reclaim the tax paid. Of course, had our violinist been in receipt of fees sufficient to take him above the limit for compulsory registration or, indeed, had he registered voluntarily, he would effectively have paid £375 less for his new instrument.

The result of all this is that HM Customs & Excise are better off to the tune of £375, all of which has been paid by the ultimate purchaser. None of the firms involved with increasing the value of the instrument has been financially affected, and the amount of tax has been calculated on the maximum value of the goods.

This example illustrates, in the simplest possible way, the workings of VAT. Of course, it is highly unlikely that any registered person would make only a single taxable supply in any tax period. The amounts remitted to, or claimed back from, HM Customs & Excise at the end of each quarter therefore usually represent the total of VAT charged to customers (called *output tax*) less the total VAT paid to suppliers (called *input tax*).

Rates of tax

There are currently two rates of Value Added Tax: the standard rate (15%) and the zero rate. The operation of the standard rate is illustrated in the example above, and it is this rate that the musician will most often encounter. Items which are zero-rated do not incur tax, but the registered person is nevertheless enabled to reclaim input tax from HM Customs & Excise, even if this results in his total input tax regularly exceeding his total output tax. Among goods and services which are zero-rated are the following:

(a) Most food (but not catering)
(b) Exported goods
(c) Fuel and power (but not most petroleum products)
(d) Most forms of transport (but not taxis)
(e) Books and music (but not stationery or manuscript paper)
(f) Certain types of advertisement
(g) Children's clothing

Exempt supplies

Exempt supplies are often confused with zero-rated supplies because both incur no liability to tax. However, the difference is of considerable importance. Whereas, as was explained above, the making of zero-rated supplies does not affect the right to reclaim input tax, making exempt supplies can mean that the registered person may not be able to recover a proportion of the input tax already paid. For example, if an instrumentalist spends a day a week teaching at a school, and this involves him in a regular journey by car, he will find that a proportion of the tax paid on petrol will be disallowed because school teaching appears on the list of 'exempt supplies'. A similar restriction may be applied to take into account private, as opposed to business, use of a car, although this restriction is applied only to petrol and not to repairs.

Neither does the amount of any exempt supplies count towards the annual taxable turnover when deciding whether or not registration is necessary.

As shown in the example above, many musicians make exempt supplies, one of the items to be found on the exemption schedule being 'the provision of education by a school or university'. This includes the work of the musician employed to teach in such an establishment. Private tuition given to individual pupils is also exempt, provided the VAT inspector can be persuaded that music is an academic subject . . .

Items to be treated as exempt include the following:

(a) The grant of an interest in land (including the sale of private houses and offices, but not including hotel accommodation, holiday lettings and parking facilities)
(b) Insurance
(c) Postal services supplied by the Post Office
(d) Betting, gaming and lotteries
(e) The provision of credit (including hire-purchase and credit sale agreements)
(f) The provision of education by a school or university
(g) Private tuition to an individual pupil in an academic subject
(h) Services of doctors, dentists, opticians, etc (but not certain practitioners, including osteopaths and psychoanalysts)
(i) Undertakers' charges
(j) Membership fees to trades unions and professional bodies

Registration

Following the 1986 budget, registration for VAT is compulsory for all persons whose taxable supplies exceed, or are expected to exceed, £20,500 during any 12-month period. The first important consideration is that it is the person, not the business, who is registered. A musician who earns only

£15,000 in a year, but increases his overall earnings by, say, working as an accountant in his spare time, is liable for registration if his income thus exceeds £20,500 in total. VAT would then be chargeable on all his business activities, provided they are not exempt. 'Person' may include an individual, a partnership (for example, a string quartet, where this is treated as a business for tax purposes), a limited company, an association or a charity.

When deciding if registration is necessary, it is important to consider future income, even though it may not be easy to estimate this accurately. Registration is compulsory if there are reasonable grounds for believing that the total taxable turnover will exceed the limit set by the government in the next 12 months. It is also necessary to register if the turnover exceeds a certain figure in the last calendar quarter, unless HM Customs & Excise can be satisfied that the taxable turnover over the next nine months will not bring the total over the compulsory registration limit. Details of the current registration limits may be obtained from any VAT office (listed under 'Customs & Excise' in the telephone book).

It is vital that 'taxable turnover' is calculated accurately. It should include income from all business activities, including amounts received as expenses, any sideline activities (letting a holiday caravan, for example) and any amounts 'passing through' which may not initially appear to be part of one's own income. If an instrument is purchased for a school or pupil with the teacher's own money, and then passed on, it has effectively been purchased and re-sold, even if no profit has arisen. This amount becomes part of the taxable turnover and may render the teacher liable for registration. (If you do not wish to register for VAT, ensure that instruments are purchased direct from the supplier by pupils.) If a cheque is received for an engagement undertaken by an ensemble, paid into an individual's bank account and subsequently partly paid out to the ensemble's other members, the total amount of the cheque counts towards the taxable turnover of the individual musician. (If you do not wish to register for VAT, open a separate bank account for ensembles or groups, and ensure that cheques are made payable to the ensemble, and not to an individual member.)

The calculation of taxable turnover should not include exempt supplies and, therefore, sums received for teaching in a school, college or university, and certain types of private teaching need not be included; it should, of course, include items which are zero-rated.

At the time of registration, VAT paid on items purchased *before* registration can be reclaimed as input tax, provided the equipment concerned is still being used for business purposes. This provision enables VAT paid on instruments to be reclaimed, even if the instruments were purchased before an application to register was made.

If a person fails to register, he will be treated as though he had been registered from the date on which registration should have taken place. VAT will, therefore, have to be accounted for, even though it has not been charged. This can prove very expensive, and it is consequently advisable to register early rather than late. Attempts to avoid registration altogether are doomed to failure since the authorities can ascertain taxable turnover easily from accounts which are submitted to the Inland Revenue for income tax purposes. There are also substantial fines for evading registration.

It is compulsory to begin keeping VAT records (see below) and charging VAT as soon as registration becomes legally necessary. This will often be before the VAT office has been informed, and usually before a VAT number has been allocated. In this case, VAT should be added to invoices for work done (although it must not be shown separately). However, full receipted VAT invoices must subsequently be sent out for this work after the registration number has been notified.

Finally, if the total taxable turnover is below the compulsory registration limit, it is still possible to apply to be VAT-registered if it can be shown that the business would suffer if registration did not take place. *Voluntary registration* is worth considering if a musician is planning expenditure on instruments or equipment, or even if large sums are spent on petrol or telephone, for example. However, once registered, it is not possible to cancel the registration for two years.

Invoicing

Once the musician is fully registered, he must issue tax invoices to all other registered persons or organisations for work done. These invoices have to show:

    (a) an identifying number,
    (b) the tax point (the date of the engagement or, if for more than one engagement, the date of the invoice or the date of payment, whichever is the earlier),
    (c) the musician's name, address and VAT number,
    (d) the customer's name and address,
    (e) a description of the work (e.g. concert 26 July 1986),
    (f) the fee for the work,
    (g) the rate of tax charged, and
    (h) the total tax payable.

It is not compulsory to issue VAT invoices to persons who are not registered for VAT, although they may ask for them.

Many organisations, including orchestras, operate *self-billing* arrangements. Under these arrangements, the orchestra prepares the invoice, thus effectively charging itself, and this is sent to the musician, usually with the payment for the engagement. This saves the orchestra the job of subsequently collecting VAT invoices from numbers of people with whom it may not be in regular contact. If a self-billing system is in operation, the registered musician must not make out another tax invoice and send it back to the organisation concerned: the self-billing invoice is sufficient and it must not be duplicated.

Records

If a musician is keeping correct records, as described in the chapter entitled **Income Tax and National Insurance,** few modifications will be necessary to take into account the requirements of VAT law. Details of all taxable and exempt supplies must be kept, such as will enable the amount of VAT charged by the musician to be easily ascertained, as must details of all input tax paid – this may be achieved by using an account book with three columns on both the receipts and the payments side: the first column will show the total amount paid or received, the second will be used for VAT and the third will be the net amount exclusive of VAT (that is, the difference between column one and column two).

Copies of all tax invoices issued must be retained, together with invoices received for purchases. Purchase invoices should be full tax invoices, unless the total VAT-inclusive amount does not exceed £50, in which case a less detailed invoice is sufficient, such as is issued by many garages for petrol.

Every three months (or monthly, if requested by HM Customs & Excise) a VAT return must be submitted within four weeks of the end of the tax period. There are fines for people who regularly send in their returns late. Completion of the return necessitates summarising VAT records for the quarter in question in a special book, or on a special page within the tax records, to be known as the *VAT account*. This must show:

(a) the total of the output tax charged,
(b) the total of deductable input tax, and
(c) the net amount payable or repayable.

These amounts are entered on the VAT return and the difference between (a) and (b) paid to HM Customs & Excise. If the total input tax exceeds the total output tax, a refund will be paid.

A visit from a VAT inspector usually follows shortly after registration to check that correct records are being kept. These visits tend to continue at varying intervals throughout the period of registration.

Cancellation of registration

If, for any reason, taxable supplies cease, then registration *must* be cancelled. However, application for registration to be cancelled voluntarily may be made if the annual taxable turnover falls below a certain limit or, more likely, if the turnover figure at which registration is required is increased by the government.

However, if registration is cancelled, HM Customs & Excise assumes that all equipment owned by the musician is sold on the day that the cancellation takes effect (provided that VAT was reclaimed on the purchase of the equipment) and tax must be paid accordingly. For example, if Mr O'Glickstein *had* been registered at the time that he purchased his new violin, he would, as shown above, have been able to reclaim the VAT paid to the shop. However, if he subsequently applied for his registration to be cancelled, he would have to account for VAT at the rate of 15% on the value of the instrument at the date that the deregistration came into effect. This can be costly, and it is often worthwhile remaining registered, even after it has become possible to cancel the registration.

Practical points

Finally, two points which often are sources of confusion need to be mentioned. First, as a general rule, VAT paid when purchasing a car cannot be reclaimed.

Second, when deputising for another musician, it is hardly reasonable to request VAT from him if he is not himself VAT-registered. In this case, the VAT must be suffered by the deputy. However, it is important that this is calculated correctly. If the fee received is £100 and the VAT rate 15%, the tax is not £15 but £13.04 – VAT is assumed to be included in the £100. In some cases, it is possible to arrange for managements to pay VAT direct to deputies, thus avoiding this problem.

The advantages of registration are self-evident: tax is collected from employers at no cost to the musician, and he is thus enabled to claim back the VAT which he is required to pay on all business expenses, such as instruments, electrical equipment, telephone and stationery, petrol and car repairs. The better records that he will be obliged to keep will facilitate preparation of his annual accounts and these, in turn, will be more accurate, resulting in lower accountants' fees and smaller income tax demands. The administration involved is not vast and could be handled by a reasonably competent home computer – the VAT on which could then be reclaimed by the musician. With more money being spent on computers than on instruments by many musicians, I would have thought that the message was obvious . . .

SAVINGS AND INVESTMENT
PETER EDWARDS

Peter Edwards was a performing musician and record producer for over 15 years. He subsequently obtained a degree in business studies, specialising in marketing and finance, and is presently an associate of Allied Dunbar, advising professional musicians on all aspects of financial planning.

We all aim to make a satisfactory return on the money we invest. However, the definition of 'satisfactory' will vary according to the circumstances, needs and wants of the individual concerned. The two fundamentals that must never be ignored when considering financial planning are *tax efficiency* and *flexibility*.

The tax advantages of the various investment media are reviewed periodically by the government, and the aspirations and circumstances of individuals will probably change with an even greater frequency. This chapter will enable the reader to assess his own requirements and it is, therefore, first worth examining in detail those considerations which will help him to design a personal investment strategy.

IMPORTANT INVESTMENT CONSIDERATIONS

Objectives Without doubt, the first question the reader should ask himself is 'what am I saving for?' The prime objective may be a new car, building up capital for retirement, or a new instrument. Almost invariably, he will have multiple objectives. It is first essential to put these into an order of priority.

Willingness to take a risk The level of risk influences the amount of likely return. The reader needs to assess carefully how comfortable he would be with high levels of risk, especially if he has future commitments which might call on the invested funds. The obvious advice is never to put all the investment eggs in high risk baskets.

Relative wealth of the investor This factor has a considerable bearing on the available options. A professional consultant would ask what the investor has already achieved, in order to assess the range of investments open to his new client. The reader must likewise consider how much can be saved out of his income, and how much of his investment strategy will involve putting existing blocks of capital into better investment boxes.

The time factor Certain investments, such as pension plans, involve locking away money for long periods. It follows that the investor needs to be sure of his needs before placing a large proportion of his savings into long-term investments. It is always sensible to have some readily accessible money in an interest-bearing account, such as a bank deposit account or a building society.

Tax The rate of income tax paid by the investor is a vital consideration. Investment income, such as dividends from shares and interest from building societies or bank accounts, is classified as unearned income. In the case of these particular investments, basic rate tax has already been paid but, if the investor's total earned and unearned income exceeds the basic rate threshold, then there will be additional higher rate tax to pay.

Pension plans reduce the amount of income tax payable and enjoy considerable tax advantages as described elsewhere in this book. Capital gains tax, which is a tax on capital appreciation, is a further consideration. In short, investment strategies cannot be designed without a thorough analysis of the tax consequences of any course of action.

Expectations Most people expect their incomes to fall when they retire. Their expenses may or may not decrease in proportion. After the experience of the 1970s, many who are close to retirement will be sensitive to the impact of inflation. Certain lucky individuals may be expecting to inherit sizeable amounts of capital, or to benefit from other windfalls. An expectation of reduced or increased income or capital needs to be considered in the personal strategy. Do not over-estimate the value of an assumed windfall; it may not even occur.

Age and health People need different incomes at different stages in their lives. Certain investments, such as life assurance, are only available to those who are insurable. The investor's outlook on life and, therefore, his view of investment may differ according to his state of health.

Family circumstances Those of us who have financial responsibilities to others must bear these in mind when choosing investments. A strategy for parents is often dominated by the need to build up funds for such things as school fees, wedding expenses and house purchase. Similarly, the desire to leave legacies may be a major concern.

THE REASONS FOR INVESTMENT

Now that the importance of analysing the individual's blend of circumstances in relation to investment has been explained, it is time to examine four factors which relate to the human condition and, therefore, to personal investment strategy. These are

(a) dying too soon,
(b) living too long,
(c) owning a home, and
(d) emergencies.

Dying too soon A man or woman who dies prematurely can, in most cases, only leave sufficient capital to provide the dependants with the kind of income to which they have grown used by taking out life assurance. It is possible to protect the family and to invest at the same time.

Living too long Life expectancy is still increasing. It is all too easy to outlive the capacity to earn, hence the importance of retirement planning.

Owing a home Buying a home is a major financial goal of many investors. It is, in a sense, their principal investment. It can be sold without liability to capital gains tax and the government will subsidise the mortgage via tax relief.

Emergencies It is only common sense to build up capital for emergencies. It is possible to borrow money, but this invariably costs more than the return on your investments. Provided you are a taxpayer, a building society account is hard to beat as an interest-bearing emergency fund. Indeed, many individuals will never have enough cash to progress beyond such an emergency fund. It is, therefore, crucial to obtain the highest rates of interest available.

These four areas of concern are common to most individuals, and are the fundamentals of a successful investment strategy. It is now time to examine investment opportunities available for any income or capital still remaining.

INVESTMENT OPTIONS

Fixed interest deposits and fixed interest securities

Fixed interest deposits are blocks of capital which are interest bearing. The rate of interest may be fixed permanently or it may be variable. The investor knows exactly where he stands in monetary terms, and his cash is usually far more readily accessible than with asset backed investments (investments linked directly or indirectly to equities and property). The last few years have seen an ever increasing variety of fixed interest deposits, the most familiar being building society accounts and bank deposit accounts. Both offer the saver a variable net rate of interest. There is a plethora of marketing jargon used to describe the merits of these accounts, and this makes it a tedious job to compare rates. In general, the following hold true:

(a) If the saver is prepared to commit funds for periods of 30 days or more, then the interest rates will be higher than those paid on basic share or deposit accounts.

(b) A commitment to save a regular monthly amount will again attract a higher interest rate. It is up to the saver to approach his bank or a number of building societies to see what is available. Often, the smaller societies will pay marginally higher interest rates, although the investor sacrifices the convenience of a branch on every corner.

The *National Girobank* and *National Savings Bank* provide other commonly used interest bearing accounts. The National Girobank is part of the Post Office, but its operations are controlled by the government. The rates of return should be compared with those of other banks and building societies, although the fact that the deposits carry a government guarantee may attract some investors.

The National Savings Bank is also government guaranteed and is operated by the Post Office as agent. Ordinary and investment accounts are available, and interest is paid gross, i.e. without the deduction of tax at source. In the case of ordinary accounts, an individual is given exemption from basic and higher rate income tax for the first £70 of interest. If a husband and wife both have an account, then they can both claim exemption up to this level. There is, however, no exemption for the higher level of interest earned on investment accounts.

National savings certificates are also guaranteed by the government. No interest is paid but, after a stated period of time (usually five years), the certificate can be redeemed at a higher value than the original purchase price. The total rate at which the value appreciates during this period is indicated on the certificate, and the capital appreciation is free from income and capital gains tax. These certificates can be used as a medium-term investment. Certain issues are index-linked to the Retail Price Index as a protection against inflation. In times of low inflation, these do not offer a particularly good return. Information regarding these certificates can be obtained from most post offices.

Local authority mortgage bonds represent borrowings from investors secured on the revenues of local authorities. They are issued with lives of up to five years, but most are for one year.

They can be bought in multiples of £1,000. Interest is paid half yearly after deduction of basic rate tax.

Certificates of tax deposit are especially designed for the self-employed who pay tax in arrears and may wish to have guaranteed funds to meet a future tax liability. The best way to keep pace with the continual changes in the interest rates applicable to these deposits is to follow the announcements in the financial press.

The main drawback to interest bearing deposits is that, if all the interest is withdrawn and there is a positive rate of inflation, the invested capital will diminish in real terms. It is essential for these investments to have a high rate of interest to remain attractive in times of high inflation.

This brings us to *fixed interest securities*, which are different from deposits as they carry a nominal rate of interest, which remains fixed, together with the potential for capital gain. These usually take the form of *British government stocks,* known as *gilt-edged securities,* and represent guaranteed borrowings by the British government or certain nationalised industries. The investor can be entirely confident that interest will be paid and the principal repaid in accordance with the terms of the loan. Gilts carry a fixed rate of interest (the *coupon*) which is normally paid twice yearly. The face value of the stock is paid at the redemption date. The current price of a stock represents the present value of this stream of future payments and so will vary as economic circumstances change, particularly those related to the strength of the pound and inflation. Gilts offer an excellent hedge against inflation. They can be short, medium, and long term according to the specific needs of the investor. However, they are complicated and most investors will be content with the professional management offered by investments in *gilt-edged unit trusts.*

In the years prior to redemption, the market value of a gilt-edged stock is directly related to current interest rates. When interest rates fall, the value of a stock rises, and vice versa. Gilts may be bought through a stock broker, the Post Office, or by application for new issues to the Bank of England.

Another form of fixed interest security is the *preference share.* These are useful for individuals who require a high rate of fixed income. They are part of the share capital of a company, and pay a fixed dividend which has priority over any dividend paid to ordinary shareholders. There is, of course, no guarantee.

Equities

Equities, or *ordinary shares,* are the ultimate risk funds of a company. If a company issues a thousand shares and an individual owns ten of these, he will be eligible for 1% of the company's success or, indeed, its failure. The investor will expect a reasonable and rising level of dividend income and, perhaps, a rise in the share price. Such shares are backed by the physical assets of companies and, to be allowed to have a stock market quotation, a company must have traded profitably for five years. Of course, the profits may not continue.

Shares can be bought and sold in two ways. Normally, one would approach a stockbroker or a bank, but new share issues can be applied for directly. Dividends are treated as having had basic rate tax paid, and any profits made on disposal are subject to capital gains tax.

Equities have an unparalleled track record over the last 60 years, the return being greater in real terms than that from fixed interest securities. Equities should form an essential part of any investment strategy.

The *personal equity plan,* announced in the 1986 budget, allows individuals to invest up to £200 per month in shares, with all dividends and capital gains being free of tax. The investor must keep the funds invested for at least one calendar year and must re-invest all dividends received.

A *unit trust* is a simple way to invest in stocks and shares. The money from all the investors is pooled together and allocated to units in a fund of shares which is managed by professionals. It is rather like an investment club, each investor being allocated a number of units directly proportional to the amount invested. It is possible to buy units by monthly premiums or with a lump sum. The units can be sold back to the trust at any time. Like shares, there is both a capital and an income gain. Whilst the units are under management, trusts are free of capital gains tax, but disposal may lead to a liability. Basic rate tax has already been paid on the income from unit trusts.

There are well over 650 different unit trusts in the UK. Each trust is designed to take advantage of a particular market situation. Some are meant to produce a high income and some concentrate on capital appreciation. It is possible to choose a trust to perform the task required with some precision. However, a word of warning: shares, unit trusts and investment bonds are medium- to long-term investments and their value in the short term may well fall. The medium to long term trend will tend to keep pace with, and even beat, inflation as they are all asset backed investments.

Investment bonds are, in most cases, collections of unit trusts packaged together with a very small amount of life cover. They are not as specific as unit trusts. Most insurance companies will offer a *managed* bond, where the underlying investment is in shares, gilts, fixed interest and commercial property, a *property* bond, with the underlying investment in equities, an *overseas* bond, being an investment in commercial property whose profits come mainly from overseas, and a *gilt-edged* bond, offering a managed fund, consisting of British government securities and providing an uncomplicated alternative to direct investment in gilts.

The main advantage of bonds is that they form a 'storehouse' of capital. The Inland Revenue allow the individual to draw 5% of the initial value of the bond each year tax free. These 5%s do not have to be taken in any particular tax year. A regular income may be drawn, and their disposal is only liable for higher rate tax, basic rate tax having already been paid.

Property

There are four ways to invest in property. First, by direct investment in residential property; second, by direct investment in agricultural land and woodlands; third, by direct investment in shops and commercial property; and finally, by indirect investment in property, by way of shares in a property company or via property bonds.

The first three direct investments are obviously for those who have substantial amounts of capital. Most individuals (after paying for their own domestic residence) could only sensibly consider the fourth option. Investors buy shares in a company which manages properties. The owners of property bonds thus have an effective investment in the properties themselves. The growth in the value of property is generally more stable than growth in equities, but the bonds are less liquid.

There is a whole host of investment possibilities which has still not been considered but, in general, most individuals could happily build a personal investment portfolio out of the various components which have been described. There is no reason, however, to exclude any area of personal expertise. Musicians will usually have the ability to make capital gains out of buying and selling musical instruments. Knowledge of antiques or paintings might also be used for profit.

To summarise, there are no immutable laws connected with investing. There is, however, a good deal to be said for taking a realistic, common-sense approach to the whole array of available options. Once the common concerns of dying too soon, living too long, home ownership and emergency funds have been catered for, anything else is icing on the cake.

It is increasingly difficult to obtain good advice with respect to changing market conditions. The press is a good source of early warning, but there is no substitute for the personal touch. Try asking friends and colleagues for the name of the person who sorted out matters for *them* so efficiently.

SECTION 4:
BOWING OUT

DISMISSAL, REDUNDANCY AND UNEMPLOYMENT

LAURENCE WATT

Since 1974, Laurence Watt has been a partner in the firm of Charles Russell & Co. in Lincoln's Inn. He acts for a number of professional musicians, including two of London's best known self-governed symphony orchestras, and was responsible for conducting the litigation which confirmed the freelance status of the members of such orchestras. He is secretary of the Council of the London Philharmonic Orchestra and is also an amateur french horn player.

Employment legislation has now been with us for over twenty years. The right to redundancy payments arose in 1965 and the right not to be unfairly dismissed arose in 1971. At its best, this legislation provides a framework in which genuine unfairness can be remedied, and out of which a measure of protection is given against the cessation of a particular job, or of the requirements of particular work, through redundancy. At its worst, it cuts across the traditional common law right of every individual or company to contract freely as to the terms, conditions and duration of employment. In addition, employment legislation, incorporating as it does so many protections and allowances in relation to union membership, has become a political football resulting in increased complexity and constant change. The Employment Protection (Consolidation) Act of 1978 sought to bring all the legislation together into more or less intelligible form under one statute – although one or two stragglers have been enacted since.

Employed or freelance?

Before discussing the provisions of this legislation as they affect the musician, it is necessary to understand that the law will only relate to those musicians who are employed under a contract of service. Neither the employment protection legislation nor the Inland Revenue and national insurance law is helpful enough to define an employed person further than saying it is someone who works under a contract of employment. However, the precise difference between someone who works under a contract *of employment/service* and one who works under a contract *for services* is vital to the operation of the benefits or otherwise sought to be given or taken away by the legislation.

Much case law has, therefore, developed which I do not propose to analyse, save by broad reference to three well reported and important cases for the musician. These involved (i) the London Philharmonic Orchestra on its own account. Following an application by a player to the Industrial Tribunal, the orchestra successfully challenged the jurisdiction of the tribunal and thus settled to the professed satisfaction of the Inland Revenue authorities and the Department of Health & Social Security (DHSS), the self-employed status of the full members not only of that orchestra, but also the other London self-governed orchestras – and, indeed, any other musical organisations structured on a similar basis; (ii) the London Philharmonic Orchestra (who agreed to be the guinea pig, having been through the hoop before) on behalf of themselves and all three other self-governed orchestras in London. The DHSS unsuccessfully sought to challenge the traditional self-employed 'freelance' status of the extras and associates of these orchestras for the purposes of the social security legislation governing the classes of payment of national insurance contributions, and (iii) the Midland Sinfonia where, again, the DHSS unsuccessfully challenged the freelance status of the players in this orchestra.

These decisions inevitably had, and will continue to have, not only important consequences to the particular organisations to which they refer, but also in relation to the profession as a whole.

On the one hand, the second LPO decision above will almost certainly cover, directly, the non-permanent personnel hired on a similar basis by all other orchestras, large or small, self-governed *or* contracted, be they independent or attached to, for example, a ballet or opera company. On the other hand, the importance of the Midland (now English) Sinfonia's decision derives from the fact that this orchestra represents a typical structure for ensembles large or small with a permanent management who gather together players on a regular basis or otherwise as and when necessary, to perform under a particular name or title. Indeed, this structure is very similar to the large orchestra (the management) bringing in its extras and associates (the musicians); it was not very surprising, therefore, when this decision followed the principles laid down in the second LPO case which immediately preceded it.

The fact that musician may sign a piece of paper which purports to govern the terms on which he plays will not *necessarily* take away the freelance or self-employed status he would otherwise enjoy, and each situation must be taken on its merits. Furthermore, the principles embodied in these decisions will extend to musicians who do part-time teaching, either privately or for colleges, depending upon the terms which govern their services.

Briefly, the primary principles which have been held to be pertinent as to employment status (in the absence of a full time contract) are:

(a) the tradition of self-employment in the profession,
(b) the control exercised over the musician being only that necessitated by the very nature of the work,
(c) taxation and national insurance arrangements,
(d) the degree of risk,
(e) whether or not the musician is carrying on business on his own account,
(f) the provision of equipment,
(g) the availability to perform other work, and
(h) the view taken by the musician and the orchestra as to their relationship.

The benefits of self employed (freelance) status lie principally in the realms of taxation and the freedom to operate as and how the musician wishes. The disadvantages are primarily the long term lack of employment security – which can be catered for at a cost – the lack of the benefit of any of the employment protection provisions set out in the legislation, the lack of any redundancy rights and, finally, the lack of any right to unemployment benefit or other benefits to which only persons who are employed or available for full time employment are entitled (see later).

The category, therefore, to which the employment legislation relates in the music profession is fairly substantially reduced and will only cover musicians who work as full contracted members of orchestras coming under the auspices of organisations such as the BBC, the Western Orchestral Society, various opera houses and others; it will also relate to those who teach or lecture under contracts of service with universities, colleges, schools and other educational institutions.

Notice

Any person who is employed under a contract of service is entitled to minimum periods of notice laid down by statute. These apply regardless of any shorter period which the employee and his employer may have purported to agree.

The periods laid down are as follows:

  (i) Continuous employment for one month or over, but less than two years, will entitle an employee to a minimum of one week's notice.

 (ii) Continuous employment for two years or more, but for less than 12 years, will entitle an employee to one week's notice for each year of continuous employment.

(iii) Continuous employment for 12 years or more will entitle the employee to not than less 12 weeks notice.

An employee cannot agree to reduce his right to the statutory minimum period of notice.

Dismissal

Wrongful dismissal will always be unfair; unfair dismissal will not always be wrongful. This conundrum will perhaps better be understood by explaining that the word 'wrongful' should be read in the context of breach of contract and the word 'unfair' in the statutory sense that dismissal, even if totally in accordance with the contract, can nevertheless give rise to an application to an industrial tribunal alleging unfairness, upon proof of which the complainant becomes entitled to compensation. Furthermore, the compensation awarded by an industrial tribunal bears little relationship to any damages that might otherwise have been awarded had there been a breach of contract. Indeed, in certain circumstances reinstatement or re-engagement orders can be made.

The other main difference of principle with which the musician is concerned is that, whereas *wrongful* dismissal can mean either termination of a contract for services or a contract of service (it simply involves breach of the terms of the contract under which the musician performs), *unfair* dismissal can only be claimed where a musician is employed under a contract *of service*.

For all practical purposes, to claim unfair dismissal an employee must have been in continuous employment for two years, be under retirement age and, with certain exceptions, be employed for a minimum of 16 hours a week. He must either (i) have been dismissed, or (ii) be working under a fixed term contract which has expired without subsequently being renewed, or (iii) have terminated the contract himself under circumstances where his employer's conduct has forced him to do so (known as *constructive dismissal*).

The legislation lays down what are called acceptable reasons for dismissal, which cover misconduct, inability, ill-health, redundancy and illegality. An employer must establish one of these grounds and then the tribunal will go on to consider the fairness of the dismissal, i.e. whether the reason given is justified, whether warnings have been given and whether disciplinary procedures have been followed.

There are three reasons for dismissal which are automatically 'unfair'. These are (i) trades union activity, (ii) pregnancy, and (iii) unfair selection for redundancy. The main remedies available from the tribunal are compensation and, much more rarely, orders for reinstatement or re-engagement.

Compensation is awarded in two layers:

(i) A basic award which follows more or less automatically on a finding of unfairness (although there *can* be reductions for contributory fault) and which is calculated precisely in the same way as redundancy payments (below).

(ii) A compensation element up to a maximum of £8,000 (at 1st April 1986) which will, at the discretion of the tribunal, be reduced by any conduct by the musician contributing to his dismissal. The sanction for the refusal by an employer to re-engage or reinstate is an additional award which, depending upon the circumstances, can be between 13 and 52 weeks pay up to a maximum (on 1st April 1986) of £155 per week, in other words, total maximum extra compensation of £8,060.

An application to an industrial tribunal alleging unfair dismissal must be made within three months of the termination of employment.

Redundancy

It is difficult to imagine circumstances where redundancy is likely to arise frequently for the employed orchestral musician. A symphony orchestra without its normal full complement of players would be like a spider with six legs – it would work, but would not be quite the same. Clearly it could happen, since the BBC could well, for instance, decide to disband one of its orchestras or, at any rate, cut down its string strength. Players so affected, and music teachers who find themselves the subject of financial stringency on the part of the education establishment, will need the following requirements in order to come within the statutory protection provisions:

(i) To have been dismissed.

(ii) To be 20 or over and below the age of 65 (for men) or 60 (for women). However, it is likely that the upper age limit for women will be increased to 65,

(iii) To have been in continuous employment for a period of two years from the first day of employment. Continuous employment means working for 16 hours or more per week (unless employed for more than five years for between 8 and 16 hours a day, in which case, for redundancy purposes, the contract is treated as being work for 16 hours a day, thus bringing it fully within the provisions).

There are various 'events' which, contrary to appearances, do not break continuity. The most pertinent of these are participation in a strike and, in certain rather complicated circumstances, where a business changes hands and the affected employee is offered the same job under the new ownership, e.g. if the Western Orchestral Society took over the running of the BBC Welsh Symphony Orchestra and kept on all the players.

(iv) To have been dismissed by reason of redundancy – in other words, for the reason that either the whole 'business' in which the musician is engaged has either ceased or is about to cease, or the requirements for the particular work carried out by the musician has ceased or diminished or is expected so to do.

There are a number of exclusions from benefit and the three important ones are

(i) employees dismissed for misconduct,

(ii) employees who are offered suitable alternative employment or unreasonably refuse such an offer, and

(iii) employees under fixed term contracts where rights to redundancy have been excluded by agreement in writing.

Claims made outside a time limit of six months from dismissal will not qualify unless within that time a claim in writing has been made to the employer direct or by application to an Industrial Tribunal or, alternatively, payment has been agreed or made. A claim for unfair dismissal within this period (noting, as stated above, that application for unfair dismissal has to be made within *three* months of dismissal) will also suspend the six month time limit.

The amount of the redundancy payment is calculated as follows:

(a) one and a half week's pay for each year of employment during all of which the employee is aged 41 or over,

(b) one week's pay for each year of employment during all of which the employee is 22 or over, or

(c) half a week's pay for the years between 18 and 21 inclusive.

There is a maximum of 20 years that can count, working back on the above scales, and the maximum *weekly* amount of pay for the purposes of the above calculations, as at 1st April 1986, is £155. During the final year before retirement age, any redundancy payment is reduced by one-twelfth for each month by which the gap closes to the 65th birthday.

An employer must always go about dealing with redundancy fairly, whether he is making one person redundant or a hundred. There are, however, recognised procedures that should be followed to ensure such fairness. Some are obvious and some are less so. Here are the most important ones:

(i) Where there is a union, recognised by the employer, then the employer must consult with the union before making anybody redundant.

(ii) The employer must give as much warning as possible to the employees concerned. Indeed, where there is a recognised union and more than ten employees are likely to be made redundant within 30 days, there must be a minimum of 30 days consultation before the dismissals take effect. There are similar extended provisions for larger redundancies.

The silver lining for the employer to the dark cloud of expense that redundancy payments may expose him to is his ability to recover 41% of his outlay from the state, provided his original payment was made under his legal obligation so to do and was not made on an ex gratia basis.

Unemployment

This subject by itself is huge and this chapter can only hope to point musicians in the appropriate direction and to endeavour to cut through the maze of regulations to the most important points.

The benefits obtainable on being unemployed will depend largely on the class of national insurance contributions being paid. However, supplementary benefit is not dependent on national insurance being paid at all – more on that later. The *employed* musician who, together with his employer, should be paying Class 1 contributions, will be entitled to the full benefits, including –

Unemployment benefit
Sickness benefit
Maternity benefit
Housing benefit
Benefit for injuries suffered at work
Various types of pension payment

The DHSS provide, through all their local offices, a very comprehensive leaflet service giving details of all the benefits available. It is wise to consult these, since the rules in relation to the payment of national insurance contributions and the entitlements to benefit are complex, littered with pitfalls for the unwary, and constantly changing.

Self-employed or 'freelance' musicians will usually be paying Class 2 contributions (and, in some cases, Class 4 contributions, although these by themselves confer no right to any benefit). Class 2 contributions entitle the musician to a number of benefits, the most important of which are:

Sickness benefit
Maternity allowance
Widows allowance
Various categories of pension (including invalidity pension, providing application follows immediately upon the receipt of sickness benefit).

Class 2 contributors are *not* entitled to unemployment benefit.

Separate from all the types of benefit referred to above is supplementary benefit, to which I have already briefly alluded. Put in its simplest form, supplementary benefit is available to all unemployed people of 16 and over living in this country and available for full-time employment. Those who qualify also have to come within maximum capital and income requirements; in other words, they are means tested.

Supplementary benefit is not related to national insurance contributions. Those in part-time employment may receive supplementary benefit at the discretion of the DHSS, providing they can show that they are eligible and that they are willing to give up part-time employment for full-time employment should it be offered. By definition, one who is self-employed cannot be what the statute defines as in full-time employment. Thus, supplementary benefit entitlement follows very closely the entitlement to unemployment benefit which, as has been discussed above, is not available to self-employed people. A self-employed musician or teacher will be entitled to supplementary benefit, provided he is prepared to surrender his self-employed status and be available for full-time employment. On applying for supplementary benefit, it will be necessary to show that such a person has ceased to be self-employed, whether or not he has any other form of employment, for fourteen days.

305

RETIREMENT – THE TIME OF YOUR LIFE

PAUL BACH

Paul Bach is Public Relations Director of Saga Holidays plc, pioneers of holidays for people in retirement. He is also editor of Saga Magazine, *the general-interest magazine published six times a year by Saga which regularly covers subjects of specific interest to the retired population.*

The thing that's wrong with retirement is the name. Consider, for example, what the *Concise Oxford Dictionary* has to say: '*Retire* . . . to withdraw, retreat, seek seclusion or shelter . . .'. 'Well', as the frail English lady (80 if she was a day) I witnessed climbing aboard an elephant in a game park in distant Nepal might have said, 'you could have fooled me!'

I offer an alternative definition for the 'eighties: '*Retire* . . . to expand one's experience of life, to look to the future, to seek and achieve fulfilment'.

If that sounds a bit high-falutin', may I say that it's based on a measure of experience in providing holidays for retired people, trying to keep up with their insatiable (and stimulating) demands for fresh horizons, seeing them in many of the world's remote corners taking great bites of life with an appetite and zest that leaves younger travellers amazed and, in between times, editing a highly entertaining (to me at least!) and enthusiastic magazine for what the publishing trade deems the retirement – that word again – market.

The message that emerges time and again from every close encounter is that, in essence, retirement is a frame of mind. Those who get it 'right', who determine that the years which follow their lifetimes' work can and shall be the best of their lives, find wondrous benefits to reap.

Those who get it 'wrong', who allow retirement to creep up and ambush them, who are unduly influenced by how they remember the roles of retired people when they were younger, who omit to plan and positively reconstruct their lives, are left at the starting post.

In this context, starting post is an apt metaphor: a former colleague who specialised in pre-retirement education used to assert that retirement was life's 'last great threshold'. He would add the encouraging distinction that, compared with those other, easily categorised sectors in life's course such as, say, infancy, the teens, even middle age, the time that we spend in retirement can with luck – aided by commonsense – span more years than any of the others.

So *that,* I think, is the first message: take a firm grip on the challenge that awaits you – and go for it! And, with the greatest respect, I offer this as a rider: avoid the trap of remembering and seeking to emulate how your parents or grandparents may have reacted when retirement came for them. There has been an enormous change in recent years not only in attitudes towards retirement, but also among the people themselves who are entering this phase. Today's average 60-year-old is an active, vigorous, alert and still-curious individual determined to make the most of the sizeable chunk of life that lies ahead.

An example from my own industry underlines the point with, I think, graphic effect. It was only a few years ago that Bournemouth and Brighton were, for over-sixties, favourite holiday destinations and, for many, going there represented an annual adventure. Today, places like Kashmir and Kenya, Samarkand and Singapore are gearing up apace to meet demand from Britain's retired population.

There are a number of key areas in your own lifestyle that will benefit from re-examination when retirement comes. And it's no bad thing to start the process some time before. Elsewhere in these pages there is expert analyses and detailed advice. But a short check-list of action points will perhaps be helpful here.

Health

Don't accept that increasing age necessarily means failing health. I've been left gasping in the wake of our seasoned travellers far too often to be surprised any more! And don't accept that chronic conditions which may develop with age inevitably cannot be treated or improved. Dr Eric Trimmer, who writes for *Saga Magazine*, recently covered memory loss from that very point of view, suggesting an easily available treatment that he knew could help in some cases. Result: one very grateful reader who wrote to say how she had benefited from his advice. 'Everyone had told me to accept failing memory at my (advanced) age,' she said. 'They were wrong . . .'.

The other important point about health care is that it's rarely too late to stop bad habits. Most of you, I'm sure, don't have them! But, just in case you're tempted to, say, stop smoking or cut down on drinking or take more exercise or improve your diet, but think there's not much point at your age – don't believe it! There are countless case histories of people who have decided to opt for a healthier way of life at quite a late stage, and who have been amazed at the very apparent benefits.

Personal relationships

Yes, husbands and wives and wives and husbands. What's that you say? You've been married getting on for 40 years and you've learned all there is to know about living with each other? Maybe so. But hold on for a moment. That's 40 years or so, if I may take the woman's point of view, of being a part-time husband. Yes, part-time. For, surely, that's what a working week of 40 hours or more has made you? You've come to terms with the idea of not being with your wife during the day (weekends and holidays excepted). And she's been able to organise her life without having you under her feet every waking moment. Now all this will change – perhaps dramatically. At its most extreme, it could mean that you will have to get to know each other all over again.

Ground rules? Just one. Try to have as much understanding of your partner's changed situation as you have of your own.

Finances

Few areas of your new lifestyle will repay – in every sense – sensible planning more than your personal finances. Budgeting is a must. It can also be good fun. And it will help you avoid the pitfalls of going into retirement with the vague idea that, yes, your income may be reduced but so will your expenditure 'and you should get by all right'.

Those who have already – and sensibly – gone through the exercise will confirm how often broad assumptions based on cursory considerations do not stand up to detailed examination. And things so quickly add up – especially when it's expenditure as opposed to income! Take food. Did you used to work for the BBC? Did you perhaps enjoy subsidised meals? If so, that's at least five extra lunches you'll need to budget for – probably ten when you discover that your stay-at-home partner who's doing the cooking sees no reason why she or he shouldn't also eat at the same time, even though it wasn't worth the effort when you were away at work . . .

The number of professional musicians who've been able to enjoy the benefits of subsidised company cars is probably considerably smaller than in other occupations. But for those who have, and who are now obliged suddenly to switch to running their own, the financial implications can be considerable. As well as running costs, there are repairs, insurance, tax, depreciation and capital outlay. A company car is worth at least £3,000 p.a. That's £3,000 you'll have to find to maintain the same standard.

Finding the most suitable – and profitable – home for your savings is, of course, of paramount importance. And, because every individual is influenced by different criteria, there is no single 'best' way. A clear understanding of what your requirements are – capital growth, regular income, guaranteed interest rates, etc. etc. – is the first step. The next is to seek professional advice. Your bank is a good place to start. A close second – for advice on Inland Revenue implications – comes your local tax inspector.

Hobbies

The whole world loves a hobby – but retirement gives you two enormous advantages over the rest of them when it comes to getting the best from your chosen pursuit. The first is that you have the time – lashings of it. The second is that you have a lifetime's acquired skills and experience to apply to a perhaps new, perhaps long-discarded, pastime. I have seen artists of breath-taking ability on special interest painting holidays who are enormously proud of the fact that, before retirement, the last time they held a brush for creative reasons was in the classroom.

Hobbies can be satisfying, fulfilling, therapeutic – even profitable. To list all the options would require a separate book. But, if the idea of starting something new rather than refining an existing favourite is what appeals, your local adult education centre is a good place to start.

There, you're likely to find courses from antiques to Zen Buddhism. And, if the idea attracts you, consider the additional benefits of taking up something you can enjoy with your partner. It may even add the stimulus of competition to your lives . . .

For many, intellectual pursuits offer the most attractive challenge. I have published letters from mature graduates of the Open University – one in his eighties – while the University of the Third Age (U3A) runs organised groups throughout the country. More information from U3A: Diane Norton, 6 Parkside Gardens, London, SW19 5EA.

Finally, consider the enormous satisfaction to be derived from teaching as opposed to learning. There's always demand for professionally qualified people with experience, especially if they can cater for the odd hours that courses often demand. What could you teach? Did someone whisper music . . .?

Where to live

The fastest-growing part of the house-building market is the quaintly-named 'sheltered housing' sector. In other words, purpose-built flat and apartment developments, usually with resident staff, which are designed exclusively for (and limited to) people in retirement. Suddenly, the trade has stumbled over the fact that far more people choose to move home when they retire than hitherto had been supposed.

The reasons for this 'get-up-and-go' phenomenon are many. One to the forefront is the realisation that, with children having grown up and moved on, the old 'family home' is both too large and too expensive to maintain. Add to that the fact that, with the mortgage probably paid up, it represents a lot of tied-up capital – and the logic in finding soemthing smaller, cheaper and perhaps more attractively located becomes difficult to fault.

Logic, however, doesn't always play a part. You may be tempted to remember the bungalow at Bridlington you rented all those years ago for that unforgettable holiday – wouldn't it be just *splendid* to buy something similar? But fond-though-fading memories of happy days in the sun can pall before the reality of a force eight gale in mid-winter bringing most of the North Sea down the high street and possibly under your front door.

That isn't to say that impulse buying of this nature (provided you're both equally enthusiastic) invariably fails. Again, I've published stories about couples who've hung on the coat-tails of fate and bought cottages in the Welsh mountains, or remote Scottish islands – and never looked back. But do weigh up the pros and cons before you leap. And do consider the year-round implications.

The key factors in deciding to move include whether you can get by if you forsake all your friends, familiar services, perhaps even family, for something new and distant, or whether your best bet – if you decide to move at all – is to do so within the location you know.

Perhaps, after all, you will decide to plump for pastures new. The south coast of England is already established as the favourite place for retirement homes – for many excellent reasons. But beware the north/south price gap, growing wider by the minute. You're likely to find that the capital realised by the sale of a substantial four-bedroomed house in, say, the north east of England may not buy even a modest semi-detached bungalow on the favoured shores of the sunny south.

Sheltered housing developments have a lot to offer and are getting better all the time, as developers take heed of the advice and experience readily available from the age group for which they are designed. Yet pitfalls remain for the unwary. The terms of some leases are questionable, as is the (happily shrinking) incidence of developments where, if you decide to re-sell, you are legally obliged to do so to the developer at the price you originally paid. One of our readers lost many thousands of pounds in only five years as prices escalated in his corner of the south-east while he was tied to such a re-sell clause.

The moral is clear: if you are considering a sheltered housing development for your new home in retirement (and there's a great deal to be said for it), ensure your solicitor checks carefully the terms of the lease or the purchase – and advises you accordingly. That, after all, is what you're paying him for.

A final word on sheltered housing. If the idea appeals, don't delay the move too long. Better to plan and execute the move (any move, come to that) early in your retirement rather than late. The idea that sheltered housing is primarily for the infirm and elderly is to be actively discouraged!

Your rights

Now, here's a minefield ... Retirement brings a range of benefits, some of which will be provided automatically, others which will have to be researched (yes, by you) and applied for, yet more that will have to be prised with great difficulty from a resistant if not to say reluctant bureaucracy.

The range of state benefits designed specifically for people in retirement is too complex (and too prone to change) to examine here. But there is an authoritative and regularly updated leaflet, *Tax and Pensions over 60*, covering retirement pensions, benefits for widows, the implications of early retirement, redundancy, earnings in retirement, self employment, supplementary pension, help with heating, health and disability, fares concessions, tax (including capital gains and inheritance). It is published by Saga Holidays and is available free as one of the benefits of subscription to the *Saga Magazine*

Club. As a special concession, we shall be pleased to make it available at no charge to readers of this book who write to Saga Magazine Club, PO Box 65, Folkestone, Kent.

Holidays

As tourism accelerates its bid to become the growth industry of the 'eighties, you can be sure that – whatever your idea of the perfect holiday – you should never be stuck for choice. And it's a thought almost as warming as the sunshine that beckons that, as a buyer, the market belongs to you. Never has the choice been so large, the competition for business so fierce, the value (in real terms) so good.

Of course, there's no irrevocable reason why, once retired, you should change your holiday habits of a lifetime. But there are a number of factors which suggests that you might.

First, you're a keeper of the most valuable commodity of all: time. You can travel – in most cases – when you like, and you can stay away for as long as you like; which, for those of you who've had to make do in the past with a couple of weeks in high summer, could be very good news indeed. Why? Because every airline or tour operator worthy of the description can fill all his high-season places with no trouble at all. But off-peak it's a different game of deck quoits. The advantages are many: holidays at times of the year when temperatures are kind without being searingly hot, less chance of crowds, hotels that are genuinely glad to see you because the business means the difference between closing and staying open – and attractive prices.

Disadvantages? Well, there won't be quite so many topless ladies around the swimming pool (perhaps that's an advantage), fewer night-long discos beneath your bedroom window, less chance of 'courtesy calls' by English football supporters. Oh yes . . . and you're likely to be weighed down by all the small change you're obliged to accept for certain essentials – like drinks – whose prices come down as the season changes.

As to where? – well, it could be almost anywhere in the world: long-haul, exotic destinations like South America, the Far East, Central Asia, India and Nepal; the ever-popular

Mediterranean where, in some cases, you can stay full board for months on end for not a lot more than it would cost you to stay at home and survive the British winter; hotels, holiday centres and universities throughout the British Isles; coach tours that criss-cross Europe and the United States; a huge and growing spectrum of special interest and discovery holidays ranging from bowls and dancing to Shakespeare and Dickens; special holidays for Christmas, for people on their own, for wine lovers, for history buffs, for walkers and for card players; and cruises on rivers and oceans all over the world.

So, what's so special about them? Well, I'll declare my interest, state my prejudice, admit my bias – and tell you anyway. They're all there to be enjoyed by the most interesting, personable, stimulating and energetic people I've ever had the pleasure of being involved with. That's right – people in retirement.

ALPHABETICAL INDEX
OF ADVERTISERS